THE BULLDOG DETECTIVE

THE BULLDOG DETECTIVE

*William J. Flynn and America's First War
against the Mafia, Spies, and Terrorists*

JEFFREY D. SIMON

Prometheus Books
Essex, Connecticut

Ⓟ Prometheus Books

An imprint of Globe Pequot, the trade division of
The Rowman & Littlefield Publishing Group, Inc.
4501 Forbes Blvd., Ste. 200
Lanham, MD 20706
www.rowman.com

Distributed by NATIONAL BOOK NETWORK

British Library Cataloguing in Publication Information available

Library of Congress Cataloging-in-Publication Data

Names: Simon, Jeffrey D. (Jeffrey David), 1949– author.
Title: The bulldog detective : William J. Flynn and America's first war
   against the mafia, spies, and terrorists / Jeffrey D. Simon.
Description: Lanham, MD : Prometheus, [2024] | Includes bibliographical
   references and index. | Summary: "The Bulldog Detective is the first
   book to tell the story of William J. Flynn, the first government
   official to bring down the powerful Mafia, uncover a sophisticated
   German spy ring in the United States, and launch a formal war on
   terrorism. As the chief of the U.S. Secret Service and then as director of the Bureau of
   Investigation (the forerunner of the FBI), Flynn would become one of the most
   respected and effective law enforcement officials in American history"—Provided by
   publisher.
Identifiers: LCCN 2023013696 (print) | LCCN 2023013697 (ebook) | ISBN
   9781633888654 (cloth) | ISBN 9781633888661 (epub)
Subjects: LCSH: Flynn, William J. (William James), 1867–1928. |
   Detectives—United States—Biography. | Government executives—United
   States—Biography. | United States Bureau of Investigation—History. |
   Terrorism—Prevention—United States—History.
Classification: LCC HV7911.F62 S56 2023 (print) | LCC HV7911.F62 (ebook)
   | DDC 363.25092—dc23/eng/20230627
LC record available at https://lccn.loc.gov/2023013696
LC ebook record available at https://lccn.loc.gov/2023013697

Printed in India

CONTENTS

INTRODUCTION

IT HAD TO BE THE WORST DECISION OF HIS LIFE. HEINRICH FRIEDRICH Albert was sitting comfortably and reading as he traveled uptown on the Sixth Avenue elevated train in New York on the afternoon of July 24, 1915. When he looked up and realized the train was at the 50th Street station and about to move on, he panicked and decided to rush from his seat, yelling to the guard on the platform to hold the door open. That was all he was thinking about—not missing his stop. As he exited the train, however, a woman sitting near him shouted out that he had forgotten his briefcase. He tried to get back into the train but was unable to do so. In the meantime, a man had taken the briefcase and also exited the train. Albert then saw the man carrying the briefcase in the street and chased him along Sixth Avenue. The man jumped onto the running board of a moving, open surface car and informed the conductor that he was being chased by a crazy man who had just caused a disturbance on the elevated train. The conductor told the motorman to keep the car moving past its next stop, leaving a frantic Albert far behind.[1]

Albert, who was the commercial attaché for the German embassy, notified two of his colleagues about the incident. They decided to place an ad in a newspaper offering a reward of $20 for the return of the briefcase and its contents, hoping that the person who took it was just a common thief and, after not finding any money inside, would return it for that meager reward. What they didn't know at the time was that no amount of money would have resulted in the return of that briefcase. It was now in the hands of the U.S. Secret Service, and the lid was about to be blown off a sophisticated German propaganda, espionage, and sabotage plan inside the United States.[2]

The person who took the briefcase was Frank Burke, a Secret Service agent and leader of an eleven-man special squad that William J. Flynn, chief of the service, had formed to uncover German espionage in America in the years leading up to U.S. entry into World War I. Burke was tailing Albert and didn't hesitate to grab the briefcase when the German left the train. When Burke showed the contents to his boss, Flynn knew he and his men had struck gold. Inside the briefcase were documents detailing Germany's nefarious plans in America, including a $27 million budget under Albert's control to fund pro-German propaganda, attacks on ships carrying war supplies for the Allies, and strikes at the docks and in munitions plants.[3]

Also involved in the espionage and sabotage activities in America were Captain Franz von Papen, the military attaché for the German embassy (and the future chancellor of Germany), and Captain Karl Boy-Ed, the naval attaché. Both were expelled from the United States in December 1915. No official action was taken against Albert, who returned to Germany when America entered the war in April 1917. Exposing the spy ring was a major triumph for Flynn, who was known as "the Bulldog" for his tenacity in pursuing leads. As one newspaper proclaimed, Flynn "probably did more than any one man to rid this country of foreign spies."[4]

Flynn was a big man. At six feet tall with a cropped mustache and weighing about three hundred pounds, he struck an imposing figure wherever he went. Often in a derby hat, he was once described by a reporter as "large, mountainous almost, up and down as well as circumferentially." Flynn worked as a plumber, tinsmith, stone carver, and semiprofessional baseball player before joining the Secret Service in 1897. He soon rose through the ranks to become one of the most respected and influential detectives and law enforcement officials of that era.[5]

Long before Eliot Ness and the Untouchables went after Al Capone and the Italian mob in Chicago, Flynn dismantled the first Mafia family to exist in America. As head of the Eastern Division of the Secret Service from 1901 until 1910, Flynn pursued the Morello–Lupo gang, who were engaged in murder, extortion, counterfeiting, and other criminal activities both in New York and around the country. He ran an intelligence operation that tracked the movements and activities of Giuseppe "The Clutch Hand" Morello, Ignazio "The Wolf" Lupo, and other members of the gang for several years, building an airtight counterfeiting case against them that resulted in long prison terms for the mobsters.[6]

The success against the Mafia made Flynn famous, with front-page stories about him in newspapers across the country. The *Boston Globe* described him as "one of the greatest detectives in the world." Understanding the value of good publicity for one's career, Flynn also published first-person accounts of his adventures. While he loved the media attention and benefited from the usually glowing stories about him, Flynn nevertheless played down the image of anybody being a supersleuth like the fictional Sherlock Holmes:

> If you want some reading that will put you gently to sleep, try a detective's record of a sensational case, just as he keeps it: "Interviewed three shoe clerks; no result. Analyst reported poison lotion to be talcum and water. Spent afternoon in subway, endeavoring to locate guard with missing tooth; no result." And that goes on for weeks and maybe years and still no result, till you have very grave misgivings about the adventures of analytical criminologists and their pale, flexible hands, not to mention their eyes that seem to pierce, etc. No it's a great bore to be a real detective, when you compare yourself with a super-detective in a novel, growing more super with every chapter.[7]

Flynn's life, however, was anything but boring. In between his exploits against the Mafia and German spies, he also attempted to end corruption and ineffectiveness in the New York Police Department (NYPD) when he was named deputy police commissioner in 1910. Flynn joined his men in raids on gambling houses, "chasing gamblers up fire escapes and across roofs and dropping down skylights." Flynn began to reorganize the Detective Bureau to make it more effective and eliminate graft in the police department but was met with opposition from his superiors and entrenched political interests opposed to any reforms within the NYPD. Calling it "a thankless job," he resigned after just six months and returned to the federal government, where he was promoted to chief of the Secret Service in 1912.[8]

Flynn and his family were targets for revenge from criminals that he put away, including the mob. While in prison, Ignazio Lupo sent out orders to members of his gang who were still free to assassinate Flynn. Giuseppe Morello's half brothers, Vincenzo, Nicola, and Ciro Terranova, debated a plan to kidnap Flynn's children. They did not follow through with the kidnapping, but when Flynn learned of this, he told his children to never venture alone more than one hundred yards from their home. Christmastime was a dangerous holiday for the family. Suspicious packages disguised as gifts and addressed to his children and wife would arrive at their home in New York. On one occasion, Flynn started to open a package addressed to him with a return address he was familiar with. But he noticed that something was just not right with the package. He ran outside, put it in the yard, and then got a bucket of water and doused it. He gave it to a Secret Service agent who confirmed that it was a makeshift bomb that would have killed or seriously injured Flynn and his family had it gone off. After that occurred, to the great dismay of Flynn's children, Secret Service agents dunked every package that arrived at the home in water before they first opened them, thereby ruining any legitimate presents for the children.[9]

Flynn's exploits against German spies and saboteurs as head of the Secret Service built up his legend and caught the attention of the movie industry. A twenty-part silent movie serial about his adventures was made in 1918 by Wharton Studio, a pioneering film studio based in Ithaca, New York. King Baggot, an international film star and a friend of Flynn's, played a fictional character patterned after Flynn, who appeared as himself in one of the episodes. Had this been the end of his career, Flynn would have cemented a stellar legacy. Incorruptible, fiercely patriotic, and determined to get results no matter how long it took, he would have left an impressive record of accomplishments that served his country well.[10]

But it was when he took on anarchists and other radicals in 1919 that his career began a downward slide. After anarchists set off bombs in seven cities on the evening of June 2, 1919, including one at the home of Attorney General A. Mitchell Palmer, Flynn was appointed director of the Bureau of Investigation (BI), the forerunner of the Federal Bureau of

Investigation (FBI). Palmer, with great fanfare, announced the appointment of Flynn to head the BI and find the perpetrators, calling Flynn "the greatest anarchist expert in the United States." With these lofty expectations, Flynn faced a difficult task. There was no blueprint to follow on how to organize an investigation into such a sophisticated attack as the June 2 bombings, which had been preceded by a nationwide package bomb attack targeting prominent government officials.[11]

Flynn therefore devised the first counterterrorist strategy and policy in U.S. history. He established a powerful federal police force along with a top-notch team of agents to aid him in the pursuit of anarchists and other radicals in the country. Palmer, though, created a new division in the BI, the Radical Division, and put a young, ambitious former library clerk named J. Edgar Hoover in charge. Hoover soon hijacked Flynn's investigation and, along with Palmer, orchestrated the infamous Palmer Raids, which involved illegally rounding up, detaining, and in many cases deporting aliens who had committed no crimes. Flynn supported the raids and never spoke up against these violations of civil liberties. Combined with his failure to solve the series of bombings, this tarnished his otherwise stellar reputation.[12]

Flynn had one last chance to redeem himself. After a horse-drawn wagon exploded on Wall Street in September 1920, killing thirty-eight people and injuring hundreds of others in the worst terrorist attack on American soil at that time, Flynn once again tried in vain to find the perpetrators. With no meaningful progress to show from his investigation, he was removed from his post in August 1921 and never again returned to government service.

For Flynn, this was an inglorious end to his distinguished career. He opened a private detective agency a couple of months later and made two of his children, Elmer and Veronica, partners. That was a bad choice, as both were alcoholics and irresponsible, overspending and upsetting clients. Flynn's wife, Anne, was also an alcoholic who made alcohol in the bathtub of their home for herself and some of their six children when they were of age to drink. The excessive drinking of the family (Flynn mostly abstained from alcohol) and the problems with his detective agency depressed and weakened Flynn, who died of heart failure on October 14, 1928.[13]

Although retirement was not a happy time for him, Flynn did launch one business venture that gave him great joy. In 1924, he edited a new fiction magazine called *Flynn's*. To make sure readers knew who was behind this publication, the words "William J. Flynn, Editor, Twenty-Five Years in the U.S. Secret Service" appeared below the title. This gave Flynn a chance to relive his glory days with the Secret Service. While most of the stories were fictionalized, some were based on actual cases that Flynn or his former Secret Service colleagues had worked on. *Flynn's* (it would undergo various name changes over the years) became one of the most popular detective magazines of its time. It continued to be published for many years after Flynn's death.[14]

"I might have become a prosperous plumber had I stuck to my shop and original business," Flynn once told a reporter, "but I'm glad I followed my bent and am now a detective." Surprisingly, there is no published biography of the man who became one of this country's greatest detectives by pursuing the Mafia, spies, and terrorists and forged a lasting place for himself in American history. He was at the center of some of the most sensational events of the early twentieth century, and yet today, very few people know his name. This book is the first to tell the fascinating, exciting, and at times tragic story of William J. Flynn. The challenges that he faced more than one hundred years ago still plague America: organized crime, espionage, and terrorism. Understanding how one man tried to tackle these issues and his successes and failures can offer us insight into these endless problems.[15]

CHAPTER ONE

Learning the Trade

THE WOMAN WAS GROWING IMPATIENT. SHE HAD BOUGHT A RUG FROM a store in New York City and had been promised that it would be delivered right away. She was having company over soon and wanted her house to look nice. But it was now two hours later, and the rug had still not arrived. Since she lived only ten blocks from the store, she could not understand why it was taking so long.

The teenage delivery boy had intended to walk directly to her house with the rug on his shoulder. Halfway there, though, something caught his attention. The police were about to make an arrest. Fascinated by police work, the boy couldn't pass up the opportunity to witness such an exciting event. He joined a large crowd that was watching three uniformed policemen and five plainclothes detectives enter a tenement house, where they had cornered three young men who the previous week had shot up a dance hall, killing a detective and wounding several dancers. He followed the detectives into the hallway but was thrown out onto the street by one of the policemen. Still holding the rug on his shoulder, the boy went to the back of the house but could not gain entry.

He returned to the front of the house and waited as the policemen emerged with their prisoners and put them into a patrol wagon. The boy raced along with the wagon to the police station, all the time still carrying the rug on his shoulder. He tried to enter the station but was not permitted to do so. He stood outside for two hours, hoping to eventually be allowed inside to see the workings of the police. Meanwhile, the irate woman who was expecting her rug had notified the shop owner that the rug had not arrived. The owner informed the police, perhaps fearing that something had happened to his young worker. The police station that the owner notified turned out to be the very same station that the boy was standing outside of. A policeman told the boy he better deliver that rug at once, which he did. The woman scolded him, and his employer fired him. "And thus ended my first job all because police activity had entirely too much fascination for me," William Flynn would reminisce years later. It was a fascination that would last a lifetime.[1]

Born in Manhattan on November 18, 1867, Flynn was the oldest of six children: three boys and three girls. His father, Michael Flynn, was a butcher who had emigrated from Ireland to the United States, and his mother, Elizabeth Stanion Flynn, was a native New Yorker. He grew up in an Irish neighborhood on 41st Street, east of Ninth Avenue, and attended a nearby public school. While he was fascinated by police work, he didn't want to just be a policeman. He wanted to be a detective for the Secret Service. His enthrallment with the service began at an early age. One day, when he was twelve years old, he watched as a policeman and a well-dressed Secret Service agent made an arrest of a counterfeiter in his neighborhood. "I was hypnotized by this mysterious quiet man of the Secret Service," Flynn wrote. "To begin with he looked to me to be more of a prosperous business man than a detective. The city detectives of those days were nothing more nor less than unharnessed bulls (rounds-men in cheap and badly fitting civilian clothes), but this Secret Service man whose name, I learned later, was Bowen, looked, as I have said, like a prosperous merchant." Flynn and his friends would gather on a stoop at night and spin tales about the great adventures of Bowen and others in the Secret Service.[2]

Flynn's school days were cut short when his father died when Flynn was fifteen years old. He had to quit school and find a job to support his mother and younger brothers and sisters. Although his first job as the delivery boy for the rug company didn't work out, he found other employment, including becoming an apprentice to a plumber when he was eighteen. When the plumber, who had a son on the police force, learned of Flynn's interest in detective work, he told him that he should learn everything he could while on the job about building construction and the strengths of materials since criminals who break into houses or banks to crack safes or steal other things have a working knowledge of those subjects. Flynn followed that advice and later said the knowledge he gained helped him with various cases he worked on.[3]

Flynn was also interested in the makeup of a criminal. He began studying the theories of Cesare Lombroso, "the father of criminology," who argued that criminals "have an innate criminality that is difficult for them to resist." According to Lombroso, habitual criminals are born that way and commit crimes because it is their nature to do so. Followers of Lombroso's theories, of which Flynn initially counted himself as one, "placed an emphasis on removing 'born criminals' from society rather than seeking to reform them." Later in his career, however, Flynn would admit that for young first offenders, Lombroso's theory did not apply: "My experience of a quarter of a century in dealing with a criminal element has taught me that many a young man has 'gone wrong' because of unfortunate association or bad environment, and that he is not always inherently a criminal."[4]

By the time he was in his mid-twenties, Flynn was still a plumber, operating a successful business on the west side of New York. As noted, he had also for a while been a tinsmith, a stone carver, and a semipro baseball player. He played for the Arlingtons, a team based in Wee-hawken, New Jersey, a township close to Manhattan. Flynn loved base-ball and spent most of his spare time as a youth playing the sport. "I became a pretty good semi-professional first baseman and pitcher," Flynn wrote, "but I was never good enough to make the big league managers barter for my services."[5]

His passion, however, to be a detective for the Secret Service never faltered. When he was twenty-one, he started trying to land a job with the agency, which was then a branch of the U.S. Treasury Department. (It was transferred to the Department of Homeland Security in 2003.) The primary task of the Secret Service at that time was not protecting the president but rather safeguarding U.S. currency and preventing counter-feiting. "I think it was the romance of the counterfeiter's life that made me lean toward this branch of criminology," Flynn wrote. "Not the least of the queersman's fascination lies in the fact that he goes ahead knowing well that he cannot continue for long without being caught." ("Queers-man" was a term once used to describe a counterfeiter.) His friends tried to discourage him, telling Flynn he could make more money by sticking to plumbing and getting big city contracts. But nothing could deter Flynn and his hopes of landing his dream job. "I may not have impressed them [the Secret Service] as being top-heavy with mental powers, but my persistency won their attention," he later wrote. "The older I grew the stronger became the desire to become a government detective."[6]

He finally got an interview with the New York office of the Secret Service when he was twenty-six years old. He was told by an agent there that he should first gain some experience by obtaining a job at the Ludlow Street Jail in Manhattan. That was where federal criminals, including counterfeiters, were held awaiting trial or sentencing, in addition to individuals being held for civil cases. The agent told Flynn that working at the jail would be a great opportunity to study firsthand the mindset and behavior of counterfeiters. "Get a job there and study them for a couple of years," the agent said to Flynn. "In the meantime I shall keep my ears open for you. And don't forget to keep your own ears and eyes open—wide open."[7]

LUDLOW STREET JAIL
Employment at the Ludlow Street Jail, like many jobs in New York then, was based on political patronage. Flynn was at a disadvantage, being a Republican and active in local politics in a city dominated by the corrupt Tammany Hall Democratic political machine. The first "boss" of Tammany Hall, William Tweed, was convicted on fraud and corruption charges in 1873. Tammany Hall nevertheless continued to run New York City politics. However, in 1894, a reform fusion ticket made up of Republicans, independents, and anti–Tammany Hall Democrats won the city elections. Flynn had worked on the campaign of one of the Republican candidates, Edward Tamsen, who was elected New York county sheriff. Tamsen rewarded Flynn by appointing him to be one of the keepers at the Ludlow Street Jail at the end of February 1895.[8]

The jail where Flynn was going to get firsthand experience dealing with counterfeiters was built in 1862 at the corner of a short city block in Lower Manhattan defined by Ludlow, Broom, and Grand streets and the Essex Market Place alley. The building was sixty feet high and stretched ninety feet along Ludlow Street and ninety feet along the alley. It quickly became known as a country club jail, with a billiards table on the main floor and prisoners allowed free rein to walk around inside from seven thirty in the morning until six o'clock at night, at which time they had to return to their cells. A story about the prison that appeared in the *New York Times* in 1868 described the cells as being very clean and the inmates bearing "an appearance of physical health not equalled [*sic*] by those of many other prisons." Cigars and newspapers were provided to those prisoners who desired them. The *Times* story concluded that if the jail officials "have sought to make prison-life almost a luxury, to be desired; rather than a hardship to be dreaded, they deserve credit for being entirely successful. A fitting sign for the front of this building would be—'Verily, the way of transgressors is *easy*.'"9

It wasn't easy, however, for those who couldn't pay for better accommodations at the jail. A reporter for the *New York Herald Tribune* went undercover there as a prisoner in 1871 and revealed that those who paid the warden $15 a week got a private cell with a bed containing sheets and a pillow with a pillowcase. For $30 a week, a prisoner was given a "nicely furnished sitting room, lighted with gas in the private part of the prison." The prisoners who paid the weekly rent were treated well by the staff, who addressed them as "Gentlemen," and were not locked up in their cells until eleven o'clock or midnight. Those who couldn't pay the rent were carted off to the top floors of the prison to cramped cells. "The food is wretched and the beds filthy," the reporter wrote. He described being attacked by "angry vermin" in his cell. He remained in the prison for a couple of days. "The agony of those two nights was indescribable," he wrote. "My sickness, the cold, cutting draught, a bed I hardly dare lie upon—for in spite of my complaints to the keepers it had not been changed—the horrible smell of the paint [the inside of the prison was being painted], a miniature open cesspool at the foot of the bed, and above all, a hungry, empty, sickened sensation, which weakened me fearfully, made existence at that time and in such a place perfect agony. How I got along till morning I hardly know."10

Things had not improved much by the time Flynn started working at the Ludlow Street Jail in 1895. A report by the Prison Association of New York that year found that "the jail has many defects." Among these were that the "prisoners complained a good deal of vermin in the cells. The condition of the plumbing and water-closets is extremely bad; the plumbing is old, worn out, entirely inadequate and dangerous to health. The jail has no decent bathing facilities." The staff also mistreated some of the prisoners. A convicted counterfeiter brought charges of brutality against two of the jail keepers, claiming they gave him an undeserved beating. He fell into such despair following the beating that he tried to commit suicide by injecting himself with poison. He stated that Flynn was the only person at the jail who treated him with respect.[11]

It would not, of course, have served Flynn's purposes to alienate the counterfeiters since he wanted to learn all he could from them. He might have been worried, however, about losing his job when his benefactor, Sheriff Tamsen, came close to being put in prison for criminal contempt. A new sheriff would have the power to replace Flynn and all the other jail keepers with his own men. Tamsen's trouble began when a sheriff's deputy ignored a court order to deliver a defendant in an extortion case immediately to the Tombs prison in New York City. The deputy instead first allowed the defendant to go to a Turkish bath before taking him to the Tombs. Tamsen faced potential criminal contempt charges for failing to have his deputy follow the court's order. But those charges were ultimately not brought against Tamsen. The sheriff was in trouble again in July 1895, though, when three post office burglars escaped from the Ludlow Street Jail. Many people called for Tamsen to be fired. But once again, the sheriff survived the crisis, and Flynn's job remained safe.[12]

The year 1895 actually turned out to be a very good one for Flynn. He had obtained the job that he hoped would put him on a path to entry into the U.S. Secret Service. He had also gotten married in September to Anne Evelyn Mackey, who had emigrated from Ireland to the United States in 1883. They would remain married until his death in 1928 and have seven children together. One child, however, died after being bitten by an insect while playing in the yard outside their home. Just as he had done when he was a teenager supporting his mother and younger brothers and sisters after his father died, Flynn provided for his large family throughout his life. His children adored him, and the family never wanted for anything.[13]

Flynn's main reason for seeking the job at the Ludlow Street Jail had been to study counterfeiters, and so he couldn't believe his luck when William Brockway, "the oldest, greatest, cleverest counterfeiter of this country," was brought to the jail after an arrest during the summer of 1895. Brockway was assigned to a cell block that Flynn was in charge of. He befriended the seventy-three-year-old Brockway, who "looked more like a benevolent old professor than he did like a criminal." "Old Bill Brockway," as he was known, took an instant liking to the young Flynn and told him all about his life in crime. "Here I was, Bill Flynn of Forty-First Street, the confidant of the biggest counterfeiter in the country—possibly the world!" Flynn later wrote.[14]

Brockway was born in Essex, Connecticut, a small village about twenty-eight miles east of New Haven, in 1822. He had a natural talent for forgery as a child and imitated his teacher's handwriting for fun. He did it so expertly and rapidly that she showed off his work to school directors. He also had a rebellious nature, using his drawing skills to create unflattering caricatures of village people he didn't like and then displaying them on the face of his father's barn. He once drew a carica-ture of the pastor of his father's church, portraying him with huge donkey ears. The pastor had denounced the youth in church for questioning the religious man's beliefs. Conflict with his father eventually led Brockway to leave home while he was still in his early teens.[15]

Brockway obtained a job with a printer in New Haven and acquired new skills that would help him in his counterfeiting career. There were reports that he attended Yale and took courses in chemistry and electro-typing, but that could never be verified. He nevertheless learned how to do electrotyping, which is an electrochemical process used for the exact reproduction of different types of objects, including printing plates. He took great pride in his work and became upset when he was described in newspaper stories as an engraver. "Flynn," he said one day when he was at the Ludlow Street Jail, "you can do me a great service if you will call all the newspaper reporters together and tell them to stop saying I'm an engraver. I'm not. I never engraved a plate in my life. I do not know how. I'm a printer. Printing is my profession. I'm proud of my work as a printer. Any one can do good work with the tools of an engraver."[16]

Brockway's belittling remarks about engravers might have been due to the fact that an engraver he worked with cooperated with the authorities in an investigation that led to one of Brockway's many arrests and convictions during his fifty-year career as a counterfeiter and forger. The counterfeit notes and bonds that Brockway produced were considered among the finest ever seen by the government. He was also creative in the ways he tried to use the counterfeit bills. One plan involved making bets of $25 at racetracks around the country with large-denomination counterfeit bills. He would then receive good money in change from the large bills. That plan failed, however, as Brockway was arrested before he could put the plan into action. After his last arrest in 1895, he was convicted and sentenced to ten years at the state prison in Trenton, New Jersey. He was paroled in 1904 and lived the rest of his life trouble-free. He died at the age of ninety-eight in 1920.[17]

Another counterfeiter Flynn came across while at the Ludlow Street Jail was Emanuel Ninger, "one of the most remarkable of counterfeiters" he had ever met. Ninger did not use plates and a printing press to make his bogus bills. Rather, he was a "pen-and-ink" counterfeiter, making the bills with "india ink, a camel's hair brush and a fine gold pen." His technique involved tracing the design of a genuine note and making minute alterations to improve his copy. His counterfeit notes were viewed by many as fine art and became collectibles when it was legal for people to possess counterfeit notes as long as they didn't use them.[18]

Ninger created bogus bills in denominations of $10, $20, $50, and $100 during his fourteen-year criminal career before being caught in 1896. Ninger was typical of the type of counterfeiter that gave the Secret Service headaches—a lone wolf with no accomplices to arrest and gather evidence from. The Secret Service had despaired of ever catching the mysterious man who was passing the seemingly perfect counterfeit notes that were fooling everybody. He was apprehended only because he got careless one day in passing bills that he had not allowed to dry properly or that used a new type of ink that was not waterproof. When the ink smeared on the bills, first in a New York City grocery store when a cashier's hands were wet and then in a downtown saloon where Ninger laid a bill down on a wet bar, the police were notified, and he was arrested and sent to the Ludlow Street Jail. He pleaded guilty and was sentenced to six years in prison in the Erie County Penitentiary. He had been facing a fifteen-year sentence for his crimes, but his lawyer successfully argued before the judge for a reduced sentence, claiming that Ninger was almost blind due to straining his eyes for so long to make the counterfeit notes.[19]

Flynn met several other counterfeiters while working at the Ludlow Street Jail. By 1897, he felt he had learned enough about counterfeiting to apply again for a job with the Secret Service. "They [the counterfeiters] told me their stories and explained their methods," Flynn would later say in a newspaper interview. "When I thought I was fairly competent to match my wit against theirs I went to my Congressman, and he helped me with the appointment."[20]

Flynn began working at the New York office of the service early in 1897. He couldn't have been happier. After years of persistence, he was finally on the career path he'd dreamed about as a child. "Bill Flynn of Forty-First Street" was now a Secret Service man.

THE SECRET SERVICE

If you mention the words "Secret Service" to most Americans, the image that comes to mind is that of men in dark suits wearing sunglasses, their guns hidden, looking suspiciously all around as they protect the president of the United States. Yet when the Secret Service was created by Congress in July 1865, presidential protection was not one of its responsibilities. Even though just a few months earlier President Abraham Lincoln had been assassinated by John Wilkes Booth, a special agency to protect the president was not deemed necessary. That function continued to be provided by a few local police officers who shadowed the president when he went out in public.[21]

It was not until 1901, after another president, William McKinley, was assassinated, that Congress gave the Secret Service responsibility for protecting the president. It took five more years before Congress allocated funds for the role. But even after that, most of the service's resources continued to be devoted to another task—namely, protecting the currency of the United States. Launching a war on counterfeiting was the reason for the creation of the Secret Service in the first place at the end of the Civil War, when approximately one-third of all currency in circulation was counterfeit. That undermined confidence in the U.S. dollar and financial system. It took several more decades after McKinley's assassination for the task of protecting the president to grow to the level of importance within the Secret Service that it has today.[22]

Before the Secret Service was formed, the task of identifying and arresting counterfeiters was the responsibility of the U.S. Marshals Service, created by the Judiciary Act of 1789. It became the first federal law enforcement agency in the United States. They continued to assist with investigations and arrests of counterfeiters even after the Secret Service was established since the service was initially a small agency staffed by just a few agents, most of whom were former private detectives.[23]

During its first year in operation, the Secret Service, with the help of the U.S. Marshals and local police officers, captured more than two hundred counterfeiters. Most of these, however, were just "shovers" (also referred to as "pushers"), individuals who knowingly passed bogus bills at stores and other places. The shovers usually made small purchases with large-denomination bills to obtain big sums of genuine money in change. The criminals who manufactured the counterfeits—the printers and the engravers—remained at large. When the Secret Service was able to reel in a major player such as Bill Brockway, who was arrested many times during his career, the person was usually given probation in exchange for turning over the engraved counterfeit plates or revealing where they were hidden. This did not sit well with the media, with the *New York Times* publishing an editorial in 1867 criticizing the practice of making deals with counterfeiters. "Why are counterfeiters thus made special exceptions to the ordinary process of punishing crime?" the *Times* editorial asked. "Can the Government punish them in no other way than by taking them into partnership? Then why not apply the same rule to other offenders? In the absence of explanations on this subject, we suggest it as a proper field for Congressional inquiry."[24]

The Secret Service nevertheless made significant progress in the war on counterfeiting over the next several decades. In 1883, it was officially recognized as a distinct organization within the Treasury Department. By the time Flynn joined the service in 1897, only $1 in every $100,000 was counterfeit, a major improvement from the early days of the service when, as noted above, one-third of all currency in circulation was counterfeit.[25]

Flynn's first assignment as a Secret Service agent was to find a counterfeiter who was producing cheaply made $5 notes. "The paper was thin and the notes were greasy—of that slickness peculiar to the bogus bill turned out by the poor workman," Flynn wrote. He figured he would find the manufacturer of the notes in one of the immigrant neighborhoods of New York, where the bills would be passed among foreigners not familiar with American currency or not discerning enough to tell that they were bogus. However, Flynn was summoned to Pottsville, Pennsylvania, where police had received a counterfeit $5 note from a butcher there. The butcher, who had a prosperous shop that catered to a wealthy clientele, told Flynn that the person who passed him the counterfeit note might have been a tall, well-dressed stranger who bought a pound of sausage. The only reason the butcher remembered him was that the man had stuffed the wrapped pound of sausage into his pocket instead of carrying it, which the butcher thought was unusual. But that was the only clue Flynn had to go on, and it led nowhere, so he returned to New York.[26]

Meanwhile, more of the counterfeit $5 notes were appearing in butcher shops throughout New York City. One butcher told Flynn that the day he received the bogus note, a tall, thin, well-dressed customer had bought sausage from him. Another told Flynn that he suspected the counterfeiter was the customer who seemed only interested in receiving change for his purchase of sausage since he'd seen the man throw the meat into a trash can outside the store. Flynn also discovered from his interviews with the butchers that the customer never wanted linked sausage but rather sausage that had to be stuffed into one continuous skin. Flynn realized this was to ensure that the butchers' hands would be greasy since they would have to grasp the sausages while snipping them to the correct length to stuff them into the skins. They therefore wouldn't notice the greasy, cheaply made counterfeit bills because their hands were already greasy.[27]

Flynn continued to search for the counterfeiter he called the "Sausage Man." Reports of greasy, $5 bogus bills came in from other eastern cities, including Philadelphia, Pittsburgh, Boston, and Bridgeport, Connecticut. Flynn tried to set a trap in Boston by having five butcher shops there put big displays of sausage in their windows to lure the Sausage Man to the stores. Flynn worked with two other Secret Service agents, taking up headquarters nearby and waiting for the butchers to notify them that a tall, thin, well-dressed man had paid for sausage with a $5 bill. They would then be able to hurry over to the store while the butcher kept the man there under some pretext. The other agents, like Flynn, were large, heavyset men. Flynn realized how foolish it would look if newspapers got wind of the story. "Think of the great Secret Service of the United States of America trying to trap a counterfeiter with pork sausage!" he wrote later. "We dreaded the day when the newspapers should get hold of the fact that we were trailing a sausage hound—three large and worried sleuths. We might have been laughed out of the service."[28]

The Sausage Man did not end up visiting any of the five butcher shops. Flynn then went to Altoona, Pennsylvania, after being informed that greasy, $5 counterfeit notes were being circulated there. But again, the counterfeiter proved elusive and was never found. Eventually, the greasy notes stopped appearing. "Maybe he retired to a farm and raised hogs and settled down to enjoy sausage," Flynn quipped years later.[29]

Failing to solve his first case did not hurt Flynn's career. He did well enough as a novice agent in New York to impress his superiors, and within a couple of years, he was promoted to chief agent for the Pittsburgh district. Flynn moved there in 1899 with his wife and, at the time, two young children. The Pittsburgh area was a thriving industrial and commercial center with urban slums populated by poor immigrants. There was also a large criminal population for whom counterfeiting was always a tempting livelihood, as phony bills and coins could easily fool unsuspecting immigrants.[30]

Flynn dealt with a diverse array of counterfeiters in the Pittsburgh district. It didn't matter to him whether they were small-time players passing counterfeit nickels or more sophisticated gangs opting for larger profits. He was determined to rid the district of all the counterfeiters he could find. In one case, like Richard Kimble in the classic television show and movie *The Fugitive*, Flynn was looking for a one-armed man. But unlike Kimble, who wanted a one-armed man for killing his wife, Flynn wanted his one-armed man for passing counterfeit nickels to newsboys, among others, in Pittsburgh. The counterfeiter would give a newsboy the bogus coin and receive four good pennies as change. (Newspapers only cost one cent in those days!) The newsboys told the authorities that the man who gave them the coins was missing his right arm. Flynn and other Secret Service agents and policemen set up a surveillance operation in downtown Pittsburgh, where the young boys sold their papers.[31]

For several days, the agents and police walked up and down the main streets looking for a one-armed man buying newspapers from every newsboy. One evening, Flynn and another agent spotted a one-armed man purchasing a newspaper on the street, but he was missing his left arm, not the right one, as the newsboys had reported. "That man has got the wrong arm off," Flynn said to himself, "but I'll follow him anyhow, just for luck." Flynn went up to the newsboy and examined the coin, determining immediately that it was counterfeit. He kept the coin and gave the boy a good nickel. Then he and the other agent caught up with the one-armed man, J. B. McCauley, who was walking slowly away. They arrested him and found in his possession fifty-six nickels and one quarter, all counterfeit, along with some good money. At McCauley's home, the authorities discovered used molds for the manufacture of five-cent pieces and unused molds for quarters and fifty-cent pieces.[32]

In May 1901, Flynn was again promoted, this time to agent in charge of the Secret Service's Eastern District, with headquarters in New York City (often referred to as the "New York office" or "New York District"). He had only been with the Secret Service for four years, yet he was already quickly moving up the ranks. He was a rising star but apprehensive about how his recent promotion might be viewed by others. "Here I was nothing more than a youngster in the game and I had been promoted over the heads of much older and very efficient men," he wrote. "However, they seemed to think I had the enthusiasm and natural cunning necessary and I would be a good man to try out in New York inasmuch as I knew the big city so well."[33]

The man he replaced in New York was William P. Hazen, under whom Flynn first worked when he joined the service in 1897. In contrast to Flynn's meteoric rise, Hazen had taken an equally fast career path downward. He was chief of the Secret Service from 1894 until 1898 but then was demoted to agent in charge of the New York office. Some in the Treasury Department wanted him fired outright. Hazen's trouble began when an audit of the Treasury Department revealed that he had been using, without authorization, funds and agents to provide protection for the president, a role the Secret Service had not yet been officially granted. There were also $100 counterfeit bills circulating that were so expertly made that the Treasury Department decided to recall the entire issue of that type of $100 note. Since this occurred under Hazen's watch as chief of the Secret Service, he was blamed for it. In addition, there were reports that the chief was heavily in debt.[34]

After serving for only three years in New York, Hazen was again demoted in May 1901. This time, he was ordered by Secret Service Chief John E. Wilkie to transfer to Buffalo and take charge of a new Secret Service office that was being established there. It is not clear what happened to warrant this demotion. Hazen was blindsided by the order, which came via letter to the New York office. Hazen pleaded for a reconsideration of the transfer in a letter he wrote back to Wilkie: "It comes to me as an utter surprise. I have lived here for Three [sic] years after breaking up a home in Washington, and accepting an agreement with the Hon. Secretary to come to New York, leaving the position of Chief. I at present am living here with my family, in a leased apartment until (Oct 1901), and if it is the final determination of the Chief to have me obey this order, I will have to place my resignation in the hands of the Hon. Secretary, rather than break up my home again and my associations here in New York City. I respectfully await the Chief's further answer as to changing my headquarters from here to Buffalo District."[35]

Hazen didn't have to wait long. Wilkie responded with a terse letter, simply stating his regrets regarding Hazen's decision not to transfer to Buffalo and ordering him to make an inventory and copies of all his files and other materials. He also sent Flynn a telegram shortly after he took over the New York office, saying that "Hazen should turn over to you the Revolver forwarded by this office. I presume he will surrender his badge and commission book on the expiration of his waiting orders, don't overlook them." Ironically, had Hazen taken the Buffalo assignment, he would have been in charge of the Secret Service in the city where just a few months later, on September 6, President William McKinley was assassinated by an anarchist, Leon Czolgosz. It was in the aftermath of that event, as noted earlier, that Congress finally gave the Secret Service the responsibility of protecting the president.[36]

The assassination of McKinley also led the new president, Theodore Roosevelt, to declare a war on anarchism. In his first State of the Union Address in December 1901, Roosevelt described anarchism as "a crime against the whole human race" and said that "all mankind should band against the anarchist." Flynn and the Secret Service, however, continued to focus on their own war on counterfeiters, whether they be anarchists, capitalists, or just basic criminals. Flynn was kept busy in New York, the counterfeit capital of the country, with its large immigrant population and urban underworld. His work pursuing counterfeiters took him around the United States as well.[37]

It also took him overseas, where he testified at the trial of a group of counterfeiters in England. The gang had been passing nearly perfect Bank of England notes for several years without any of the notes being detected as counterfeit. But when they decided to expand their activity to the United States, their troubles began. One of the members of the gang tried to pass Bank of England ten- and fifteen-pound notes for exchange in U.S. money at the State Bank on Grand Street in Manhattan in January 1902. The clerk told the man, Jacob Stern, that it would take about an hour to obtain the U.S. bills and that he should come back then. Even though the bank officials examined the notes and believed them to be genuine, they nevertheless called their foreign broker to confirm their finding. The broker declared the notes to be counterfeit, although he praised them as "a beautiful piece of work." The bank officials called the Secret Service, and when Stern returned for his money, Flynn was there to arrest him.[38]

Flynn learned the identities of two other members of the gang. He communicated that information to Scotland Yard detectives, who eventually arrested most of the counterfeiters. Several pleaded guilty. Others stood trial and were convicted. The maker of the notes received immunity for testifying against the others. Flynn traveled to London to testify at the trial, and when asked by reporters on his return to the United States how everything went, he said that he was impressed with "the celerity with which the wheels of British justice move." He could not, though, get used to the British tradition of answering questions from a judge with "Yes, m'lord" and "No, m'Lord." "'Yes, sir,' and 'No, sir,' were good enough for me," the native New Yorker said.[39]

The majority of the counterfeiters Flynn came across during his career were male. But he was always intrigued by the occasional female counterfeiter. According to Flynn, women counterfeiters were better than men at avoiding capture. "It's much harder to track a woman counterfeiter, because women criminals are more secretive than men," he wrote in a 1911 newspaper piece. "They make fewer confidants, paradoxical as that fact may seem." It was also more difficult to convict a female of counterfeiting than it was to convict a man, "partly because of the sympathy for women."[40]

One of the more notorious female counterfeiters Flynn arrested was Stella Frauto. She was the leader of a group of twenty counterfeiters who were responsible for at least 75 percent of molded counterfeit coins circulated in New York in the early 1900s. In May 1902, Flynn traced the bogus coins to Frauto, an Italian immigrant who had been convicted years earlier in both Italy and then the United States of similar activity. After learning that Frauto's group was producing the coins at a plant in Hackensack, New Jersey, Flynn and several other agents raided the plant. They arrested two people who were there and retrieved the equipment used to make the coins. The raid led to information regarding the whereabouts of the rest of the gang, including Frauto, who was arrested soon afterward. Two other members, Salvatore Clemente (Stella's husband) and Andrea Romano, managed to escape before they could be apprehended.[41]

Frauto had designed a clever plan in which her husband's eighty-two-year-old mother, who likely didn't arouse suspicion due to her age, took the bogus coins frequently from Hackensack, where they were made, to a barber shop in New York City that was owned by Clemente and another man. From there, the coins were carried to a saloon owned by Romano, where they were sold to shovers at thirty-five cents on the dollar.[42]

Flynn eventually tracked Clemente to Toronto and Romano to Niagara Falls. Both men were arrested. Clemente, who was running a counterfeit operation in Toronto, was turned over to the Canadian authorities. Flynn was elated by these arrests. "At last we have run to earth the remaining members of the Stella Frauto band of counterfeiters," he told reporters.[43]

Flynn was wrong, however, in assuming he had heard the last of the Frauto gang. One of its members would resurface years later and play a surprising and important role in Flynn's battles against the Mafia. But his pursuit of the Frauto gang was further indication of what would be the trademarks of his long career. "He had identified twenty counterfeiters," historian Thomas Hunt notes, "and he did not rest until twenty were in custody. He had been required to deal with police agencies in two U.S. states [New Jersey and New York], numerous local communities and a Canadian province, and to lead raids from New Jersey to Niagara Falls. He never lost his focus."[44]

By the beginning of 1903, Flynn was well established and respected in his job as head of the Eastern District for the Secret Service. He was building a reputation for honesty and hard work. He had cracked some difficult cases and made arrests of major players in the counterfeit business. But one of his biggest challenges lay ahead, and it would involve not just counterfeiting but also extortion, robbery, and murder. Flynn was about to do battle with the first Mafia family in America. It would be a battle that would consume him for the rest of the decade.

CHAPTER TWO

Bringing Down the Godfather

SAY THE NAME "CORLEONE" TO MOVIE BUFFS, AND THEY WILL THINK OF just one thing: *The Godfather*. In that iconic film, Vito Corleone, played by Marlon Brando, was the godfather (i.e., leader/boss) of the fictional Corleone crime family. His last name was taken from the town in Sicily, Italy, where he was born. Although the movie, based on the novel with the same title by Mario Puzo, is fictional, the town of Corleone is very real. And it has a long history of Mafia activity.

Situated on high, rocky ground along the main road from the Sicilian capital of Palermo to the southern port of Agrigento, Corleone was once a fortress town built with narrow streets to guard the route to the coast. The town's name translates in English to "Lionheart." Its strategic location gave it an influential role in trade and communication in Sicily, an island in the Mediterranean Sea between North Africa and the Italian mainland. However, Corleone was also vulnerable to criminals since it was located next to the Ficuzza forest, the largest wooded area on the island that became a favorite hiding place for bandits.[1]

Crime was rampant in Corleone, with many men choosing that life over one of toiling for little pay in poor working conditions as laborers on the estates of the wealthy residents of the town. Murder was a common occurrence, facilitated by the narrow, winding streets and a maze of alleyways that aided in the escape of perpetrators and made pursuit of them difficult. It was not just Corleone that was plagued by crime. Other towns and cities in Sicily also experienced criminal activity. By the nineteenth century, small private armies known as "mafie" exploited the violent and chaotic conditions on the island by extorting protection money from the landowners. The Sicilian Mafia was thus born "as a collection of criminal clans or families."[2]

One of these called themselves the "Fratuzzi of Corleone," or the "Brotherhood of Corleone." It was founded in 1884 by Luca Patti, who recruited others to his gang until it grew to forty members over the next five years and became the largest Mafia group in Sicily. Like other similar groups, it would eventually be known as a "family," comprised of "a leader, advisers and lieutenants, and a larger group of ambitious minor thugs to carry out his [the leader's] orders." Not surprisingly, there was internal strife within the Corleone Fratuzzi, as there would be in subsequent Mafia families in both Italy and America, as rivals challenged one another for leadership of the group.[3]

One of the members of the Corleone Fratuzzi was Giuseppe Morello, a young man with a deformed right hand. A birth defect had left him with only an elongated pinky finger that was bent downward like a claw. Having to use his left hand, however, was an asset for somebody who was destined for a life of crime and wanted to evoke fear among all who came in contact with him. According to Italian superstitions, left-handedness was equated with evil and considered "the hand of the devil." Morello's physical deformity earned him the nickname "the Clutch Hand." He learned about the life of a mafioso at an early age from his stepfather, Bernardo Terranova, who was also a member of the Corleone Fratuzzi. Morello rose rapidly in the ranks of the organization, becoming a lieutenant by the age of twenty-two. He was intelligent, literate, and a fine organizer. He was also cunning and ruthless.[4]

In 1889, Morello's boss, Paolino Streva, ordered him to murder Giovanni Vella, an incorruptible police officer who was about to arrest Streva for cattle rustling, a major and lucrative activity of the Corleone Fratuzzi. Morello and another mafioso dutifully obliged, shooting Vella as he walked home one night. A witness told police that he saw Morello hide a gun under a pile of garbage in the area where Streva was shot. The police found the gun, a large-caliber revolver, and determined it had been recently fired. They then arrested Morello. He was soon released on bail,

though, after the gun, the main evidence against him, mysteriously disappeared from the police lockup, likely the work of a bribed policeman.[5]

But Morello had a more serious problem. Another witness, Anna Di
Puma, who was a neighbor of Vella's, recognized Morello as one of two
men who had been standing in the area before Vella was killed. After she
heard the shots, she ran there and found Vella mortally wounded. She
then made the mistake of telling her friends what she'd seen and how she
would be willing to speak with the police and testify in court. It didn't
take long for Morello and Streva to learn about Di Puma's intentions.
The poor woman was soon after shot in the back by an unknown assailant
as she sat on the front steps of a friend's house.[6]

With no witnesses left willing to testify against him for the Vella
murder, Morello was no longer in danger of having to stand trial for the
killing. The Corleone Mafia fixed it so that a political opponent of Vella's,
Francesco Ortoleva, was framed for his murder. (Ortoleva was convicted
and sentenced to life in prison.) Morello was, however, arrested for the Di
Puma murder since he was the main beneficiary of her death. But since
there were no witnesses to that murder (or at least no one willing to come
forward and talk with the police), Morello was let go.[7]

Perhaps leery of killing again and getting caught, he decided it was
time to turn to a new business venture: counterfeiting. Making and
distributing bogus money was attractive to Morello and his Mafia associates because counterfeiting was not at that time a federal offense in
Italy. Therefore, the job of preventing it was the responsibility of small-
town police officials, who were not equipped to deal with this type of
sophisticated crime. Despite this, Morello's operation lasted for only a
few years. In 1892, the Corleone police issued a warrant for his arrest on
counterfeiting and fraud charges. Not wanting to take his chances with
a trial, Morello fled Sicily for the United States, settling in New York
around September of that year. The Italian authorities tried and convicted
Morello in absentia two years later and sentenced him to six years in
solitary confinement.[8]

The conviction and prison sentence in Italy didn't worry Morello.
There was little chance that U.S. authorities would learn about it and
deport him. Communication between American and Sicilian law

enforcement agencies at that time was basically nonexistent. Furthermore, an immigrant was immune to deportation after three years in the United States. All Morello had to do during that time was not get in trouble. He therefore resisted at first any temptation to resume a life of crime in his new country, instead working with his stepfather (who came to America in March 1893 along with Morello's wife and child, mother, sister, half sister, and three half brothers) at legitimate jobs, including plastering (despite his deformed hand).[9]

Employment, though, was temporary, and like most recent immigrants in New York, the Morello–Terranova family had a difficult time making ends meet. To make matters worse, the economic depression of 1893, whose impact on industry and employment "was on a par with the Great Depression of the 1930s," led to despair throughout the country. Unemployment in New York reached 25 percent by the end of the year.[10]

Morello decided to move to Louisiana, where relatives and friends from Corleone lived, in search of work. The rest of his large family soon followed him there. His first job was selling lemons from a bag he carried on his back. Then he and his stepfather worked on a sugarcane plantation. After about a year, the family moved to Texas, where they found employment planting and picking cotton. They stayed there for two years but returned to New York in 1897 after every member of the family became ill with malaria. Morello's wife, Maria, died one year later. He remarried in 1903 and would remain with his new wife, Nicolina, for the rest of his life.[11]

Having saved about $500 from his earnings in Louisiana and Texas, Morello purchased a coal basement in Little Italy, an area in Lower Manhattan where many Italian immigrants lived. That business, however, failed within a year. He then tried several other ventures, including operating a date factory and two saloons. Those also failed and had to be closed or sold. Realizing that he would never make it as an honest businessman in America, Morello returned to a life of crime beginning in 1899. He picked up where he left off in Corleone, starting with a counterfeit money operation and expanding to extortion, blackmail, and murder.[12]

Morello tapped into the large community of exiled criminals from Corleone that he knew from the old country who were living in all parts of the United States, including Kansas City, New Orleans, Seattle, and New York. He installed a small printing press in an apartment in an area in Upper Manhattan known as Italian Harlem and began making $2 and $5 counterfeit bills. He then hired Italian and Irish workers to seek out buyers in New York City for the phony money at a discount of 60 percent. After several of Morello's men were arrested in 1900, one of them informed on Morello, stating that he was the mastermind of the counterfeiting operation. Morello was arrested, but nobody else would betray him when they all appeared in court. Charges were therefore dropped against Morello (the authorities also could not find the printing press), but the others in his group all received prison sentences.[13]

Morello continued to build his criminal network from his base in East Harlem and benefited when Vito Cascio Ferro, an influential Sicilian mobster, came to New York in September 1901. At that time, there were other Mafia families scattered across the country, but Ferro helped "unite them into a national network with Morello installed as boss of bosses to oversee operations and resolve any disputes." Ferro stayed in the United States for a while and was arrested in May 1902 along with a group of counterfeiters but was never prosecuted. He went back to Sicily about a year later after being suspected of involvement in a murder in New York.[14]

One of the most important additions Morello made to his organization was bringing in Ignazio Lupo ("Lupo the Wolf"). Lupo became not only a member of the crime family but also a part of Morello's actual family when he married Morello's half sister, Salvatrice, in 1903. He was Morello's most trusted associate and involved in a wide range of criminal activity. "I give you my word," William Flynn would later write, "Lupo needed only to touch you to give you the feeling that you had been poisoned."[15]

Lupo the Wolf was ten years younger than Morello. He was born in Palermo in March 1877, the son of Rocco Lupo and Onofria Saietta. He grew up in a middle-class family with three brothers and one sister. He enjoyed a comfortable life, thanks in part to his family's ties to the Palermo Mafia, which gave them influence in the city. His life of crime started early when he was still just a young boy. First, it was crimes such as simple robbery and theft. But then, at the age of eighteen, he shot and killed Salvatore Morello (no relation to the Clutch Hand) while working at a clothing and dry goods store that his father had bought for him in Palermo. Lupo claimed that Morello had come at him with a knife during an argument and that he'd shot him in self-defense.[16]

Charges were filed against the teenager, but before he could be arrested, his parents helped him flee Palermo. Lupo first went to Liverpool, where he sold fruit for about three or four months. Business wasn't good, however, so he moved to Montreal. He stayed there for only a month and then went to live with relatives in Buffalo. He eventually moved to New York City, arriving in 1898. A year later, based on the testimony of clerks who'd worked for him at his store in Palermo, Lupo was tried and convicted in absentia "of a deliberate and willful murder" and sentenced to twenty-one years in prison. Lupo would later claim that he was never even aware of that conviction and sentence from the Italian court.[17]

Lupo started several businesses during his first few years in New York. One was with a cousin on the Upper East Side, where his relative would tend the store while Lupo went outside selling merchandise and trying to attract customers. However, after a falling-out with his cousin, he moved to Brooklyn and became an importer of oil, cheese, and wine from Italy. He then went back to Manhattan in 1901 and opened a wholesale grocery store in Little Italy. That business grew, and he soon owned several retail stores. He also owned an import store and ran a saloon across the street. Morello owned a restaurant in the back of this building. Lupo was a smart businessman but also a counterfeiter, extortionist, blackmailer, and murderer. He built his own criminal network and preyed on Italian immigrants in Little Italy. He eventually merged his criminal organization with Morello's, giving birth to the Morello–Lupo gang.[18]

Among the group's terror tactics was sending threatening letters to local, wealthy Italian businessmen, extorting money in exchange for not doing harm to their businesses or to them and their families. These came to be known as "Black Hand" letters because each note had a black hand symbol drawn on it, interpreted as "pay or die." The symbols varied in design, from an open hand to a closed fist or a hand grasping a knife. Most recipients of these letters didn't hesitate to pay. Those who did hesitate or refused to pay suffered the consequences. In one case, a butcher received a Black Hand letter demanding $1,000. He was instructed to place the money inside a loaf of bread and give it to a man who would come to his store the next day, raising a red handkerchief. The butcher refused. A couple of days later, he was shot dead by two men in his shop.[19]

In another case, reminiscent of the famous scene in *The Godfather* where a Hollywood film producer would not give a role in his movie to a singer who was close to the Corleone family and woke up to his favorite horse's bloodied head next to him in bed, Morello and Lupo targeted an Italian who owned a stable with several excellent horses. These horses were rented out daily to contractors and others who needed strong work-horses. The Black Hand letter that Morello and Lupo sent demanded $500, or the stable owner would find some of his horses dead. He refused, and a couple of weeks later, one of the gang's men went into action. He stood across the street from two of the stable owner's horses that were attached to a wagon parked outside a Lower East Side store. The mafioso told a boy who was walking down the street that the horses liked apples and asked if he'd like to give half an apple to each horse. The boy said yes and ran across the street to feed the horses. A few minutes later, the driver came out of the store and started to drive away, but after just four blocks, the horses collapsed and died. They had eaten a poisoned apple.[20]

Morello and Lupo did not come up with the idea for Black Hand letters. These had been used many years before by the Mafia in Sicily. And when they started appearing in many different cities in the United States, a myth arose that there was a central organization, a "Society of Black Handers," terrorizing innocent people. Newspapers tended to attribute the term "Black Hand" to any crime committed by an Italian. The *San Francisco Call* reported in 1905 that there were thirty thousand members of the organization stationed in a dozen cities. The public, however, was more fascinated by than fearful of this society. After all, it was Italian immigrant criminals targeting other Italian immigrants and not, for the most part, anybody else. Adding to the public's intrigue was that some of the letters, as reported and reproduced by the media, showed, in addition to the Black Hand symbol, "crude drawings of skulls, revolvers and knives dripping with blood or piercing human hearts." The Black Hand letters reinforced the general public perception of Italian immigrants as uncivilized and not worthy of living in America.[21]

Although Morello and Lupo didn't initiate the practice of sending Black Hand letters, they nevertheless added some innovations to the extortion method, which was also being used by ordinary criminals for their own personal gain. After mailing a Black Hand letter to a merchant, Morello would wait near the victim's store and watch as the mailman delivered the letter. Then, as the victim was reading it, Morello would appear in the store and see the alarm on the merchant's face. He would ask the poor man what the problem was, and the merchant, knowing that Morello was a high-ranking Mafia member, would show him the letter. The merchant would beg him to find out who sent it and negotiate a lower price to ensure that his store would not be bombed or he and his family killed. Morello would take the letter (thus eliminating any possibility that the merchant could go to the police with it and the letter then possibly be traced back to Morello) and tell the merchant that he'd see what he could do. Morello would then come back in a few days and tell the merchant he had some good news. He had been able to locate the sender of the Black Hand letter and had reasoned with him to obtain a reduced monetary demand. The merchant was then quite content to give Morello the money to deliver to the Black Hander and thus end the matter, never suspecting that he had just himself paid the extortionist.[22]

While Morello and Lupo were building their criminal enterprise, another man was building his reputation on the other side of the law. The Mafia didn't know it yet, but they were about to meet their nemesis, a man who would not rest until he brought them to justice.

ENTER THE BULLDOG

William Flynn had only recently assumed his position as head of the New York office of the Secret Service when Morello and Lupo began terrorizing and exploiting their fellow Italian immigrants in Little Italy and elsewhere. According to Flynn, they made a good team. "Morello was the rough, bearish and hairy-looking monster, cruel as a fiend, and always unshaven," Flynn wrote, while "Lupo was the well dressed, soft-spoken, slick-looking 'gent' of pretended refinement. He, too, was cruel and heartless. Lupo was the business man of the two. Morello had in his make-up more of the cunning of the born criminal. He was cautious like the fox and ferocious like a maddened bull."[23]

In 1902, Flynn and the Secret Service noticed a flood of counterfeit $5 bills appearing in New York. What was new was that these bills were not American-made. An analysis of the paper and inks indicated that they had been manufactured in Italy and smuggled into the United States. The shovers of these bills were known associates of Morello and Lupo. But the Secret Service was baffled as to how the counterfeit money had gotten through customs.[24]

It turned out that Morello was using Lupo's import business, which included olive oil, to smuggle in the bogus bills. Morello would send the printing plates to Italy, where he figured the counterfeit money could be made without the Secret Service knowing about it. He would then arrange to have the bills stuffed inside the empty cans that always accompanied the larger barrels of imported olive oil. The usual procedure was that an importer would pour the large barrels of olive oil into the smaller cans so they could be sold to customers in various stores. Since these shipments were not carefully inspected by customs at the New York City piers, Morello and Lupo had devised a clever scheme.[25]

But the Secret Service, working with the Bureau of Customs, eventually figured it out, but not before more than $10,000 in counterfeit bills found its way into New York and was then distributed in Manhattan, Pittsburgh, Yonkers, and other cities. A raid of Morello's restaurant uncovered some of the cans stuffed with phony $5 bills. Morello and several accomplices (but apparently not Lupo) were arrested and brought to trial. The jury, however, decided the evidence was not strong enough to link Morello to the counterfeit money. "He was the only one of the gang which I had arrested who had escaped conviction," a frustrated Flynn wrote.[26]

Having once again escaped being sent to prison, Morello felt confident he could continue to evade the law no matter what he did. He was crafty and had loyal and scared followers who knew that if they gave any information to the authorities about his criminal enterprises and activities, they would wind up dead. His own men would be killed if they talked to friends or other people about their connection to Morello and his illegal operations. And the godfather would make sure it was a grisly enough murder to send a message to everybody else in the organization.

That is what happened to Giuseppe "Joe the Grocer" Catania. The Brooklyn grocer, a member of Morello and Lupo's counterfeit ring, tended to drink too much and, when drunk, not keep quiet. Morello learned that Catania, while drunk, had revealed to others his association with the counterfeiting operation. Morello decreed that Catania had to go. The last person seen with him before his murder in the summer of 1902 was Lupo, but the authorities could not conclusively link him to the crime. Other leads went nowhere, and the investigation was eventually ended. Catania's body was discovered by two boys swimming in the East River. They noticed two potato sacks on the shore. Hoping they might contain something valuable, the boys opened them and to their horror found in one sack blood-soaked clothes and in the other Catania's body, his throat cut from ear to ear, his head nearly decapitated. Leaving the body in an open area where it was sure to be discovered was what Morello intended. He had sent his message: "Weakness and lack of discipline meant inevitable death."[27]

That Morello and Lupo again avoided having to pay for their crimes upset Flynn. Although he strongly suspected that they were responsible for the Catania killing, his hands were tied because it wasn't his responsibility to investigate homicides. The Secret Service went after counterfeiters and had to leave the job of pursuing murderers to the police. But if he could get Morello and Lupo on counterfeiting charges, then he could at least put the mobsters away in prison for a while. But catching the leaders of the organization was proving difficult. Morello and Lupo were careful and usually covered their tracks, having others risk arrest by passing around the counterfeit bills. Flynn's dilemma was how to break the members' code of silence and their dreaded fear of their leaders the next time some of the Morello–Lupo gang were arrested. Flynn had an idea, and he put it into practice early in 1903.

On December 31, 1902, several members of the Morello–Lupo organization were arrested in Yonkers, New York, as they were passing around counterfeit $5 bills. The bogus money displayed the imprint of the National Iron Bank of Morristown, New Jersey. The case therefore became known as "The Morristown Fives." Flynn and the Secret Service discovered that these notes had been imported from Italy as part of Morello and Lupo's scheme of having counterfeit money printed overseas and then shipped to New York.[28]

When the Yonkers police brought the suspects to Flynn's office in New York, he recognized them as members of the Morello–Lupo gang. (Their photos and information were already in the Secret Service files.) He then put his scheme into operation. He tried to work two of the counterfeiters, Giuseppe DePriema and Isadoro Crocervera, against each other in the hope of implicating Morello and Lupo:

> When Crocervera and DePriema were brought to my offices I knew in advance that neither of them would talk, having had the characteristics of the men recorded long before they were arrested. However, in order to give Crocervera the impression that DePriema had told me a lot of the workings of the gang, I hit upon the idea of keeping DePriema in my inner office for several hours while Crocervera remained in an outer office. I was timing my effort for a purpose. As DePriema was leaving, I stepped to the door with him and shook his hand warmly and patted him on the back in order that Crocervera, seeing the performance, might gain the impression that DePriema had confessed all he knew about the gang. Naturally, the object of this move was to tempt Crocervera to talk and give information important to the government.[29]

Crocervera didn't talk, but when another suspect in the Morristown Fives case was subsequently arrested, Morello's outfit was convinced that DePriema had indeed betrayed the organization. DePriema would have to pay for this with his life. Morello, however, faced a problem. DePriema was now in the Sing Sing maximum-security prison in Ossining, New York, about thirty miles north of Manhattan, after being convicted of the Yonkers crime. Realizing it would be too difficult to breach security there, Morello followed the Sicilian custom of selecting a blood relative for revenge. But as DePriema had no blood relatives in the United States, the Mafia instead chose the next closest relative, his brother-in-law, Benedetto Madonia.[30]

Madonia, also a member of the Morello–Lupo counterfeit operation, lived in Buffalo and was unaware that a death sentence had been imposed on him. He apparently was also unaware of the suspicions the Mafia had that his brother-in-law had betrayed the organization. Otherwise, he surely wouldn't have gone to New York to seek Morello's help in getting DePriema transferred from Sing Sing to a prison closer to Buffalo. He also had a dispute with Morello over money that he wanted to resolve. The godfather was only too willing to have a sit-down with Madonia at his restaurant in Little Italy. It would be Madonia's last meal on earth.[31]

Morello's restaurant was a dingy, windowless room in the back of Lupo's tavern on Prince Street. It consisted of a single stove; an old, rusted sink; several tables and chairs; and a floor strewn with cedar sawdust. Past three in the morning on April 14, 1903, Madonia was sitting at one of the tables, eating a plate of beans, beets, and potatoes. Morello hadn't shown up yet. There were a few members of the organization present, standing against a wall and talking with each other in low voices that Madonia couldn't hear. Madonia had just finished his meal when another group of people entered the room. Madonia recognized two of them. One was Tommaso Petto, nicknamed "the Ox" for his strong build. The other was Morello. The sight of Morello made everybody in the room nervous. Nobody made eye contact with him.[32]

The Clutch Hand gestured with his good left hand, and two of his men sprang into action. They picked up Madonia by the arms and held him as he tried in vain to fight them off. Morello then approached him and made another gesture, signaling the men holding Madonia to drag him across the room to the sink. Madonia's head was pulled back by the hair as a third man thrust a fourteen-inch-long stiletto dagger into his throat. Madonia collapsed, but the mobsters picked him up again as Petto the Ox, his own knife in hand, moved closer to the doomed man and with one forceful swipe severed Madonia's throat and jugular vein, almost beheading him.[33]

Morello wanted the mutilated body of Madonia to be found. Otherwise, the message to all who might betray him would be lost. Similar to leaving the body of Giuseppe Catania in a potato sack on the shores of the East River, this time Morello decided to leave the body right in the middle of a street in Little Italy. And instead of a potato sack, Madonia was stuffed into a three-foot barrel. Morello's men, however, couldn't get the entire body to fit. One arm and a leg protruded out. So they put an old overcoat over the exposed parts and moved the barrel to a horse and wagon waiting in an alley outside the restaurant. They then rode to East 11th Street and Avenue D and left their package on the sidewalk.[34]

The first person to notice it was Frances Conners, an Irish cleaning woman, as she walked to a nearby bakery to buy breakfast rolls. It was around five thirty on a drizzly morning. Her curiosity getting the better of her, Conners lifted the overcoat from the barrel and then let out a terrifying scream that woke up the entire neighborhood. A crowd immediately ran to the scene and was horrified by the sight of Madonia's arm and leg hanging over the barrel and the dead man's nearly decapitated head, covered with blood and sawdust, clearly visible to them. Some of the women joined Conners in screaming hysterically.[35]

A policeman arrived and rolled the barrel over to pull the body out. He blasted his whistle, and several more policemen came to lend assistance. By 6:15 a.m., the crowd around the barrel had grown so large that a squad of police reserves from nearby station houses was needed to keep the curious onlookers away from the body. It wasn't long before newspaper reporters appeared, eager to get details and photographs of what promised to be a sensational story. While murders were common in New York, like in other large cities, not every day was a body with a nearly severed head found in the street, stuffed inside a barrel. Newspapers throughout the country quickly labeled this the "Barrel Murder Mystery," as the identity of the victim was not yet known.[36]

Solving the crime became a top priority for the NYPD. Thousands of officers were immediately put on the case. Nobody could "remember a time when so great a proportion of police resources had been devoted to a single case." Informants were questioned, and "every nook and corner of New York [was scoured] in an effort to learn, first of all, the identity of the victim." The coroner's surgeon even allowed a photographer from the *Evening Journal*, a popular newspaper in the immigrant community in

New York, to take a picture of the body as it lay on a slab in the morgue. The authorities were hoping somebody would recognize the face.[37]

Since this was a murder and not a counterfeit case, there was no reason for the police to bring in the Secret Service to help in the investigation. William Flynn therefore arrived at his office at nine that morning, unaware of what had transpired earlier on East 11th Street. It looked to him like this was going to be another routine day, following up on leads about counterfeiters in New York and the surrounding areas. He and his men had been watching Morello and his associates and had noticed a stranger standing under a lamppost while members of the group met inside a butcher shop in Little Italy on the evening of April 12. Flynn knew by sight most of the members of the local Mafia, but he didn't recognize the new person. He was given the code name "#11" in the Secret Service files.[38]

It wasn't until he read about the murder in the newspapers and saw the photo of the dead man in the *Evening Journal* that Flynn thought it might be the stranger he and his men had seen with the Morello gang two nights earlier. He sent two of his agents to the morgue to confirm this, and they called him at six thirty that evening to report that the dead body indeed resembled that man. Flynn then went to the morgue later that night to make sure. "The murder was not within my province," he wrote, "yet I wanted if possible to solve it, partly for my own satisfaction, partly because every fresh fact I learned regarding the organization I was after could be used by me to advantage."[39]

Something, however, bothered Flynn. The dead man in the morgue was wearing a blue suit, while Flynn and his agents remembered him in a brown suit. He thought that perhaps it was an optical illusion that had made the blue suit appear brown. The stranger had been standing beneath a flickering streetlight, and the slanting electric light had made it difficult to make out all the details of his suit. So the ever-curious detective summoned for the dead man's clothing to be brought to his office. Flynn examined it under a light he'd rigged up over his desk to simulate the streetlight. When he shone the light down on the clothes at an angle similar to the angle of the streetlight, the suit looked brown instead of blue. Flynn was now certain that the dead man in the barrel was the man he and his men had seen the other night.[40]

He called Inspector George McClusky, head of the NYPD's Detective Bureau, who came to Flynn's office in the Treasury Building around midnight. The police were eager to learn of any clues in this sensational murder. Flynn briefed them on what the Secret Service knew about the Morello organization—the names of the mobsters, the nature of their operation, and, most important of all, that they had been observed in the company of the dead man two evenings ago. The meeting at his office ended at 1:15 a.m. "They were very much elated with the information I gave them," Flynn gleefully wrote in his daily report.[41]

Flynn could indeed be proud of himself and his agents. It looked like their countless hours of surveillance of the Morello–Lupo operation might now be paying off. If the leaders of this group could be put away with long prison sentences for murder, then their counterfeiting operation would be dealt a severe blow. Inspector McClusky was anxious to make arrests that very day (April 15), but Flynn was worried that the police were moving too soon. He felt there was not enough evidence yet to link Morello, Lupo, and others to the murder, and he also felt further investigation might yield more conclusive results that would stand up in court. Murder, however, was a police matter, and there was little he could do to dissuade the inspector from going through with his plans. The NYPD needed Flynn and his men to accompany them as they searched for the suspects since they didn't know what Morello and his gang looked like. It was left to the Secret Service agents to point them out when they spotted them in the streets or in other places in New York. McClusky wanted Morello to be the first one arrested.[42]

It promised to be dangerous work since most of the Sicilians were expected to be armed. Morello wasn't spotted until the evening when he went into a pastry store in Little Italy. McClusky and Flynn decided it would be too dangerous to arrest him there because a shootout inside or even right outside the store could result in innocent people being killed. So Flynn went to a spot on Delancey Street that he knew from prior surveillance Morello would pass on his way home. With Flynn were two of his agents and four of McClusky's detectives. When he saw Morello pass by around eight o'clock, he signaled to the detectives. Just at that moment, Tommaso Petto appeared. Flynn hadn't known that Morello would be walking home with Petto the Ox. It didn't matter, as the four burly police detectives pounced on the mobsters before they had a chance to draw their weapons. Morello was knocked to the ground, and Petto was punched between the eyes, causing him to fall too. Morello had a .45-caliber revolver and a knife tucked in the waistband of his trousers, while the Ox carried a pistol in a holster and a stiletto in a sheath. With Morello arrested, the Secret Service agents and police detectives following the other members of the group throughout the city then made their arrests. All told, eleven suspects were captured that night, including Lupo the Wolf, who was arrested at his home around midnight, the last one to be taken.[43]

All the suspects' residences were searched, but no evidence linking them to the barrel murder was uncovered. Flynn at least had hoped he would find counterfeit money or the equipment to make bogus bills and coins in some of the prisoners' dwellings, particularly those of Morello and Lupo, so he could get them on those charges, but none was found. A barrel similar to the one in which the dead man had been stuffed was discovered in a search of the basement of one of the Morello gang's hangouts. But with no smoking gun yet uncovered, the prospects for convictions of the mobsters looked dim.[44]

There was also still the mystery of who the dead man in the barrel was. The prisoners were taken to the morgue and questioned as to whether they knew him. Each feigned ignorance, with Morello shrugging his shoulders and saying, "Don't know," and another responding, "No understand." None of the prisoners would admit to having ever seen the man before. "We then hoped that relatives or friends would claim the body and thus establish the victim's identity," Flynn wrote, "but for all we could tell after days of waiting he had died without a single friend, with no relative to care whether he went to potter's field [a cemetery for poor or unidentified people] or not."[45]

Fearing he might never learn the identity of the dead man, Flynn tried one last gambit. He requested that Joseph (Giuseppe) Petrosino, the NYPD's top Italian detective, go to Sing Sing prison, where the counterfeiters arrested in January for passing the "Morristown Fives" were serving time. Petrosino brought with him a photo of the dead man and showed it to the prisoners. One of them, Giuseppe DePriema, told Petrosino that the man was his brother-in-law, Benedetto Madonia. When DePriema asked what happened to him, Petrosino replied that he was murdered. DePriema "cursed the murderers in his cell, he shook his fist against the bare walls, and he swore a vendetta against the men who had slain his relative by marriage." He told Petrosino that Madonia had lived in Buffalo and had been connected with a group of counterfeiters in New York. He described a watch chain that was found in one of Madonia's pockets and provided other information, including details of a scar on Madonia's face, to convince Petrosino that DePriema had indeed identified the barrel murder victim.[46]

Petrosino returned to New York with the good news. Flynn, however, must have realized then that his earlier ploy to make it appear that DePriema was cooperating in the counterfeiting investigation had backfired and probably gotten his brother-in-law murdered. Meanwhile, Flynn and Petrosino went to police headquarters to examine the evidence in the barrel murder case. They found a pawn ticket for a watch among the possessions of Tommaso Petto. Madonia's wife was interviewed, and she gave details of certain markings and engravings on her husband's watch that exactly matched the watch Petto had pawned.[47]

This evidence resulted in a grand jury indicting Petto for first-degree murder. He was held in the Tombs prison for several months, but his lawyer successfully argued that he be released on his own recognizance since even with the pawned watch, there was not sufficient evidence to bring him to trial with any expectation of a conviction. Petto the Ox promptly left New York, and the Secret Service traced him to Pittston, Pennsylvania, where an unknown assassin, presumed to be a blood relative of Madonia's, shot him dead in his home in October 1905. A dagger was also thrust into his heart.[48]

The case against the other suspects in the barrel murder also fell apart. A magistrate determined that there was not enough evidence to hold them on a murder charge, and they were all released. These developments clearly disappointed Flynn. He had spent endless hours tracking down the Morello–Lupo organization since becoming chief of the New York office of the Secret Service in 1901. Now, two years later, the top dogs of the group were still free. He knew, however, that he'd have more opportunities to nail Morello and Lupo because they were unlikely to voluntarily give up their life of crime. The Bulldog was determined that the next time he arrested them, he would catch them with sufficient evidence to hold up in court. Flynn was a patient man, and it didn't matter to him how long this would take. "Steady hammering," he once told a reporter. "That's my doctrine and advice. It doesn't do to drop a case under pressure of a new matter. Reserve a place for it in the back of the head. Think of it. Hammer away at it, here a little, there a little until the men you are after are either apprehended or dead."[49]

THE FEARLESS POLICEMAN

Flynn was not alone in wanting to bring down the Morello–Lupo gang. He had an important ally in the NYPD. Joseph Petrosino also wanted the mobsters apprehended or dead. Petrosino was a rarity, an Italian in the Irish-dominated NYPD. Like Flynn, he rose rapidly in his career and garnered glowing media attention. He was described by the *New York Times* as "the greatest Italian detective in the world" and became known as the "Italian Sherlock Holmes."[50]

Short of physical stature—he was only five feet, three inches tall and wore lifts in his shoes to compensate for his height—Petrosino was nevertheless built like a stevedore. He weighed nearly three hundred pounds, most of that being muscle. He had large shoulders and a thick, strong neck. His face bore the pockmarks of a childhood bout with smallpox. He projected an image of toughness, often wearing a Prince Albert coat, black suit, black shoes, and black derby hat. He was a master of disguises, a necessity for the well-recognized detective who was policing the Italian immigrant community in New York. Among his disguises were a laborer, a Catholic priest, an Orthodox Jew, a Board of Health bureaucrat, a gangster, and an organ grinder with his monkey. He sometimes spent entire days as a beggar, clad only in rags. He was so good at disguises that his friends often passed him by without recognizing him.[51]

An immigrant himself, Petrosino was born on August 30, 1860, in Padula, a village in the province of Salerno in the Campania region of southern Italy known for a famous Carthusian monastery. His father was a tailor, and his mother, who died when he was a young boy, was a housewife. He had one younger brother and one younger sister. The family grew after his father remarried and had three more children. Seeking a better life, as was true for most Italian immigrants, the Petrosinos left Italy in 1873 and arrived in New York after a twenty-five-day journey.[52]

Petrosino was enrolled in the city's public school system, where he began to learn to speak English. He also learned how to fight, as street brawls between the Irish and Italian kids were common in Lower Manhattan, where Italians were beginning to move into neighborhoods dominated by Irish immigrants. This caused resentment and anger on the part of the Irish, and the Italian schoolchildren often experienced the brunt of this hatred. "When the Italian kids emerged from the front door [of the school]," writes author Stephan Talty, "a howl rose up from the nearby tenements, echoing off the cobblestones as one Irish mother after another pulled up the sashes on their windows, leaned out, and shouted at their sons below to '*kill the dagos!*' The fair-skinned boys heard them, picked up rocks, and sent them spinning at the heads of the Italian boys and girls, who fled the school in packs. Small gangs charged at the dark-haired children and attempted to cut off the stragglers. If they cornered one, they beat him until his blood flowed."[53]

One Italian boy who never ran away was Petrosino. The other Italian children looked up to him for protection as they walked home each day after school. He would lead them into the streets, and as soon as a rock was thrown, he would charge at the perpetrator and start beating him up. He often returned home with his shirt bloodied, a sort of badge of honor. "Over time," writes Talty, "a small legend began to grow up around his name." Like many Italian immigrants, he had to quit school after the sixth grade to help support his family. He worked many different jobs, including shining shoes and being a butcher's assistant, railroad crew timekeeper, hat store worker, stock brokerage runner, and street cleaner. But he wanted to become a policeman, and since the police ran the sanitation force, the street-cleaning job provided him with an opportunity to make some contacts to hopefully fulfill that dream. He worked hard, impressed his superiors, and soon was in charge of the barge that towed the garbage out to sea, where it was dumped into the water. A police inspector was impressed with Petrosino's commanding presence and leadership skills and helped him get on the force, even though he did not meet the minimum height requirements. The police saw the potential value in having Petrosino join them—an Italian who knew the customs and dialects of the growing Italian population in Lower Manhattan.[54]

On October 19, 1883, Petrosino was given shield number 285 and officially became one of the first Italian policemen in the department. It was a proud day for the young immigrant from Padula. He probably expected some hostility and discrimination from the overwhelmingly Irish force. But it's unlikely he was prepared for what greeted him from his own people the day he left his apartment in Little Italy, proudly wearing his brand-new blue police uniform and domed felt helmet and carrying a locust wood nightstick by his side. He was the target of insults and obscenities from his neighbors, while street peddlers shouted out warnings to local criminals that a policeman was approaching. To the Italians from southern Italy and Sicily, anybody wearing a uniform represented "a corrupt and antagonistic enemy." Many (but not all) Italian immigrants believed that Petrosino, by joining the police, had betrayed them and that it signified "an extreme and deliberate affront" that would not be forgotten. He soon received death threats in the mail and was forced to move to a small apartment in an Irish neighborhood.[55]

It was a lonely time for the young bachelor, but the hostility Petrosino received from some of his countrymen did not dampen his enthusiasm for his new job. He quickly began making arrests, and despite the discrimination he would face throughout his career, he nevertheless earned a reputation in police circles "as a man of great intuition" who could easily identify criminals who'd emigrated from Italy. He eventually won over the vast majority of law-abiding Italian immigrants who were proud that one of their own was trying to protect them from the criminal element in their community, which would soon include the Morello–Lupo outfit and the numerous Black Hand extortion threats. While Petrosino caught his share of murderers, arsonists, and robbers, not all of his arrests were of hardened criminals. One in particular delighted those who read about it in the newspapers.[56]

It occurred in April 1894, when Petrosino was sent by his captain to enforce a law prohibiting, among other things, the wearing of costumes on Sundays. The statute "Crimes Against the Person and Against Public Decency and Good Morals" was known as the Sunday laws and included bans on haircuts and newspaper delivery, as well as operating telegraph offices and other businesses on a day people were expected to go to church. Petrosino's assignment was to attend a benefit at which Frederick Israel, a nineteen-year-old actor with dreams of pursuing a vaudeville career, was scheduled to perform a one-person comic song and dance routine on a Sunday evening using the stage name "Frederick Ward." It was the young actor's first gig, and he wanted to make the most of it.[57]

Israel came onto the stage wearing burnt cork makeup, a white check coat with a red waistcoat underneath, a pair of white beaver plaid trousers, a dilapidated hat, a red wig that looked like a piece of buffalo rope, and green whiskers. He also carried a large walking stick. Petrosino was sitting inconspicuously in the audience in plain clothes when he saw Israel take the stage. The weird costume at first startled him, but he then rushed down the aisle, went through the stage door, and tapped Israel on the shoulder as he was receiving his first applause of the evening. "You are my prisoner," Petrosino boomed out. "Those whiskers are against the Sunday law." Half the audience erupted in laughter and applauded Petrosino, thinking this was part of the act. The newspapers had fun with Petrosino, calling him "an Italian copper who has Thespian ambition himself" who had "dropped in as a police critic" for Israel's performance.[58]

It was when Israel was escorted off the stage that the audience realized the actor had actually been arrested. Petrosino told him he could not allow him to change out of his costume into regular clothes because the costume was evidence of Israel violating the Sunday law. Even the green whiskers had to stay. Petrosino then began walking with his prisoner down Broadway to the station house, attracting a crowd of nearly a thousand spectators along the way. They shouted a mixture of cheers and jeers for the young actor and his captor. Petrosino hailed a Sixth Avenue car and jumped aboard with Israel to avoid the throngs of people. That did not deter the crowd, which was clearly enjoying the spectacle. They ran after the car and continued to shout and cheer loudly. When Petrosino and Israel got out near the station, the crowd followed them right up to the station's doors. Reserves were called in to keep people at bay. Israel was locked in a jail cell, and all the bewildered young man could say was "I really didn't expect to arouse such a fuss. I'll know better next time."[59]

Petrosino's career was helped by an important backer: Theodore Roosevelt. The future president became head of the New York Board of Police Commissioners in 1895 and pledged to reform the police department. He wanted policemen hired on the basis of ability, not party affiliation or other types of favoritism. He took an immediate liking to Petrosino, of whom he would later say, "He didn't know the name of fear." Roosevelt promoted him (in July 1895), making him the first Italian detective sergeant in the country. Petrosino was savvy enough to keep the important relationship going, praising Roosevelt whenever he could in his dealings with reporters or with other policemen. The two men became good friends and saw each other often.[60]

With each passing year, Petrosino's legend continued to grow. He was always in the news, making arrests and garnering glowing stories. In one case, he saved an innocent man from the electric chair at the last moment by getting a confession from the real killer. In another, he came down from the skylight of a building using a rope to rescue a little boy who had been kidnapped. By the time Petrosino worked with William Flynn on the barrel murder case, he was a celebrated detective not only in the United States but in other countries as well, particularly in Italy, where stories of his exploits were reaching his home country.[61]

Like Flynn, Petrosino was not happy that the Morello–Lupo gang had gotten away with murder. And like Flynn, he also vowed to keep after them and bring them to justice no matter how long it took. He knew he couldn't continue to be a one-man police force trying to keep law and order in Little Italy. Since the Italian immigrants didn't trust the Irish cops, Petrosino wanted a special force made up of just Italian policemen to tackle crimes perpetrated by and against the Italian immigrant community.[62]

After some resistance from the top brass at the NYPD, Petrosino got his wish in September 1904, when Police Commissioner William

McAdoo told him he could have his special force, to be known as the Italian Squad, with Petrosino as its leader. That was the good news. The bad news was that there was no budget for the squad, and although Petrosino requested twenty men, he was allowed to pick only five from the ranks of the NYPD. There weren't a lot of qualified candidates to choose from, as the NYPD had approximately ten thousand policemen in 1904 but fewer than twenty could speak Italian. And of those twenty, even fewer could speak Sicilian. But it was a start, and that's all Petrosino needed to get the ball rolling.[63]

Petrosino would eventually be allowed to recruit more men, and by 1906, the Italian Squad was comprised of forty policemen. The squad's methods were brutal but effective. In what amounted to targeted harassment, they would follow Mafia members and other criminal suspects around the streets of New York and throw them up against a wall as they questioned them about their activities. They broke noses, jaws, and collarbones. Petrosino made no apologies for these actions. "If the courts send these criminals back into the streets we'll make life so tough for them that they'll have to clear out whatever way they can," he once told a reporter.[64]

In one celebrated incident (in 1908), Petrosino went mano a mano with Lupo the Wolf. Wanting to confront the mafioso over a series of recent extortion activities and threats that Lupo had made, particularly one where he told others that he was going to hurt Petrosino unless the detective left him alone, Petrosino one day walked into one of Lupo's grocery stores. He started inspecting stacks of hams and cheese and then walked over to Lupo, who was standing nearby in one of his tailored suits. Petrosino said something to him in a low voice and then punched him, causing Lupo to fall to the ground. He proceeded to give Lupo "a severe beating." There were eyewitnesses to the incident who spoke with the *New York Times*. As time went on, the story became embellished. One account claimed that in a move reminiscent of the barrel murder that Petrosino, William Flynn, and others were convinced Lupo had been a part of, Petrosino had picked up the unconscious Lupo from the ground, stuffed him in a barrel, and left it in the middle of the street.[65]

Petrosino, who had been promoted to lieutenant of the Italian Squad in November 1906, became frustrated with what he viewed as the bottomless pit of Italian criminals continually immigrating to America. "The United States," he wrote in a syndicated newspaper article in February 1908, "has become the dumping ground for all the criminals and banditti of Italy, Sicily, Sardinia, and Calabria." He called for a "Special Bureau of Inspectors," whose job would be to focus only on Italian immigrants. He also wanted Italy's cooperation with his plan. "It would be an easy thing to obtain from the Italian government a description and record of all criminals who are suspected of having left for America," he wrote, "and with the aid of this the inspectors could prevent a great many of these men from ever entering the country." To highlight the importance of this, he put the above passages in capital letters.[66]

NYPD Commissioner Theodore Bingham liked Petrosino's ideas and took them even further. He created a secret police force early in January 1909 and put Petrosino in charge. This squad was to be made up of only half a dozen men "whose identities would be known only to the commissioner and would never testify in court." Bingham would pay their salaries out of a secret fund, and they would report only to him. For one of its first missions, Bingham wanted Petrosino to travel to the lion's den in Sicily with three objectives. First, he was to check judicial records for anyone who had served time in Italy and then immigrated to the United States. These former prisoners could be deported back to Italy if they had been in the United States for less than three years. Second, Petrosino was to gather the names of the most dangerous criminals currently incarcerated in Italy. This would enable U.S. immigration inspectors at Ellis Island to turn them away if they tried to enter the country after being released from prison. And third, Bingham wanted Petrosino to establish a spy network in Italy of trusted local agents who could continuously feed the NYPD the names of any Italian criminals, whether or not they had served time in prison, who were attempting to immigrate to the United States.[67]

It was, to say the least, a dangerous mission for any law enforcement official. But it would be particularly risky for Petrosino, enemy number one to the numerous Italian criminals he had put away. Many had friends and relatives back in the old country, and some of the criminals had already returned there either via deportation or simply leaving the United States to go home. Petrosino also had just recently humiliated Lupo the Wolf, giving him a beating in his own store in front of other people. Since the Morello–Lupo gang had ties with the Mafia in Sicily, if word got out about this secret mission, Petrosino's life would be in jeopardy. It would probably be easier to catch Petrosino by surprise and assassinate him there than in New York. Petrosino didn't know the streets and criminals of Sicily like he knew those of Manhattan. Furthermore, Petrosino was so famous that any disguise he might try to use to keep his identity secret would probably not work since his face was as recognizable in Italy as it was in the United States.[68]

How, though, could Petrosino say no to Bingham? His life's work involved tracking down Italian criminals victimizing fellow immigrants in America, and now he had a chance to make some significant progress in the battle against them. It would also not look good if it became known that the tough detective, who had preached to others to stand up to criminals, would not go to Sicily because of personal risks. But if there were ever a time in his life when he should have placed his personal life over his professional one, this was it. After a lifetime of loneliness, at the age of forty-seven in January 1908, he married Adelina Saulino, the daughter of the owner of an Italian restaurant he frequented. They had their first child, a girl, also named Adelina, that November. He was happy for the first time in his life. He would rush home after work to be with his wife and play with the baby. Always a lover of opera, he would have musicians drop by his apartment after dinner to play some of his favorite arias. But he was soon going to leave all of this behind as he prepared for his dangerous mission.[69]

Petrosino was scheduled to be in Italy for around three months to carry out his work. Those he told about his impending trip begged him not to go. One of the priests at St. Patrick's Cathedral, where he had been married, said to him, "Do not go to Italy because I am afraid you will not return." Petrosino replied, "Probably not, but it is my duty, and I am going." Clearly aware of the risks he faced, Petrosino signed over power of attorney to his wife so she could control his affairs in the event of his death and collect his remaining salary. A fellow detective who went to the pier to see him off warned him of the risks he would be facing in Sicily. "Watch out boss," he said. "Down there, everything's Mafia."[70]

On February 9, 1909, Petrosino (using the alias Simone Velletri) set sail for Genoa, Italy, on the steamship *Duca di Genova*. His cover story to anybody inquiring was that he was a businessman. He was not, however, in disguise, and the ship's purser recognized him from his numerous photos in newspapers. He was excited to meet the famous detective and told him not to worry, that he would keep his identity a secret. "You can rely on my discretion," he told him. Petrosino did not seem worried at all. In fact, he spent several hours talking with the purser about some of his most memorable cases.[71]

It is not clear why Petrosino was so careless, but perhaps once on board the ship, he decided not to worry about his identity and felt he would be able to take care of himself. What he didn't know then was that his secret mission had already been revealed in the newspapers. By the time he arrived in Genoa on February 21, there had been stories the day before published in the *New York Times*, *New York Sun*, *New York Herald*, and other outlets, including the Italian American paper *L'Araldo Italiano*, regarding the secret police force Bingham had formed with Petrosino as its head and hints that the detective was on his way to Sicily on a special mission. When reporters asked Bingham where Petrosino was, since he had not been seen in New York for some time, the commissioner glibly replied, "Why, he may be on the ocean, bound for Europe, for all I know." The *New York Times* article also revealed that the paper had learned from a source "that a part of Petrosino's work is to study conditions here and in Italy, with especial reference to the Black Hand methods. The Italian Government has expressed its willingness to aid in every way the efforts of the New York Police Department in running down men who have been blackmailing wealthy Italians here at various times." The article stated that Bingham had given Petrosino the general orders, "Go ahead and wipe out the blackmailers."[72]

Petrosino took a train from Genoa to Rome, where he met with Italian government and police officials. He also went to Padula to visit his brother. He then took a train to Naples and from there a boat to Palermo, where he arrived on February 28. For the next two weeks, he went about his mission, gathering copies of penal certificates from the Palermo courthouse and from records offices in nearby towns. He compared the names on those certificates to a list of criminals living in New York that he'd brought with him to Italy. He obtained hundreds of such certificates and sent them back to Bingham to begin working on deportation procedures. He also started disbursing money from his secret police fund to build up a network of local informants who would remain in Sicily and regularly report back to him and the NYPD once he returned home. While taking some steps to ensure his safety, such as checking into a hotel under an alias and wearing a disguise when he went outside of Palermo to gather records, he made several foolish mistakes. These included opening a bank account in Palermo in his own name and revealing his true identity to waiters at the Café Oreto, where he regularly had dinner. He even began walking around Palermo without his gun.[73]

The police commissioner of Palermo, Baldassare Ceola, offered to supply Petrosino with a bodyguard, feeling it would be too dangerous for the detective to wander around town alone. Petrosino refused, telling Ceola that the presence of a policeman would hamper his meetings with informants who didn't trust the police. Many would refuse to meet with him if a policeman were present. He also said that he had friends in Palermo who would protect him. It may also have been hubris that explains Petrosino's refusal to have a bodyguard. He was the great American detective who always liked to project an image of invincibility in his dealings with criminals. The last thing he perhaps wanted known was that he couldn't take care of himself and needed a foreign policeman to escort him around town.[74]

Petrosino was making progress on his trip when, after a brief thunderstorm on March 12, he walked from his hotel to the Café Oreto around seven thirty in the evening. He sat at his usual place in the restaurant, a corner table, with his back to the wall so nobody could attack him from behind. There are differing accounts as to what happened next. According to one, two men, whom the waiters could not identify, joined Petrosino for dinner. After finishing his meal and paying the bill, Petrosino said goodbye to the men and walked out the door. In another account,

Petrosino ate alone until the same two unidentified men came into the restaurant, walked up to his table, and had a brief conversation with him. They then left the restaurant, followed by Petrosino, who quickly paid his bill and didn't wait for any change. What is not disputed is that Petrosino took a different route than normal to walk back to his hotel. Instead of turning left once outside the restaurant's door as he always did, he walked straight ahead, crossing a road, and began strolling around the Piazza Marina. Police later surmised that he was probably going to some spot to meet up again with the two unidentified men from the restaurant whom he apparently trusted.[75]

At 8:50 p.m., three shots rang out near the northwest corner of the piazza. Then, after a short pause, a fourth shot was heard. A sailor waiting for a streetcar ran over to the area and found Petrosino just as he was collapsing to the ground. He saw two men he was never able to identify emerge from the shadows and vanish into the night. He then heard a carriage drive away. A medical officer from the sailor's ship arrived about fifteen minutes later and could tell right away that Petrosino was dead. He examined the body and found that the detective had been shot at close range, with wounds to his right shoulder, cheek, and throat. Among his belongings were his NYPD badge, a notebook, and a picture postcard addressed to his wife, Adelina, on which he'd written, "A kiss for you and my little girl, who has spent months far from her daddy."[76]

Petrosino's death made front-page headlines in newspapers around the world. There were calls for revenge against his assassins. The *World*, a New York City newspaper, ran the headline "War on Black Hand in All America for Murder of Petrosino." His murder "caused a country-wide order for the police of all cities to dragnet for Black Hand miscreants." Inspector James McCafferty, head of the NYPD's Detective Bureau, tele-graphed chiefs of police throughout the United States, requesting that they round up all known Italian criminals in their jurisdiction. There were even calls by some to end all immigration from southern Italy.[77]

In Palermo, the police began the dauntless task of rounding up suspects. In an area of the world where the Mafia was so prevalent and where Petrosino had so many enemies, Police Commissioner Ceola knew he was going to have a hard time finding the culprits. He would have to deal with the omertà, the Mafia's code of silence, and the fear of people in Palermo and other places in Sicily of incurring the wrath of the Mafia by cooperating with the authorities. The police arrested scores of suspects, of which Ceola believed about a dozen or so were involved in the murder. In a communiqué he sent to the Ministry of the Interior and the chairman of the Chamber of Indictment on March 27, Ceola wrote that most of the suspects had been in New York but had returned to Sicily: "It is certain they all knew Petrosino, and knew of his presence here, such a profound hatred they had against him for the steadfastness and tenacity with whom [sic] he persecuted members of sicilian [sic] criminal underworld in New York, that his coming to Palermo must have scared them, and [they] decided to safeguard themselves and their accomplices in America, and also to take revenge for what he had done against them, to kill him."[78]

The main suspect was Sicilian Mafia boss Vito Cascio Ferro, who had been implicated in the 1903 barrel murder and had helped establish Giuseppe Morello as leader of the Italian underworld in the United States. Ceola received a series of anonymous letters from New York tying Morello, Lupo, and other members of their organization to conceiving of the murder plot, with Ferro carrying it out in Palermo with the help of his wide network of criminals. The two suspected triggermen were Calogero (Carlo) Costantino and Antonio Passananti, both employed in Brooklyn as managers of two of Lupo's grocery stores. The two Mafia members had traveled to Sicily within days of Petrosino's voyage to Italy, their fares paid for by the Morello–Lupo family. It would later be learned that Lupo, on hearing the news of the assassination, turned to another member of the group and said with a smile, "Petrosino has been killed. It was successful!"[79]

Nobody, either in the United States or in Italy, was ever convicted for the crime. All charges were eventually dropped due to lack of evidence despite the fact that Ferro had been seen by a witness in Palermo on the day of the murder. A powerful politician who was also a nobleman, Domenico De Michele Ferrantelli, supported Ferro's claim that he had been staying at Ferrantelli's home in Burgio many miles away at the time of the killing. "The murderers of the detective will never be brought to justice," journalist Frank Marshall White wrote a little more than a week after the assassination. "It's better the population of New York resigns itself to this fact." White argued that the police in Palermo "have done and will do everything in their power to protect not only the murderers of the detective, but all Italians of America, whose criminal past was precisely the object of his investigation. This does not necessarily mean that the police in Palermo have been actual accomplice[s] to Petrosino's murderers, but it means that they . . . [do not] dare to raise a finger against them." The one police official who vigorously tried to investigate the crime, Ceola, was removed from his position and forced into retirement four months after the assassination.[80]

Petrosino died a hero, and New Yorkers gave him one of the largest funerals in the city's history on April 12. Mayor George McClellan had declared a public holiday. Following the hearse as it moved along the streets were a thousand mounted and on-foot police, two thousand schoolchildren, and sixty Italian associations in uniform. More than two hundred thousand people lined the sidewalks to watch the procession. A monument was erected at his grave site in Calvary Cemetery in Queens in 1910, and then, almost eighty years later, a park near Little Italy was renamed "Lieutenant Joseph Petrosino Park." There was also a movie made about his life in 1990 starring Ernest Borgnine as Petrosino. But the detective would probably not have liked the picture. Labeling it "a real disappointment," *New York Times* film critic Howard Thompson wrote that the movie "barely touches on the insidious complexities of the Mafia's operations" and said it did not "convey the organized crime scourge of the century," something that Petrosino fought hard against and ultimately paid for with his life.[81]

COMITO THE SHEEP

At the time of Petrosino's death, William Flynn was still investigating the Morello–Lupo counterfeiting operation. He had spent the ensuing years since the 1903 barrel murder tracking the mobsters and gathering information that he hoped would one day finally put the gang away for a long time. He was similar to Petrosino in his unswerving desire to destroy them and all other criminals preying on the Italian immigrants. Flynn was always aware that whatever evidence he gathered and actions he took had to stand up in court and not be used by the defense to get charges dismissed or sway a jury to an acquittal.

Flynn also knew it would be counterproductive to arrest the lower-tier members of Morello and Lupo's criminal enterprise. "Past experience with these Morello–Lupo counterfeiters had taught me not to make an arrest until I had the net completely woven around the men who made the money," Flynn wrote. "It is futile to arrest the 'pushers-of-the-queer'—that is, the men who distribute the bad money among the little Italian grocery stores and shoe shops, small merchants, and the like. The arrest of these men only serves to warn the manufacturers of the bad money that the Secret Service is on the trail." The counterfeiters would then shut down their factory and move it to another location. Flynn also knew that even if he arrested these individuals, he would obtain little information of value from them. "As a rule," Flynn wrote, "all that a 'pusher' or distributor can tell is where he got the bad money," which would not be enough to lead to the arrests of the main players in the counterfeit operation.[82]

After all the suspects in the barrel murder case, including Morello and Lupo, were released by the police magistrate due to insufficient evidence, the NYPD, with the exception of Petrosino, could not continue with their investigation. There were too many other murders, robberies, and various crimes being committed in New York for them to focus just on this case. Flynn, however, made sure that every suspect was shadowed by a special Secret Service agent. This amounted to "life surveillance." Every few months—he didn't have the resources and personnel to conduct a permanent, twenty-four/seven operation—an agent would follow members of the group and keep Flynn posted on where they lived and what they were up to. He was practicing his philosophy of "steady hammering," never letting a case go even as he had to move on to other matters.[83]

One of those other matters involved uncovering a plot in 1906 by a sixty-four-year-old New Yorker to finance a revolution in Venezuela with counterfeit money. Captain George B. Boynton, who described himself as "a fair, square and honorable soldier of fortune," was the son of a distinguished New York surgeon and born with a yearning for adventure. There wasn't a revolution or war anywhere in the world that the Civil War veteran didn't want to be a part of, whether by selling weapons and other materials to one side or the other, running blockades, or undertaking a whole range of other risky endeavors. In his adventures, he participated in revolutions and uprisings in Cuba, Chile, Haiti, and the Dominican Republic. He also got involved in the Franco-Prussian War of 1870–1871 and in conflicts in the Balkans. He claimed that he never made much money from his activities, but it was said that "he can't help getting mixed up in a good scrap, although he has always tried to get on the side whose success meant most for the country affected."[84]

Deciding it might be time to settle down, the aging thrill seeker took a job as manager and director of the Orinoco Corporation in Venezuela in the mid-1890s. The company held a concession from the Venezuelan government covering practically the whole Orinoco Delta, with its valuable timber, asphalt, and mineral deposits. The government of President José Cipriano Castro Ruiz wanted to end this monopoly. The Orinoco Corporation therefore intended to finance a revolution against the Castro regime. Boynton went to New York in May 1906 to raise money in order to buy the dyes and silver bullion necessary to start the process of making counterfeit Venezuelan "bolivar" silver dollars. He planned to purchase these items in New York, while the actual manufacturing of the bogus money would take place in the Orinoco Delta in Venezuela.[85]

The Secret Service learned of this scheme from a person who had been approached by Boynton's friend and lawyer, Lewis M. Thomson, to advance them the necessary funds. Flynn then had one of his agents pose as a possible investor in the counterfeit operation. When the agent gathered enough evidence against Boynton, his lawyer, and a couple of other accomplices, they were all were arrested. But to Flynn's astonishment, James Ridgway, U.S. commissioner of the Southern District of New York, released the defendants, stating that he had no jurisdiction since the actual counterfeiting was not going to take place in the United States.[86]

Flynn, however, didn't give up and took the case to a federal grand jury because there was a federal law making it a crime to counterfeit the coin of another government. When the grand jury issued indictments in September, everybody but Boynton, who had gone to Trinidad, was arrested again. Believing that Boynton "appreciated loyalty above everything else," Flynn sent an unofficial but very clear warning to Boynton's new lawyer stating that unless Boynton came back to New York to stand trial, his accomplices would be dealt with very harshly by the courts. It worked, as Boynton, not wanting to see his friends receive long prison sentences, wrote back, "Will be in court to plead guilty on Monday with my grip packed and ready to go to jail." True to his word, the dapper fugitive returned, pleaded guilty, and was sentenced to six months of hard labor. His accomplices also pleaded guilty but were only fined and then released. Boynton left the court smiling and seemingly unconcerned as he was escorted by a deputy to the Kings County Penitentiary. Three months later, President Theodore Roosevelt pardoned him, impressed that he had voluntarily returned to the United States knowing that he would be sent to jail.[87]

Among Flynn's other responsibilities during this period was helping to protect Roosevelt, whom he was friends with, whenever the president visited New York and the surrounding areas. Flynn was also sent along with other Secret Service agents to Portsmouth, New Hampshire, in the summer of 1905 to provide protection for the Russian and Japanese delegations at a peace conference aimed at ending the Russo-Japanese War. Things didn't get off to a good start, though. The State Department car that was taking Flynn, Sergei Witte (head of the Russian delegation), and one other Russian diplomat to their hotel on their first night in Portsmouth ran out of gas, leaving everyone stranded on an isolated, dark road. This was not exactly a situation the Secret Service was happy about. However, another State Department car was summoned, and Flynn and the diplomats arrived safely at their destination.[88]

Despite all his work with the Secret Service since the time of the barrel murder, bringing Morello, Lupo, and the other top Mafia figures to justice was still Flynn's main goal. He tried everything he could to make that happen, including placing one of his Italian-speaking agents, Peter Rubano, within the inner circle of the gang. Rubano began undercover work in 1905, hanging around saloons and other places in Little Italy. He gradually won the confidence of Lupo the Wolf, but the latter never revealed anything to him about the gang's counterfeit racket. Flynn also recruited five Italian former counterfeiters as informants. To protect their identities, Flynn would meet with them in secret, making sure nobody, not even his own men, ever saw him speaking with them.[89]

For several years, there was little progress in uncovering evidence that would send Morello and Lupo to prison. In May 1909, however, the Secret Service was contacted by bankers and storekeepers in New York, Philadelphia, Pittsburgh, Buffalo, Boston, Baltimore, Chicago, Cincinnati, and other cities regarding counterfeit Canadian $5 bills and American $2 and $5 bills that they were receiving. These notes all appeared to be from the same manufacturer and had been passed by Italians. Morello and Lupo, who were in desperate need of cash due to failing businesses, had begun producing the bogus money in December 1908 at an old stone house in Highland, New York, a farming village about fifty miles up the Hudson River from Manhattan. It wasn't until May 1909 that the counterfeit bills were ready for circulation.[90]

Flynn eventually traced the rash of new counterfeit money to the Highland plant, but by the time his agents got there in late September, there was nothing to be found. The counterfeiters had suspended their operation and dismantled the printing press. They had also buried the counterfeit plates and ink in the woods about two hundred feet from the farmhouse where they made the bogus bills. But Flynn had learned that the person in charge of distributing the counterfeit notes was Antonio Cecala, a high-ranking member of the Morello–Lupo outfit. He was often seen by the townspeople of Highland with Salvatore Cina, another member of the gang who owned a farm somewhere near the village. Flynn also learned that Lupo had visited there. Further investigative work led to a grocery store in Manhattan that was once owned by Lupo and where Cecala, Morello, Lupo, and others were seen meeting. Flynn devised a scheme in which he used an informant to purchase counterfeit bills from one of the members of the gang who was working for Cecala. The good money was marked by the Secret Service so that if and when Cecala was arrested, they might find these marked bills on him since he would likely be collecting all the money from his underlings. This in turn would link Cecala to the counterfeiting operation.[91]

Flynn decided it was time to make a series of arrests even though he still didn't have the "smoking gun" he so desperately wanted—namely, somebody from within the gang who would testify against Morello and Lupo. He was worried he might never find such a person. Better to make the arrests now, he thought, as the Secret Service had so many members of the Morello–Lupo group under surveillance. So, on November 15, Flynn's men, along with detectives from the NYPD's Italian Squad, raided several locations around Manhattan and other areas, arresting fourteen members of the gang, including Morello. Lupo, to Flynn's dismay, had eluded surveillance and wasn't caught that day. It wasn't until January 1910 that Secret Service agents were able to arrest him in connection with the Highland counterfeiting operation.[92]

Prior to the Morello raid, Flynn instructed one of his young agents, Thomas Callaghan, who was only seventeen years old, to locate the apartment where Morello lived. Flynn knew the address of the building but not the exact apartment. He didn't want to raid the wrong place and thereby give Morello a chance to escape. He also wanted to make sure Morello would be in the apartment when the raid began. Callaghan, who for weeks had been keeping tabs on Morello by working as a shoeshine boy in Morello's neighborhood, waited until he saw Morello walking down the street with his two of his half brothers, Vincenzo and Ciro Terranova, and another man, and then he entered the four-story building before they did. He sneaked up to the second floor, hoping he could see or hear Morello enter an apartment on the first floor. But Morello and his group climbed the stairs, forcing Callaghan to quickly go to the top floor. Callaghan figured he could still see or hear Morello enter an apartment on either the second or the third floor. But the group continued up the stairs to the fourth floor, where Callaghan was hiding. He knew his only hope was to walk down the stairs nonchalantly and hope Morello wouldn't become suspicious. Callaghan came face-to-face with Morello in the stairwell, the youngster's heart "thumping like a pile driver." For unknown reasons, the godfather didn't question the presence of the teenager in the building. Morello simply said, "Scusa, please," and stepped aside to let Callaghan pass.[93]

Callaghan wasn't able to tell which apartment on the fourth floor Morello entered, but the knowledge that Morello was now at home and on the top floor was still valuable intelligence. Flynn himself led the raid on Morello's apartment. He found the godfather asleep with, according to Flynn, four loaded revolvers under his pillow. Another one of Morello's half brothers, Nicola Terranova, was also asleep in the apartment, with five loaded revolvers under his pillow. Morello and Terranova didn't have time to draw their weapons as the Secret Service agents and detectives pounced on them and placed them under arrest. But Morello's wife, Lina, came from another room with her infant daughter in one hand and a knife in the other. The agents and detectives were able to get the knife away from her, but she managed afterward to hide some incriminating evidence in her baby's diaper when she was allowed to leave the room to put her daughter to sleep. One of the agents saw this, and the baby was taken from her and the diaper removed. Hidden there were three letters Morello had written to Mafia leaders in other cities. The agents also found Black Hand extortion letters inside Lina's apron pocket.[94]

A raid at the apartment of two brothers of the group, Pasquale and Leoluca Vasi, yielded $3,600 in counterfeit $2 notes. Agents also arrested Cecala, Morello and Lupo's close associate, as he walked from his apartment to the Bowery. He was brought to Flynn's office, where he was searched and found to have $221 in genuine money on him. But of that sum, there were two $1 notes and one $2 note that Flynn had previously marked and given to his informant to purchase counterfeit money.[95]

Having Morello in custody was especially good news for Flynn. He couldn't help but get a dig in against the godfather when he was in his office after being arrested. He called Callaghan in and asked Morello, "Ever see this young lad before?" Morello shook his head, "Never." Flynn then told him that Callaghan had been following him for a long time. "Do you remember meeting anyone when you were going upstairs to your apartment last night?" Flynn asked. Morello said, "Yeh—a boy. A little boy." Flynn then said, pointing to Callaghan, "This is the little boy." Morello became incensed, stared angrily at the teenager, and said, "If I know this last night, I cutta your throat."[96]

Flynn received a congratulatory telegram from Secret Service Chief John Wilkie the day after all the arrests. But Wilkie had one pointed question for Flynn: "What kind of a case do you think you have on Morello" [no question mark in the original]. Flynn wrote back, "Got some damaging letters on Morello and have a possible chance to land him." But it is unlikely Flynn truly believed that the Black Hand letters seized from Morello's apartment, as well as the letters he had sent to other Mafia figures in the country, would be enough to convict him. Flynn had been down this road before, with Morello and his cohorts continually beating the raps and always being released due to lack of evidence. What Flynn really needed was what he had always wanted: somebody from within the group brave enough to defy the Clutch Hand and tell all he knew about the Morello–Lupo gang in return for favorable treatment from the government.[97]

He finally found such a man when, in January 1910, agents arrested Antonio Comito, an Italian immigrant who had been forced to work for the Morello–Lupo group as a printer of counterfeit notes. He had been hiding from both the Secret Service and the Mafia for several months, fearful of arrest by the former and death by the latter, who always viewed him as weak and expendable. They often mocked him and treated him harshly. After being arrested, he told Flynn he was willing to testify against Morello, Lupo, and all the others. That was the good news for Flynn. The bad news was that he was known as "Comito the Sheep" because of his timid nature. Why couldn't his moniker be "Comito the Lion," Flynn probably said to himself. Could such a person actually have the courage to defy the Mafia in court as they stared at him and their attorneys relentlessly attacked his testimony? Flynn had to take that chance when the trial began on January 26.

He knew from Comito's confession that if "the Sheep" could withstand the pressure and fear of being in the same courtroom with Morello and Lupo, Flynn had "a witness who could fasten guilt upon almost every man of the band I was running to earth." He felt sorry for Comito, who "was not at heart a criminal nor had he profited at all by the counterfeiting scheme." Working to Flynn's advantage was that Comito "had vivid, almost perfect recall and an apparently compulsive need to recount his experiences in detail." His story was one of a poor Italian immigrant who had gotten caught up with the Mafia and had no way to get out.[98]

Comito came to New York from Catanzaro, the capital of the Calabria province in southern Italy, in the summer of 1907. He had previously lived for seven years in Brazil, where he worked as a printer, teacher, and assistant to the Italian consul in Rio de Janeiro. The only work he could find in New York, however, was short term: jobs at two print shops. By August 1908, he was unemployed and depressed regarding his financial situation. But when he was offered a printing job in Philadelphia by a man he did not know whom a fellow member of the Sons of Italy fraternal organization had introduced him to, he gladly accepted. On the journey to that city with his mistress, Katrina Pascuzzo (Comito had a wife in Italy), and his new employer, they took a detour, and Comito found himself at the farmhouse in Highland, New York. The kind stranger who'd offered him the job turned out to be the mobster Antonio Cecala. Comito and Katrina were now prisoners of the Morello–Lupo gang.[99]

When Cecala finally told him that his job would be to print counterfeit money, Comito protested, saying that was not his kind of work. Cecala grabbed him by the shoulders and said, "Don Antonio, you are the person who must execute this work under my direction and the guidance of some one else that you will know in the future. *Your life would be lost if you should reveal our secret to any one.* We are twenty men banded together in this affair, and we will respect you as one of us. Caterina [*sic*] will be respected as well, and when we are done we will give her a sum of money to go to Italy; but you must remain with us for life." Comito realized he had no choice but to do as Cecala said. "The voice of the 'Black Hand' Society had spoken," he wrote in his confession. "I was the unwilling tool. To refuse meant death. So I resolved to play my part as well as I could and merely answered that I would do what they asked but not to expect perfect work as I was not a practical plate printer, and had never seen counterfeit money before nor printed it."[100]

Comito and Katrina remained in Highland until work was suspended in the summer of 1909, when a new batch of counterfeit notes had been printed and was ready for distribution. Printing yet another new batch of notes was scheduled to resume in a few months. Comito was allowed to return to New York with Katrina but became alarmed after reading in the newspapers about the November 15 arrests of several members of the Morello–Lupo gang: "I became frightened, thinking that these fellows might think that I had said something to the police as they knew I was dissatisfied with the treatment they had given me. Losing no time I packed my things and went to live with an American family in Dominick Street." He stayed there until January 4, 1910, when he was arrested by six Secret Service agents and brought to Flynn's office, where he confessed and told his story of being forced to work with the gang.[101]

Flynn kept secret from the media that he had another member of the Morello–Lupo group under arrest. He and his men provided round-the-clock protection for their star witness, often having Comito sleep at Flynn's office. When the trial began, Secret Service agents were placed throughout the packed courtroom and in the corridors. As Comito, "a thin, nervous youth," was being sworn in as the prosecution's first witness, there was shock on the faces of the eight defendants, including Morello, Lupo, and Cecala. They apparently had not learned that Comito had fallen into the hands of the Secret Service. They now realized this was not going to be like previous trials, where there was always insufficient evidence to convict them. The government had finally found somebody from within their group who was going to tell all.[102]

During three days of direct examination, Comito talked about how he was forced to join the group and recalled in stunning detail all the activities of the Morello–Lupo gang at the farmhouse where they made the counterfeit money. He never once looked at the defendants, who were trying to intimidate him with their glares. Instead, he just stared at a window as he testified. He was then subjected to relentless cross-examination for two more days by the defendants' lawyers. He gained more confidence as the proceedings continued, even sparring with the lawyers and eliciting chuckles from the spectators in the courtroom. On one occasion, he was asked in cross-examination how much one of the defendants he'd seen at the farmhouse weighed, a question aimed at obtaining a wrong answer to show that Comito was not being accurate in his testimony. Comito simply said, "I never weighed pigs in a slaughter house, so I can't tell." On another occasion, Charles Le Barbier, one of the lawyers for the defendants, demanded to know why Comito did not look at him when answering his questions. Comito "replied in a torrent of eloquence in his native tongue that he did not like the looks of Mr. Le Barbier's face, because it reminded him of the faces of the Sicilian thugs who had forced him to print the counterfeits."[103]

Comito the Sheep performed like a lion on the stand and won the praise of the reporters in the courtroom. The *New York Times* wrote that Comito "gave evidence that he is not going to be terrorized by the prospect of getting in the way of a thin, sharp stiletto or stopping a revolver bullet some dark night." The *New-York Tribune* described how "one of the counsel for the defense, Mirabeau L. Towns, tried to connect him [Comito] with the counterfeiting plot, but the witness could not be made to deviate from his first story." Flynn was also impressed with Comito's performance, writing to Chief Wilkie after the trial was over that Comito "proved a remarkable witness and not once did he make a single mistake, and without a memorandum."[104]

Several witnesses who lived in Highland provided additional damaging testimony against the defense, stating that they'd seen Morello, Lupo, and the other defendants in town at different times and together. These included the village's hardware dealer, postmaster, butcher, grocer, telephone operators, and barbers. The defense case was weak, with Morello choosing not to testify and Lupo and the others offering flimsy alibis. As the trial drew to a close, Flynn felt confident of a conviction. "Up to this time," he wrote to Wilkie, "the Defense has not offered any testimony upon which an acquittal or even a mistrial could be expected, and at recess one day last week [defense] Attorney La Bara [*sic*] told me this was the best case he had ever seen presented in the United States court."[105]

The jury deliberated on February 19 for just over one hour before returning guilty verdicts for each defendant on all six counts of the indictment. Judge Thomas Ray pronounced a sentence for the first two counts—the making of counterfeit $2 and $5 notes—and suspended sentencing on the remaining four lesser counts. But before doing this, Ray cleared the courtroom of all the spectators except for reporters and government officials. One by one, he called each defendant to the bench. What happened next shocked everyone present in the courtroom.[106]

When Morello's name was called, the godfather trembled as he rose and nervously approached the bench. When Ray asked him if he had anything to say, Morello held up his right hand, stating that he had been born deformed and that he had a large family to support. He asked the judge to suspend sentencing, promising to move back to Italy immediately. Ray would have no part of that and sentenced him to twenty-five years in prison. Morello looked stunned and went into convulsions and fainted. He had to be carried out of the courtroom. Lupo the Wolf began crying "long and bitterly" when his attorney begged for mercy, claiming that his client had always been an honest and generous man. Lupo, who in his testimony admitted to killing a person in Italy in self-defense, told the judge that he would return to his native country if allowed to do so and "face my accusers." Judge Ray replied, "It is my conviction that Lupo and Morello were at the head of this enterprise and that they are justly convicted." He then sentenced the Wolf to thirty years in prison. Lupo "stood, seemingly catatonic," on hearing the sentence. The remaining six defendants also received lengthy prison terms, ranging from fifteen to seventeen years. They all sobbed on hearing their fate. At the time, the sentences were the longest ever imposed for counterfeiting. At the end of the day, the total stood at a combined one hundred and fifty years and $7,600 in fines. "That will help some," Flynn said to reporters with a half smile as he walked out of the courtroom.[107]

The once-powerful Morello–Lupo gang had been reduced to weeping and pathetic figures. They were led out of the courtroom for the short walk outside to the Tombs prison, manacled and surrounded by scores of deputy marshals, Secret Service men, detectives, and policemen needed to keep order and prevent any rescue attempt by the prisoners' friends and relatives. The marshals held up traffic in the street, and a crowd of sobbing relatives watched as Morello, Lupo, and the others were marched into the Tombs. A couple of days later, they were transferred to the U.S. Penitentiary in Atlanta to serve their sentences.[108]

The *New York Times* exulted in their fate:

> The spirit of Giuseppe Morrello [*sic*], the chief of the Black Hand, is broken. Lupo (the Wolf,) the proud and haughty one, the carrier of the

mandates of the dread society, has been seen to throw himself upon his face in despair and weep. The gang that gathered about them is dispersed, broken in fragments and without a head. For not only have their chiefs been sent to Federal prisons, but along with them eight most active lieutenants.

So is broken up an organization that has terrorized half of the United States, a gang at the door of which are laid such crimes as the notorious "barrel murder" in New York and, assassination of Lieut. Petrosino in Italy. So are removed the men who have dominated thousands of Italian-Americans through fear, and are believed to have collected tribute in a thousand cases.

The crime of counterfeiting has at last been proved against these men. For a decade they have escaped punishment largely through intimidating witnesses. But now they are in prison for long terms in every case. So ends a romance of lawlessness which had but few parallels in the history of the nation.[109]

Flynn and his men were praised by the media for their "untiring efforts" against the Morello–Lupo gang. Flynn's boss, Secret Service Chief Wilkie, wrote him a personal letter of appreciation: "The admirable cooperation of all your assistants where everybody pulled together heedless of personal comfort and convenience; the days and nights of tireless activity in giving to every detail of the work intelligent and painstaking care and the inspiration of your splendid enthusiasm and direction made only one result possible—a perfect case." He praised Flynn even more later in the letter: "I don't mind saying to you that in my opinion if this division during its last ten years had accomplished nothing else than the successful prosecution of the Lupo-Morrello [sic] gang the total appropriation for the ten years would have been well spent. From every side there come congratulations on the success in this case. The Secretary's office is particularly gratified, and I know from information that has reached me that the very large and respectable class of citizens of Italian extraction express the highest satisfaction at the punishment which has been meted out to these criminals."[110]

Years later, in a book he wrote about the barrel murder, Flynn used the successful outcome of the trial to encourage Italians to stand up to the Mafia:

The reason for the fear in the mind of the honest, and even the most intelligent, Italians is born of the thought that such leaders as Morello and Lupo, were more than human in their craftiness, and had dark and mysterious ways of avoiding the best detectives in this country, and that they could even commit murder and laugh in the teeth of the police. The answer to such a thought is the sentence imposed on Morello, Lupo and the other members of the gang now confined in the federal prison. If there are other leaders of less magnitude than these two, and who have caused any Italian fear through threat or otherwise, I invite such Italian to tell me what he knows. There are cells unoccupied in many prisons.[111]

Several months after the trial, Flynn learned from an informant that Morello's half brothers, Vincenzo, Nicola, and Ciro Terranova, were debating a plan (that they ultimately rejected) to kidnap Flynn's children as a way to force him to support an appeal of Morello's conviction. (Separately, Lupo had given orders from prison to two of his associates to have Flynn assassinated.) The informant was none other than Salvatore Clemente, a member of the Stella Frauto gang (and Stella's husband) who Flynn arrested for counterfeiting in 1902, as discussed in chapter 1. Clemente was arrested again in October 1910 and this time reached an agreement with Flynn to turn informer on the Morello family (he was a close friend of the Terranova brothers) in return for not having to go to jail and for a small retainer. Clemente would remain a trusted informant for Flynn in the years ahead.[112]

Morello's twenty-five-year sentence was commuted to fifteen years in January 1918, making him immediately eligible for parole, which was denied. However, he received a good-conduct release in March 1920. He then became an adviser to a second generation of Mafia bosses but was murdered by a rival faction in August 1930. Lupo was paroled from prison in June 1920 and obtained a conditional commutation from President Warren G. Harding in October 1921. The commutation stated that Lupo would be returned to the penitentiary and required to complete the remaining years of his sentence if he became involved again in any unlawful activity. But the career criminal could not go straight. Although he did not resume his counterfeiting operations, he did become engaged in racketeering and extortion activities. Having violated the terms of his conditional presidential commutation, President Franklin D. Roosevelt ordered that Lupo be returned to the Atlanta prison in July 1936 to serve out the remaining years of his original sentence. His health failing, Lupo was finally discharged from prison in December 1946 and died of natural causes three weeks later.[113]

Antonio Comito remained enemy number one to the relatives and friends of the Morello–Lupo gang. Flynn moved him out of New York and placed him in a safe house on the Mexican border. Comito returned for a brief time in the summer of 1911 to receive $150 from the Secret Service for a steamship ticket back to Italy. He sailed on July 1, 1911, but eventually left Italy to live in South America, where, Flynn later learned to his delight, Comito the Sheep became a very prosperous businessman.[114]

The Morello–Lupo case cemented Flynn's legacy as "one of the greatest detectives in the world." His "steady hammering" had brought about the downfall of a powerful crime syndicate in New York. He knew this didn't mean the end of the Mafia, which would continue to grow and expand throughout the country with new generations of criminals vying for control of the huge profits to be made from organized crime. But Flynn had done his part in the battle against those who exploited and terrorized innocent people. His only regret probably was that Joseph Petrosino, whom he respected very much, was not around to see the successful end of the long struggle against Morello, Lupo, and their accomplices.[115]

By the end of 1910, Flynn had been with the Secret Service for more than thirteen years. He had come a long way from his first assignment—finding the "Sausage Man" passing counterfeit $5 bills at butcher shops in cities along the Eastern Seaboard. He had failed in that mission, but now he had attained worldwide fame for bringing the Morello–Lupo gang to justice after a decade of pursuit. The Bulldog felt satisfied but also restless. He was ready for a new challenge.

CHAPTER THREE

A Thankless Job

ON JANUARY 18, 1895, AN INVESTIGATIVE COMMITTEE HEADED BY State Senator Clarence Lexow issued a bombshell report that shook up the police, politicians, and the public throughout New York City. After nearly a year of investigations and six hundred and seventy-eight witness testimonies, it found that corruption within the police department was so widespread that it could be found "from the highest down to the lowest [officials]." This included interfering and helping to fix elections on behalf of the corrupt Tammany Hall political machine, receiving payoffs for protecting houses of prostitution and gambling, using excessive force on people they arrested, and engaging in blackmail, extortion, and other illegal activities. Promotions within the police force were also often bought and not earned. The committee stated that this "establishes an indictment against the Police Department of the City of New-York as a whole."[1]

The more than ten-thousand-page Lexow Committee report was one of the most scathing repudiations of the police ever seen in the United States. The city needed somebody quick, somebody with name recognition to put a better face on the department and attack the corruption the committee had identified. They found that man in Theodore Roosevelt, a bright, young, ambitious public servant with a reputation for initiating reforms in the federal civil service from when he served for several years on the U.S. Civil Service Commission. Mayor William L. Strong appointed him to head the New York Board of Police Commissioners in May. This was an ideal job for Roosevelt since it would provide him an opportunity to keep himself in the public eye and, if successful, accomplish reforms in the largest police department in the nation. He saw this job as a potential stepping stone to higher national office one day.[2]

The newspapers lauded Roosevelt's appointment, with one syndicated story praising "his vigor, his dash and his disregard of precedents." Roosevelt started immediately introducing reforms throughout the department. He began hiring and promoting policemen based on their abilities and not on their contacts, payments, or party affiliations. One of the men he promoted was Joseph Petrosino, whom he made a detective sergeant. Roosevelt ordered regular physical exams and firearms inspections for all members of the police department. He visited precincts often to make sure everybody was performing their duties and reassigned or fired those who weren't. He even took walking tours of the streets after midnight to catch officers by surprise and, to his dismay, found policemen sleeping while on duty or visiting cafés and saloons. Many of these men received official reprimands.[3]

Roosevelt, however, faced a backlash from the public for one of his reforms when he tried to enforce a New York State law prohibiting the selling of alcohol in saloons on Sundays. He claimed that he was doing this to end police blackmail of saloon owners, in which an owner was allowed stay open on Sundays in return for a payoff. Roosevelt hoped his enforcement of the law would send a clear message to the police force that no bribes or blackmail would be tolerated. The problem was that Sunday was the only day off for most workingmen, and they looked forward to having a relaxed time at their favorite watering holes. It was estimated that 95 percent of New York City residents favored saloons being kept open for at least part of the day on Sundays.[4]

Roosevelt resigned his post in April 1897, when President William McKinley offered him the job of assistant secretary of the navy. He then became governor of New York in 1899 and ran as the vice-presidential candidate in McKinley's successful reelection campaign in 1900. He became president in 1901 following McKinley's assassination. Years later, Roosevelt reportedly said that being police commissioner of New York was more difficult than being president of the United States. But he viewed his brief time as commissioner as a success:

The result of our labors was of value to the city, for we gave the citizens better protection than they had ever before received, and at the same time cut out the corruption which was eating away civic morality. We showed conclusively that it was possible to combine both honesty and efficiency in handling the police. We were attacked with the most bitter animosity by every sensational newspaper and every politician of the baser sort, not because of our shortcomings, but because of what we did that was good.[5]

Once Roosevelt was out of office, "the city returned to its bad behavior." Tammany Hall, which had lost the elections in 1894 to a reform fusion ticket, regained control of New York with the election of its handpicked candidate, Robert Van Wyck, as mayor in November 1897. Van Wyck, a city court clerk, had agreed that if he won, he would allow Richard Croker, the boss of Tammany Hall, to control who received the forty thousand patronage jobs. Meanwhile, all the police officers who had been dismissed from the force during Roosevelt's tenure as commissioner were reinstated with back pay due to successful court appeals.[6]

Tammany Hall's return to power resulted in its control once again of the police, with Boss Croker helping to put in place William Devery as chief of police, a man the muckraking journalist Lincoln Steffens labeled "a disgrace." Devery had been in charge of a police station house on the Lower East Side of Manhattan and one time told his men, "If there's any grafting to be done I'll do it. Leave it to me." As police chief, Devery "blessed gambling, prostitution, and after-hours drinking all over town . . . for a shakedown price."[7]

While Devery was running the police department, the number of policemen under his control grew when the five boroughs of New York (Manhattan, Brooklyn, Queens, the Bronx, and Richmond [later renamed Staten Island]) were consolidated in 1898 into one single metropolis to be known as the "City of Greater New York." Each borough's police force was merged into one department with more than six thousand men, giving birth to the "New York Police Department." There had been several different names since 1845, including the "Municipal Police Force," the "Metropolitan Police Force," and the "New York Police Force."[8]

For the next decade, New York "seesawed back and forth . . . between cops who take and cops who don't." Roosevelt blamed the "system" for any corruption. "There are no better men anywhere than the men of the New York police force," he wrote in 1913, "and when they go bad, it is because the system is wrong." It took a reform mayor in 1910 to make yet another attempt to fix this "system." But Mayor William J. Gaynor needed a Roosevelt-type figure to help him, somebody honest and strong-willed with name recognition who would generate public support for what Gaynor intended to do. He didn't have to look far to find that man.[9]

CALLING ON FLYNN

At eleven o'clock in the morning on April 18, 1910, William Flynn walked into Mayor Gaynor's office at City Hall. Word of the unannounced meeting quickly spread and sent reporters into a frenzy as speculation immediately arose that the famed Secret Service agent was going to quit his job to become police commissioner of the NYPD. Flynn denied this when asked later by reporters. "The Mayor sent for me several days ago," he said. "No position was tendered and I asked for none. What we talked about I do not care to say. Let him tell that if he desires. I am not looking for a job being perfectly satisfied where I am. My advice, however, is always at the Mayor's disposal."[10]

Gaynor also did not reveal the nature of the meeting to reporters. It was known, however, that Gaynor wanted to reorganize the NYPD's Detective Bureau and have it operate separately from the uniformed force. He also wanted detectives to be selected carefully and chosen for merit alone, as was the case with Secret Service agents. What better man to take charge of this than the head of the New York office of the Secret Service?[11]

In all likelihood, Gaynor probably did offer Flynn the job of police commissioner or deputy police commissioner or at least let him know that the job was his whenever he wanted it. And even though Flynn told reporters that he was "perfectly satisfied where I am," the challenge of shaking up the NYPD and making them operate like the Secret Service had to be appealing to him. He still had follow-up work to do with the remnants of the Morello–Lupo gang, who would soon be tried, convicted, and given long prison sentences. But by October, he decided to leave the Secret Service and accept an offer from Gaynor to become second deputy commissioner of the NYPD. He was authorized by Gaynor to work independently of the police commissioner and answer only to the mayor.[12]

Gaynor, just like Flynn, was an "honest, tireless and incorruptible public figure." But unlike Flynn, the mayor was "hot-tempered and irascible and had no patience whatever with stupid men." He was born in 1851 to a farming family in Whitestown in Oneida County in central New York State. Although he loved farm life, he didn't think that would be a good career choice. Instead, he wanted to become a Roman Catholic priest. He attended Whitestown Seminary; Assumption Academy in Utica, New York; and then Christian Brothers College in St. Louis. But he changed his mind about the priesthood and moved to Boston, where he taught public school. He later returned to New York and studied law, gaining admittance to the bar in 1875. He practiced law in Brooklyn until 1893, when he was elected to the New York Supreme Court. After serving on the bench for fourteen years, Gaynor was reelected in 1907 to a second term as a justice.[13]

He resigned, however, two years later to run for mayor of New York. What was surprising about that decision was that he ran with the backing of Tammany Hall. Gaynor had earned a reputation for honesty, independence, and reform, the exact opposite of what the Tammany political machine was known for. Gaynor "will have to tell the public how he, who has always fought political corruption and fought bosses and machines, could lend himself to the most corrupt machine and one of the worst bosses [Tammany boss Charles Murphy]," one newspaper wrote. And it is unclear why Tammany wanted to nominate him for mayor. Perhaps they believed the popular Gaynor was likely to win on whatever ticket he ran on, and so in nominating him, they could then try to manipulate him once he became mayor. But he made it clear before the election that he was going to be his own man. He went to the Tammany Hall building on East 14th Street for the first time in his life and addressed a group of district leaders gathered there, saying, "So this is Tammany Hall. But if this is really Tammany Hall, where is the tiger? [The tiger was the cartoon symbol newspapers and magazines used to depict the powerful

Tammany organization.] That tiger which they say is going to swallow me up. . . . If there happens to be any swallowing, it is not at all unlikely that I may be on the outside of the tiger."[14]

Gaynor proved indeed to be independent of Tammany Hall once he became mayor. He began filling appointments and promotions to city jobs based on numerical order from a competitive list. No money or influence was allowed to interfere with this process. He had been in office just a little over seven months, however, when tragedy struck. On August 9, 1910, the mayor was shot from behind as he was about to board a ship for a vacation to Europe. The bullet entered the back of his neck, below his right ear, and became lodged in his throat. The shooter was a disgruntled former city employee, James J. Gallagher, who had been a night watchman employed by the New York Department of Docks. Gallagher was dismissed from his job a few weeks before the shooting for failing to report to work on time and for disrespecting his foreman. He petitioned the mayor's office for reinstatement but was told by Gaynor's secretary that there was nothing the mayor could do for him. Just before firing his pistol, Gallagher shouted at the mayor, "You have taken my bread and butter away from me." The wound was believed at first to be fatal by everyone at the pier, including Gaynor, who on the way to the hospital said to one of his aides, "Say goodbye to the people."[15]

Gaynor survived, but being shot left a lasting effect on him both physically and psychologically. The bullet that was lodged in his throat could not be safely removed, leaving him weakened and haggard for the rest of his life. He was always in pain, and for a long time, he could hardly speak above a whisper. Psychologically, the assassination attempt depressed him. "I am sorry for the worry I have caused you all," he wrote to his sister on September 3. "You remember my dog 'Spot,' when we were children. He got hurt once, and crawled under a pile of logs and lay there for more than a week before he came out. Well, when any trouble happens to me, I feel just like poor 'Spot'—I would like to crawl under the log pile and stay there." But at the same time, the experience of almost losing his life made him even more fearless than before the incident. He was urged by supporters to run for governor, and there was speculation that he intended one day to also make a run at the U.S. presidency. He wrote an emphatic letter to one of his supporters denying any interest in either position but emphasizing that it wasn't because he was afraid of the tasks and responsibilities of higher office. "When a man has gone down into the Valley of the Shadow," he wrote just a month after being shot, "and looked the spectre Death in the face, and said to it, 'I am ready,' nothing in this world looks very large to him, as I can assure you."[16]

William Flynn didn't need a near-death experience to know that there was nothing in the world too large or too difficult for him to deal with. Always confident and self-assured, he reported for his new job on October 21, 1910, eager to begin the task of reorganizing the NYPD's detective force. At the same time that Flynn became second deputy commissioner, Gaynor appointed James C. Cropsey, a lawyer, to be commissioner and Clement J. Driscoll, a former newspaper man, to be first deputy commissioner, with the task of cleaning up the vice and gambling that was prevalent in the city. But it was Flynn who garnered the most media attention. Newspaper reporters were downright giddy about his appointment and showered him with praise and effusive stories about his career. "Flynn Is to Give New York a Real Detective Force" was the headline of a story in the *New York Times*, while the *Brooklyn Daily Eagle* exclaimed, "Backed by Real Detective Experience, W. J. Flynn, Head of City Service, Brings Terror to Evildoers." Other papers wrote stories about Flynn's new job with headlines like "New York Bad Place for Crooks Now" and "Flynn Revolutionizes the Detective Bureau."[17]

The "revolution" started during Flynn's first month on the job. It was more like a massacre, however, for the many detectives who had enjoyed the easy life before Flynn arrived, the "incompetents who had been made first-grade detectives through 'influence' with the idea of getting the $2,500 salary without doing any noticeable amount of work." Flynn had several hundred young and ambitious patrolmen appear before him at police headquarters and answer questions regarding their qualifications to become detectives. "As soon as I decided on the number of young detectives I wanted," Flynn wrote, "an equal number of the old timers were measured for blue uniforms, exchanged their golden badges for nickel ones, and resumed their acquaintance with the delights of walking post." These "slow moving bodies" did not fit into Flynn's plans, which included establishing a detective force that would resemble and be as effective as the U.S. Secret Service and Britain's Scotland Yard. "Nothing will count with me," he told a reporter, "so long as I am here except fitness and ability."[18]

After demoting the old-time detectives and replacing them with a fleet of young eager beavers, Flynn abolished all the branch Detective Bureaus in the city. Every detective was placed under Flynn's control, with the Detective Bureau granted total autonomy from the rest of the NYPD by Mayor Gaynor. Detectives were no longer part of the local precinct commands, even though they would be placed in station houses throughout the city. They would now be working independently of the uniformed police, which was how Scotland Yard detectives operated. Also, Flynn instructed his men to gather all the evidence in a case but to let the uniformed policemen make the arrests whenever possible, again similar to Scotland Yard's methods. This was to keep the identities of the detectives unknown to the criminals, who in many cases didn't realize that they had been under surveillance. The detectives could thus work future cases without their identities being revealed through word of mouth by the arrested criminals or being spotted by the arrested criminals themselves when they eventually got back on the streets after serving their sentences.[19]

Flynn also required his detectives, numbering about five hundred, to file daily reports accounting for everything they had done in the preceding twenty-four hours, just like he had to do when he was a Secret Service agent. This was a tedious and somewhat time-consuming process for the detectives, but it ensured that everybody was doing their jobs as instructed. It worked with the Secret Service, and Flynn expected it to also work with the police. The Detective Bureau under Flynn was also not going to be used to deal with minor crimes such as prostitution, solicitation, gambling, petty theft, and so forth, which Flynn felt should be left to the uniformed police and to First Deputy Commissioner Driscoll, who had responsibility for those matters. Instead, Flynn wanted his men to concentrate on detecting and tracking down murderers, kidnappers, and other similar criminals. Flynn's men also became a Secret Service–type force of detectives, with the local precinct police captains where they were stationed never knowing the cases that they were working on. Even Commissioner Cropsey was kept out of the loop by Flynn, who was concerned about leaks coming from the police department that could threaten the safety of his men and compromise their investigations.[20]

One of his early investigations involved the kidnapping of children by criminals who sent "Black Hand" letters to the victims' families. The end of the Morello–Lupo gang had not resulted in an end to the use of this type of blackmail and extortion, where groups of criminals would pretend to be part of the Black Hand society and send letters adorned with different types of death symbols to Italian merchants and wealthy families, ordering them to "pay or die." In the case of the kidnappings, it was their children's lives that were in danger. Some families paid and got their children back; others did not, and their children were killed. The children who were returned home after payment had been told to never give any details about the ordeal or what their captors looked like, or else their families would be killed. Some of the kidnapped children bore scars on their wrists from ropes and straps that had been used to restrain them, and one child had burn marks on his body. For some of the survivors, the emotional trauma was overwhelming. One kidnapped child was emaciated when returned to his parents, and his eyes were described as having "the haunted look of a scared child."[21]

On November 19, 1910, eight-year-old Giuseppe Longo was playing in front of his father's grocery store in Brooklyn when a stranger wearing a slouch hat asked him if he would like to go with him to see a movie. The boy said yes, and the stranger took him to an elevated train for what the boy thought was the ride to the movie theater. When he asked the man where the movie was, the only reply he got was that it would be a good movie. Their destination, however, turned out to be a five-story tenement building on East 63rd Street in Manhattan. When they arrived at the building, Longo was scared and didn't want to go inside. The kidnapper then put his hand over the boy's mouth, carried him upstairs, and placed him in a room in one of the apartments. There was a woman there with her two small children. She gave Longo some bread and warned him that if he tried to escape, he would be killed.[22]

A couple of hours later, Michael Rizzo, Longo's cousin and one year younger than him, was brought into the room. He told Longo that a man had approached him that same day in front of his house in Brooklyn.

He'd persuaded Rizzo to join him for a trip to a movie and promised to buy him candy. Instead, he took him to the tenement building. Rizzo was kept in the locked room with Longo until December 3, when a member of the kidnapping gang moved Rizzo to another location. Both boys' families were wealthy and received Black Hand letters demanding large sums of money or their sons would die. "If you wish to see your dear son again, you must send $15,000," the kidnappers wrote to Longo's father, Francisco. "If you do not do this, the head of your boy will be sent to you in a postal package." A similar letter was sent to Nicola Rizzo, Michael's grandfather: "We have phoned you and now we send you the present letter and tell you that you must pay us $5,000 if you want your boy. If you don't have the cash, we must send you your boy's head." Each of the boys' families refused to pay and instead turned the letters over to the police.[23]

As soon as Flynn learned of the kidnappings, he chose three of his best Italian detectives to go after the criminals and rescue the boys. He didn't want the case to be dismissed in court due to a lack of evidence, so he instructed his team to not make any arrests unless they saw the kidnappers with the children. Flynn realized that he was sending the young detectives on a dangerous mission. He told them that they would be matching wits with crafty and desperate criminals and that they might have to risk their lives in order to apprehend them. The three detectives chosen were Ralph Machelli and Rocco Cavane from Manhattan and Charles Carrao from Brooklyn. They wore a variety of disguises as they mingled around neighborhoods in Manhattan known to be centers for Italian criminals using Black Hand extortion methods. One posed as an organ grinder, another a peddler, and still another a roustabout. They were taking a page out of Joseph Petrosino's playbook, the famed detective having used similar disguises early in his career.[24]

For nearly three weeks, Machelli, Cavane, and Carrao worked day and night trying to locate the boys and their kidnappers. The big break came on December 8, when Flynn received a tip from somebody he had befriended while working at the Secret Service. The tipster, who might very well have been an informant Flynn was still using, told Flynn that a "strange" boy had been seen in a tenement building at 330 East 63rd Street in Manhattan. Flynn sent about a dozen more detectives that afternoon to assist Machelli, Cavane, and Carrao in surrounding the building and making a raid once they could verify that one or both boys were inside. Michael Rizzo's twelve-year-old brother was brought along to help make the identification.[25]

When they arrived at the tenement, Machelli, Rizzo's brother, and a number of other detectives quietly entered the building and proceeded up the stairs to a room on the second floor, where they believed the kidnapped boys might be. There was a transom over the door, and the detectives didn't have a ladder on which one of them could climb and look into the room. So Machelli asked Rizzo's brother if he would be afraid to stand on Machelli's shoulders and look in. "Not a bit," he told Machelli. "I am ready." Machelli lifted him, and the boy saw his cousin, Giuseppe Longo, but not his brother Michael in the room. "Hello Joe," he said, but Longo was in such a state of fright that he did not recognize his cousin. He retreated to a corner of the room and began to cry. At that point, the detectives broke down the door. Machelli picked up Longo and told him not to cry. "I am not going to hurt you," he said. "I am a policeman, and I am going to take you home." The boy then stopped crying and told Machelli that "this place is full of bad men, and they are all black hand [criminals]."[26]

The detectives then searched the rest of the building and two adjoining ones. They didn't find Michael Rizzo but were able to arrest several members of the kidnapping gang. One of them tried to flee through a window and a fire escape but was caught by the detectives with their guns drawn. It took several of them to subdue the man, who "fought like a wild beast." Maria Rappa, who'd kept watch over Longo and was an important member of the group, was arrested as she returned to the tenement building from work. A total of ten members of the kidnapping ring were apprehended that day.[27]

Later that night, Michael was found standing alone and shivering in front of a bonfire on East 107th Street, having been let go by other members of the kidnapping gang after they learned of the arrests of their partners. Flynn rushed to the police station house where the boy had been brought and drove him around in his car to see if he could remember anything about locations and the people who kidnapped him. Flynn bought the boy a bright new red sweater, which delighted the youngster.[28]

The scene the next day at the Brooklyn courthouse where all the prisoners were scheduled to be arraigned was pandemonium. The angry crowd outside shouted insults at the kidnappers. An elderly woman tried to strike them with her cane. There were cries of "Let me get at them" from the crowd, and the police nervously got all the prisoners inside the courtroom safely. Longo's mother told reporters of her anguish while her son was in the hands of the kidnappers: "Every day I have been waiting. In the morning, no little Joe to dress, after school no little Joe, when we went to bed, no little Joe. I wanted to kill myself. And they cut his hair and sent me some of it, telling me that they would cut off his head if we did not pay money. . . . Do you wonder that I wanted to kill myself?"[29]

Before the trial began, Maria Rappa, who the authorities believed was ready to confess in open court, was visited in jail by an associate of the leader of the gang, Stanislao Pattenza. (Pattenza had also been arrested.) She was told that if she revealed any details of the gang's operations, she would be killed. She therefore denied knowing anything about the kidnapping during the trial. She was convicted and sentenced to a term of not less than twenty-five years and not more than forty-nine years and ten months in prison. Pattenza received the same sentence. The judge declared that he wished he could have imposed the death penalty. He told Pattenza, "You were the brains, the leader, and acknowledged chief, the king of the Black Handers. . . . Criminals of your class should never have been admitted to the country. No worse men are allowed to live than Black Handers. Men of your habits should be punished as severely as those guilty of murder. I regret that the law does not provide the death penalty for such crimes."[30]

But it was during his sentencing of Rappa, a mother of two children, that he expressed the feelings of most people regarding her role in the abductions:

> It is almost unbelievable that you . . . could have held these two crying, broken-hearted children, knowing as you must have known, the terrible suffering of their distracted parents. Your own children lived with you in the very room where you kept Giuseppe Longo a prisoner. The part that you have taken in this crime shows that you have not the spirit

or instinct of a mother. . . . The unnatural part you took in this crime stamps you as an undesirable member of society.[31]

The convictions and sentencing of Rappa and Pattenza were yet another feather in the cap of Flynn. He was meeting all the high expectations that the public and others had placed on him when he joined the NYPD. He had been in office less than two months and had already achieved a major success by apprehending a group of kidnappers and bringing their captives back home safely. Flynn received death threats afterward from friends of the kidnapping gang who sent him letters adorned with death hieroglyphics. It didn't faze him a bit. "They are so funny," he said, "that I want to read them. I don't believe a word in them, so they only afford me amusement."[32]

Although successful in the Longo and Rizzo case, Flynn was realistic about his ability to solve all the crimes that came his way. He believed the public was spoiled by reading detective yarns in which the fictional supermen detectives could do no wrong and always got the bad guys. "As supermen we are practically useless," Flynn wrote years later. "I've spent months on a case, chasing every clue and half-clue, and then never solved it." Flynn kept hoping he would find a detective novel that reflected real-life situations: "I used to read the new detective novels quite hopefully, thinking I might come across some sub-supersleuth, who had to give up a case, but now know that I never shall."[33]

One major case that he wasn't able to solve while he was with the police was the disappearance of Dorothy Arnold, an attractive, wealthy, and studious-looking twenty-five-year-old socialite who somehow vanished in broad daylight on Fifth Avenue, never to be seen again. The case became one of the most sensational of its time, covered extensively in the media and followed daily by a rapt public. Private detectives in addition to police departments around the country were active in the search for the young woman. Reports that she might be in Europe resulted in detectives and newspaper reporters traveling there to follow up on various leads. "There was nothing that could be done that was left undone," Flynn reminisced, "either by the police, private detectives retained by the family, or by the newspapers."[34]

It all began late in the morning on December 12, 1910, when Dorothy told her mother that she was going to shop for an evening gown to wear to her younger sister Marjorie's debutante party, which was going to be held in a few days. Her mother asked if she would like for her to go along, but Dorothy said no. She told her that if she found a dress she liked, she'd telephone her mother so she could come to the store to view it before Dorothy bought it. Dorothy began walking from her home on East 79th Street and stopped along the way to buy a half-pound box of chocolates, charging it to her family's account. She did the same at a bookstore, where she purchased *Engaged Girl Sketches*, a series of love stories that had appeared in *Ladies' Home Journal* magazine. The bookstore was located on Fifth Avenue and 27th Street, meaning that Dorothy had walked more than fifty blocks on a wintry day in New York. But she liked to walk, and the distance was no problem for the young, healthy woman.[35]

Thus far, there was nothing unusual about her demeanor. Later, it would be theorized that perhaps she committed suicide, depressed over a rejected manuscript that the aspiring writer had burned in the family's fireplace. But workers at the stores where she stopped and neighbors and other people who remembered her walking along the streets said that she looked cheerful that day and didn't seem to be worried about anything. Outside the bookstore, she ran into a friend, Gladys King, who by coincidence had with her an acceptance note for Dorothy's sister's debutante party that she was going to mail. Gladys handed the note to her, joking that she now wouldn't have to pay for postage. Dorothy laughed, and the two friends chatted for a little while and then said goodbye. It was now almost two o'clock. That would be the last time anybody remembered seeing Dorothy. She never made it to any dress stores.[36]

When she didn't return home for dinner, her parents became worried. She had always let them know beforehand if she was going to skip dinner. When she was still missing the next morning, they were frantic but did not call the police. Dorothy's father, Francis R. Arnold, a wealthy perfume importer and a very private man, didn't want the police involved. Instead, after first using a family friend to make inquiries, he hired Pinkerton's National Detective Agency to lead the search for his missing daughter. Pinkerton officials, despite Arnold's reluctance to involve the police, sent descriptive circulars about Dorothy to police departments throughout the country. Although Flynn and the NYPD undoubtedly received these circulars, they could not launch an official investigation until the Arnold family appealed directly to them for help. This did not occur until January 22, 1911, nearly six weeks after Dorothy's disappearance.[37]

When they met, the always savvy Flynn urged Arnold to immediately hold a news conference. Flynn knew better than most the power and influence of the press and how the media could be useful at times such as this, getting the story out and perhaps leading somebody, somewhere, to recognize the missing woman. Arnold resisted this idea for a few days but finally agreed to call reporters into his office and tell the world the story about his daughter's disappearance.[38]

It was a story that made reporters salivate. This was not yet another foreigner who had been kidnapped, a suspected Black Hand operation, but rather a young American heiress who apparently had everything going for her and just happened to vanish one day while going shopping. It had all the makings of a sensational story that the newspapers could milk as long as possible. Arnold told the reporters that he feared his daughter was dead. "Assuming that she walked up home through Central Park," he said, "she could have taken the lonely walk . . . along the reservoir. There, because of the laxity of police supervision over the park, I believe it quite possible that she might have been murdered by garroters, and her body thrown into the lake or the reservoir. [Such] atrocious things do happen, though there seems to be no justification for them."[39]

The police searched the bushes and shrubbery of Central Park and dragged the lake there but did not find a body or any clues. The search extended throughout the country and to Europe. Thousands of letters were sent to the family, to the police, and to Flynn, people claiming to have seen Dorothy. Many were crank letters, certainly spurred by reports that there was no limit to what the Arnold family would pay for Dorothy's safe return. "Anything that savored of a clew," Flynn wrote, "no matter what we thought of its improbability, we ran down."[40]

Dorothy was never found. There were naturally many theories as to what might have happened. As noted earlier, suicide seemed improbable since she appeared happy on the day she disappeared despite her previous disappointment over a rejected manuscript. Murder seemed the most likely explanation, but Flynn didn't think that had occurred since there was no evidence of foul play, and no motive was ever uncovered for why someone would want her dead. Another theory was that she slipped and fell on the icy pavement on her way back home from the bookstore, suffering a concussion that caused amnesia. But somebody would surely have seen her fall on the busy New York streets. Also, no hospital in the area reported treating a young woman with a concussion or suffering from amnesia that day. Somebody would also have seen her seized by kidnappers on the busy streets, although an abduction in isolated areas of Central Park was a possibility. However, no credible ransom notes were ever received by the family. It was also suggested by some that she might have been kidnapped by "White Slavers," but again, no evidence of that crime ever turned up.[41]

One tantalizing theory was that Dorothy, for whatever reason, simply wanted to disappear and start a new life. Perhaps she felt her family was too controlling—her father would not allow her to move out of the house and take an apartment in Greenwich Village, even though she was in her mid-twenties—or she was simply tired of being the rich girl and wanted a new identity. Writing about the case in the summer of 1925, Flynn admitted he was still baffled: "It seems incredible that a highly educated young woman such as Dorothy Arnold could vanish from human sight without leaving a tangible trace behind. Yet so far as could be learned, that is exactly what happened fifteen years ago next December. No fiction was ever more unbelievable."[42]

TROUBLE WITHIN THE TROIKA

As Flynn continued to reorganize the Detective Bureau and deal with crimes such as kidnappings, murders, and major robberies, he was given a new responsibility: cleaning up the city of its illegal gambling establishments. That was originally the job of First Deputy Commissioner Driscoll, who proved not up to the task. All forms of gambling were thriving under his watch. It is not clear who directed Flynn to begin raiding gambling houses, but since he reported only to Mayor Gaynor, it was probably the mayor who wanted Flynn to take care of this problem. Flynn wasn't happy about this, viewing it as a waste of his time and that of his men. He believed that detectives should focus on gathering evidence of crimes and building airtight cases against criminals before making any arrests, not raiding gambling or prostitution houses, which should be left to the uniformed policemen. Nevertheless, he went at this task with his usual unbridled determination and energy.[43]

Flynn's gambling raids "were unceasing and effective; the gamblers never knew where the lightning was going to strike next." It wasn't just the gamblers who were caught by surprise. Flynn's detectives also didn't know what their missions were going to be until the last moment. This was in line with Flynn's style of secrecy, ensuring that there would be no leaks or discovery by the criminals of an impending raid. Flynn's first raid on December 19, 1910, was spectacular, hitting three gambling houses on the same day. His method of attack had not been seen in the city for a long time.[44]

He had given orders to thirteen detectives to meet him in the afternoon at a subway station on 50th Street in Midtown Manhattan. They were not told the purpose of the meeting. A few minutes after they gathered, a car drove up, and out came Flynn and one of his top detectives. Flynn then told the group that they were going to raid a gambling house in the area and gave them the address of the building. But that is not all that Flynn gave his men. He distributed axes and crowbars to the surprised detectives, and then, like Eliot Ness and the Untouchables, who raided bootlegging operations in the 1920s, they all marched quickly and determinedly to their destination. It must have been a sight to behold, a group of tough-looking men carrying axes and crowbars in the streets of New York. People who saw them surely wondered whether this was a gang of thugs about to knock off a bank or a jewelry store.[45]

When the detectives reached the first gambling house, some of them went to the roof and others to the rear exits to block off all routes of escape. Then the remaining detectives entered the building and climbed the stairs to the attic, where the gambling was taking place. A heavy door blocked their entry, so they battered it down with their axes and crowbars. They found seventy-five men inside and arrested seventeen for whom they had warrants. Once Flynn saw that the raid was successful, he hurried to his car and raced to another rendezvous point in Manhattan where several more detectives were awaiting his arrival. He also gave this group axes and crowbars and told them the address of a second gambling house to be raided. After smashing down several heavy doors inside the building, the detectives found a large group of gamblers and arrested nine for whom they had warrants.[46]

Thus far, the raids were going along without a hitch. But the third one in Lower Manhattan turned violent, as several of the gamblers fought with Flynn's men in an attempt to escape. Many in the crowd of more than two hundred gamblers became panic-stricken when they saw several detectives crash into the room from a skylight above and heard the sounds of axes and crowbars from the other detectives who were breaking down doors from the outside. Fourteen gamblers who had warrants were arrested. All in all, it was a very successful day for Flynn and his men. The message had been sent throughout the city that gambling houses would now be attacked relentlessly by the NYPD.[47]

For the next several months, Flynn continued raiding gambling establishments, hitting more than eighty while he was in office. These raids were met with widespread public approval. In one raid in Harlem, a large crowd gathered to watch Flynn's men at work and shouted and jeered at the gamblers as they were led away in patrol wagons. Many in the crowd came forward to tell the detectives the names and addresses of those gamblers they recognized. Flynn pretended to be a worker at the establishment after the gamblers were arrested. The phones were still ringing with bettors wanting to place wagers on a racetrack. Flynn took the bets and got the names and phone numbers of the bettors, useful information for future arrests.[48]

But Flynn wasn't happy spending 70 percent of his time raiding gambling houses. It wasn't what he'd signed up to do when he joined the NYPD. He was also having problems with Commissioner Cropsey. The two men were not on speaking terms by early 1911. Cropsey was undoubtedly jealous of Flynn, who was getting continual and extensive favorable publicity in the newspapers for the job he was doing, ranging from arresting kidnappers and bringing their victims back home safely to initiating a war on gambling in New York. Flynn received "more newspaper notice than all the rest of the department together, and printed praise is meat and drink to all public officers." But what really irked the commissioner was Flynn's secrecy. Flynn would not reveal to Cropsey who his detectives were or what their secret missions involved. A frustrated and angry Cropsey demanded that Flynn do so, but Flynn told him that Mayor Gaynor had given him total autonomy from the rest of the police department when he joined in October 1910. He added that he feared his detectives' lives would be in danger if the nature of their secret work was revealed, a not-too-subtle hint that he didn't trust Cropsey to prevent leaks from his office. Flynn also said that he intended to protect his men no matter what since he alone was responsible for their safety and the success of their missions. Flynn's men loved him for his loyalty and refusal to buckle under the pressure from Cropsey.[49]

Gaynor called the feuding commissioners into his office in February in an attempt to patch things up. The mayor "advised Commissioner Cropsey in a kindly way that he must not interfere with the former Secret Service officer in his management of the Detective Bureau." But Flynn apparently had had enough. He continued in his job for two more months but then handed in his resignation on April 15, to take effect on May 1. The cover story from the Gaynor administration was that he had "borrowed" Flynn for only six months from the Secret Service, and now that the time was up, Flynn was returning to his old job.[50]

When pressed by a reporter for the real reason he was quitting, Flynn revealed the frustration and anger that had been building up inside him for months:

> I am sorry that I have to talk about this thing at all. I am very reluctant to do so. Frankly, I am quitting the department because I found conditions to be greatly different from what was promised. I came here to do detective work, pure and simple. I wanted to reorganize the whole Detective Bureau and put it on a good working basis. I expected to be able to do this, because I have been a detective most of my life, and thought I was familiar with the work. Well, I had not been here long before I found that conditions were not going to be the way they had been promised. I found that a lot of people were working against

me. Just when I was getting into my stride I found that I was being saddled with a lot of extraneous matter. They handed to me the work of the Bureau of Repairs and Supplies for instance. This hampered me greatly. Then I was suddenly saddled with this gambling business. I did not want to do this work because it had been given to another Deputy. Then, many promises were made which were not kept. Things gradually were being run in a way to which I couldn't submit. The deputyship is a thankless job, and things reached such a pass that I became disgusted and decided to quit and go back to my Secret Service work.[51]

Flynn's friends told reporters that he had been assured by Gaynor that he would eventually be made commissioner of the NYPD, but he learned that there was never any intention on the part of the mayor to give him that post. His friends also said that Flynn was convinced that Cropsey and Driscoll were working against him and "that a systematic campaign to discredit him had been started and that outrageous stories were being circulated about him." Flynn also questioned the honesty and competency of many of those working in the police department. "It is the crookedest layout I have ever known," he reportedly told his friends. "Men, both high and low, who have shown themselves to be incompetent and unworthy of trust have been continued in their positions until it is absolutely impossible to get results."[52]

Flynn's resignation was front-page news in many papers, with head-lines clearly showing whose side the media was on. "Flynn Harried into Quitting the Police," the *New York Times* wrote, while "Flynn Is Glad to Quit His 'Thankless Job'" was the headline in the *Brooklyn Daily Times*. The *New York Times* praised Flynn for "doing more within six months to clean up the city of gamblers and crooks and solve important crimes than any other person in years." The *New-York Tribune* lamented that Flynn's resignation "is a loss to the city and a blow to the Gaynor administration."[53]

Flynn resumed his job as head of the New York office of the Secret Service on May 23. For the next year, he chased down counterfeiters both in New York and in other states, making a number of major arrests. One of these was the capture in October 1911 of Albert Leon, a Russian political refugee and leader of a gang of counterfeiters passing bogus $10 notes. Flynn and his men arrested Leon in New York just as he was about to board a ship bound for Dutch Guinea in South America. In another incident, Flynn and his agents were on a ferry to New York with a counterfeiter they had earlier arrested when the prisoner opened a window in the cabin where he was being held and jumped into the Hudson River. He refused to grab life buoys that were thrown his way, choosing to drown himself rather than spend any time in prison. He was not in handcuffs because the Secret Service did not like to attract public attention by escorting suspects in restraints.[54]

When he wasn't busy dealing with counterfeiters, Flynn spent his spare time writing stories for newspapers about his past adventures with the Secret Service. One of these was about the barrel murder mystery and his pursuit of the Morello–Lupo gang. That story was read by Ignazio Lupo (Lupo the Wolf), who was serving his sentence for counterfeiting in the U.S. Penitentiary in Atlanta. An angry Lupo (or his attorneys) wrote a scathing letter to U.S. Attorney General George W. Wickersham, accusing Flynn of "self-advertising" and writing the story only to enhance his career. Lupo claimed that he was not involved with the barrel murder and that Flynn's story prejudiced public opinion against him.[55]

Meanwhile, conditions within the NYPD deteriorated after Flynn's departure. Gaynor was embarrassed and angered by Flynn's resignation and blistering attack on the management of the police department. He soon forced Commissioner Cropsey to resign—Cropsey had failed to follow Gaynor's policy of using the exact numerical order of the civil service list to hire new policemen—replacing him with Rhinelander Waldo, the city's fire commissioner, who was later found by an investigative committee to be "incompetent and unfit to perform the duties of his office." George Dougherty, superintendent of Pinkerton's National Detective Agency, left his job there to become head of the NYPD's Detective Bureau but proved unable to match Flynn's effectiveness in dealing with the various crimes that plagued New York.[56]

By August 1911, "a reign of terror" was occurring in the Italian communities in Manhattan, with bombings, murders, and kidnappings becoming almost a daily occurrence. The Italian consul general, Signor G. Fara Forni, blamed the police, claiming that they were not doing enough to protect the victims of these crimes. Reporters flocked to Flynn to get his view on the deteriorating situation in New York. "The trouble is almost altogether with the management of the detectives," Flynn said. "The department ought to have men, not a great many, just a few capable men, who specialize in looking out for bomb throwers and kidnappers." Flynn stated that such a group of detectives should not be given any other assignments that could interfere with their work: "The various methods of the blackmailing bomb throwers and kidnappers should be A, B, C's to them. Then they would get results." Flynn cited his unit at the Secret Service as an example of the benefits of specialization: "Take my own department here, for example. We are here to stamp out counterfeiting. They must do that, and they must study counterfeiting until they know all the distinguishing tricks of the business. They know their work, and are expected to know it, no matter if they know nothing else. The result is that we have reduced counterfeiting to a minimum."[57]

As bad as things were for the NYPD in the summer of 1911, it got much worse the next year, when one of the biggest scandals in the department's history occurred. The head of the department's vice squad, Lieutenant Charles Becker, a notoriously corrupt cop, secretly went into business with a gambler, Herman Rosenthal, investing in Rosenthal's gambling house in Midtown Manhattan and offering protection for 20 percent of the profits. Payoffs to the police by gamblers, owners of houses of prostitution, and others weren't that unusual in New York; the Lexow Committee had uncovered such activities in its investigation in the 1890s. But what made this front-page news was what Becker allegedly did to prevent his actions from becoming publicly known.[58]

Commissioner Waldo received several anonymous reports that Becker was corrupt. Waldo met with his lieutenant, who denied any wrongdoing. To prove his "honesty," Becker decided to raid Rosenthal's club in April 1912. This upset Rosenthal, who then went to District Attorney Charles Whitman and accused Becker of numerous shakedowns and accepting payoffs. Whitman didn't believe Rosenthal; after all, he was just an angry gambler trying to get revenge on the police. But when Rosenthal went to the media and told his story, the resulting newspaper headlines forced Whitman to act. He convened a grand jury, with Rosenthal scheduled as the star witness beginning on July 16.[59]

Rosenthal, however, never made it to the courtroom. After dining at the Metropole Hotel in Midtown Manhattan on the evening of July 15, he was shot dead by four men as he left the hotel around two in the morning. The gunmen fled in a gray Packard sedan but were eventually arrested. So too was Jack Rose, a gambler who claimed that Becker had enlisted him to hire a gang of mobsters to kill Rosenthal. Becker was taken into custody and tried for Rosenthal's murder, while Rose was granted immunity for his testimony. The trial was followed closely by people throughout the country. Whitman now saw the political value of launching a vigorous prosecution of Becker, which he would use success-fully as a stepping stone to the governor's office.[60]

Becker was convicted of murder, but it was overturned by the appeals court, which ruled that the verdict was "shockingly against the weight of evidence." The judge in the case, John Goff, was also found to be biased in favor of the prosecution. A second trial, however, resulted in another guilty verdict. Becker was sentenced to death and on July 30, 1915, became the first policeman in America to die in the electric chair. The four gunmen had suffered the same fate a year earlier after being found guilty in a separate trial.[61]

In the aftermath of the Rosenthal murder, the New York City Board of Aldermen created a special committee in August 1912 to investigate the NYPD due to the "intense public excitement and indignation" police involvement in the killing had caused. The Curran Committee, named after its chairman, Henry H. Curran, needed a leader for the investiga-tion who was beyond reproach for his honesty and integrity, someone the public could trust to conduct a thorough investigation. The obvious choice was William Flynn, but he was a busy man with the Secret Service and, given his experience with the NYPD, might want to stay as far away as possible. It is not known why he accepted the temporary assignment, but it could be that he was persuaded to do so by Secretary of the Treasury Franklin MacVeagh, Flynn's ultimate boss, as the Secret Service was part of the Treasury Department. Curran visited MacVeagh in Washington on August 21 to plead his case for "borrowing" Flynn for the investigation.[62]

The news that Flynn was going to be the chief investigator for the committee "caused a sensation in police circles." It was reported that

Flynn's investigation would "trace the course of graft from the dives and gambling halls to the policemen, or other collectors and from them to their superiors in the department and to the politicians who act as the real protectors of the law breakers." Flynn, however, did not last long with the committee, resigning in November due to Mayor Gaynor's withholding of payment for his services. It was probably Gaynor's way to get back at Flynn for embarrassing him when he suddenly resigned from the police department and criticized those who were in charge. The committee continued its work until March 1913 and issued a final report in June, which, like the 1895 Lexow Committee report, was a scathing indictment of police corruption and graft in New York City.[63]

Flynn returned to his old job and was promoted in December to chief of the Secret Service. John Wilkie had left that position to become chief supervising special agent of the U.S. Customs Service. For Flynn, his promotion was a dream come true. He was now in charge of an organization that he loved and anticipated spending many more years keeping America safe from counterfeiters. Soon, however, he and the Secret Service would be called on to keep America safe from a new type of adversary, one that would pose a serious threat to national security.

CHAPTER FOUR

On the Trail of
German Spies and Saboteurs

ANYBODY WHO GROWS UP IN NEW YORK IS TAUGHT FROM EARLY CHILD-hood that there is no other place in the world like the Big Apple. William Flynn was no different. He was a New Yorker through and through. "He was reared there," wrote Walter Bowen, who worked at the Secret Service after Flynn left and became its official historian by congressional appointment. "His family was reared there; his best friends were there. He and his family had breathed its tangy atmosphere for so long and loved the looks of its skyline so much that there was just no other place, no other people, to match New York. Roots ran deep, too deep to be wrenched up without permanent damage."[1]

Flynn didn't want to move to Washington, D.C., which he would have to do in order to be chief of the Secret Service. He had an idea, however, for how he could have his cake and eat it too. He met with Treasury Secretary MacVeagh on December 16, 1912, the day before the official announcement of Flynn's promotion was scheduled to be made. He had a proposal for MacVeagh. Instead of Flynn moving to Washington, why not move the Secret Service headquarters to New York City? Only somebody of Flynn's stature—and a true New Yorker—would make such a bold request. MacVeagh, of course, turned that offer down, telling Flynn it would be detrimental to the Secret Service to have its national headquarters anywhere else but Washington. The two men, though, reached a compromise. The headquarters would remain in

Washington, but Flynn could continue to live and operate in New York, making frequent commutes to the nation's capital at his own expense. Flynn and MacVeagh agreed that the arrangement would necessitate a $500 reduction in Flynn's yearly salary of $3,600.[2]

As expected, the media exulted in Flynn's promotion. He was approaching mythical status in terms of the public's perception of his abilities. One newspaper's headline gushed, "Why Counterfeiters Can No Longer Sleep," and the story declared that Flynn "can detect a bad coin or bill with both hands tied behind his back." But counterfeiting was not all that Flynn had to deal with in his new position. When he was head of the New York office, he had been responsible for protecting presidents when they visited the city or surrounding areas. Now, though, he had to safeguard their lives wherever they traveled in the United States or abroad. Foreign trips by presidents particularly worried the Secret Service since they would have to operate in unfamiliar environments.[3]

Such a trip occurred the day after Flynn took office, when President William Howard Taft traveled to Panama to conduct an inspection of the Panama Canal. Flynn sent three agents to accompany the president on this trip. The agents got jittery when, during a reception for Taft at the palace of the president of Panama in Panama City, they heard a loud explosion nearby. Rumors had been circulating earlier that an anti-Taft demonstration was planned for that night. Two of the agents immediately left the reception to investigate, using the decorated and glittering horse-drawn carriage that had brought Taft to the reception to take them to Cathedral Square, where they thought the explosion might have occurred. As they traveled through the streets, many people thought the official-looking carriage was carrying Taft and saluted and bowed as the vehicle passed by. The startled agents simply bowed back. When they arrived at the square, they found a large crowd of Panamanians making a lot of noise and having a good time. Whatever explosion took place was not related to any threat to the president.[4]

Flynn also had to worry about the upcoming Inauguration Day scheduled for March 4. Both President Taft and President-elect Woodrow Wilson would be in the same place at the same time, always a high-risk situation for the Secret Service. As was procedure, Flynn brought in agents from all over the country to assist in preparations for the ceremony and also take up posts along the parade route and other areas. He was also receiving reports from field agents in other states regarding the backgrounds of groups and organizations that were boarding trains for Washington to attend the festivities. It was a stressful day for Flynn, but it passed without incident to the great relief of the new chief.[5]

As busy as Flynn was dealing with counterfeiters and protecting presidents, he still found time to write. Like he did in 1911, he wrote a series of articles for newspapers in 1914 recounting some of his Secret Service adventures. One of these, which was reprinted in many papers across the country, dealt with the "Black Hand" methods of the Morello–Lupo gang. An Idaho newspaper reprinted the story on June 28, 1914, under the headline "Black Hand Secrets Revealed by Chief of Secret Service." As coincidence would have it, on that very day, thousands of miles away, another group with the name Black Hand was involved in one of the most famous assassinations in history, an event that sparked World War I. While the United States would not be drawn into that conflict until 1917, there would soon be war-related activities occurring in the country. And the main perpetrators would be highly trained and well-financed German agents carrying out a secret war against America.[6]

FOR THE FATHERLAND

There is something about the name "Black Hand" that has been attractive to criminals, terrorists, and revolutionaries. The Italian criminals whom Flynn dealt with in the United States adopted that name, even though there was never a central, organized Black Hand society in America, just mafiosos, criminals, and others taking advantage of the fear that name evoked in its victims. That was not the case in Serbia, where the Black Hand, also known as "Unification or Death," was an organized terrorist group dedicated to ending Austro-Hungarian rule in the Balkans and creating a pan-Slavic empire under Serbian control.[7]

Toward that end, Gavrilo Princip, a nineteen-year-old Bosnian Serb nationalist who had been trained and armed by the Black Hand, shot and killed Archduke Franz Ferdinand, heir to the throne of the Austro-Hungarian Empire, and his wife, Sophie, as they rode in a car through the streets of Sarajevo, Bosnia and Herzegovina, during a visit there on June 28, 1914. Princip believed this would be the first step in uniting the South Slav peoples. Instead, the assassination set off a sequence of events that soon led to World War I. Austria-Hungary declared war on Serbia, triggering various alliances to come into play. Russia, France, and eventually Britain (the Triple Entente) joined with Serbia, while Germany and Italy were aligned with Austria-Hungary (the Triple Alliance), although Italy at first remained neutral and then later switched sides, entering the war in 1915 with the Triple Entente.[8]

The United States was determined to remain neutral. On August 19, 1914, President Wilson proclaimed U.S. neutrality in a message to Congress, concluding with the following words:

> I venture, therefore, my fellow countrymen, to speak a solemn word of warning to you against that deepest, most subtle, most essential breach of neutrality which may spring out of partisanship, out of passionately taking sides. The United States must be neutral in fact, as well as in name, during these days that are to try men's souls. We must be impartial in thought, as well as action, must put a curb upon our sentiments, as well as upon every transaction that might be construed as a preference of one party to the struggle before another.[9]

The Germans, however, did not view U.S. actions during the early war years as neutral. The powerful British navy had imposed a blockade of German ports, thereby cutting off supplies to Germany from the outside world. But U.S. trade with Britain continued, and America "became the main supplier of arms, munitions, military and civilian goods for the enemies of Germany and her allies in early 1915." The Germans didn't wait until then to set up a clandestine group in the United States with the purpose of organizing, financing, and implementing the German strategy for America, including sabotaging U.S. trade with Britain. The secret group was established in late August 1914 and comprised of diplomats, businessmen, secret agents, and propagandists. New York was chosen as its base of operations since it "was the center of American political and economic power by the fall of 1914." It was also a beehive of foreign intrigue: "During the first months of the war, the city bristled with foreign agents of all colors and backgrounds vying for financial backing, political influence, and intelligence on the opposition."[10]

The man put in charge of the intelligence network in America was the German ambassador, Count Johann Heinrich von Bernstorff. A tall, dashing, and charming diplomat, he had been the ambassador to the United States since 1908 and was therefore very familiar with American politics and culture. He also had an American-born wife, and the couple was active and popular in Washington, D.C., social circles. Von Bernstorff was highly intelligent and received numerous honorary degrees from U.S. universities. With his military background, having served for eight years in a Prussian artillery unit, he was the perfect man to be the secret head of the foreign agents. He could combine his understanding of military strategy with the skills of a diplomat and maintain the cover of his ambassadorship to deny any knowledge of the network's activities if they became public.[11]

Von Bernstorff placed his three top aides in different buildings in Lower Manhattan, "in convenient proximity to both Wall Street and New York Harbor." Franz von Papen, the military attaché, created an intelligence center at 60 Wall Street that was disguised as an advertising agency. Karl Boy-Ed, the naval attaché, worked out of the German consulate at 11 Broadway, a structure overlooking the harbor, which allowed him to keep track of U.S. and other nations' ship movements. And Dr. Heinrich F. Albert, the commercial attaché, operated out of the Hamburg-American Building at 45 Broadway. Von Bernstorff also worked frequently in New York, maintaining a suite in the Ritz-Carlton hotel and a Long Island summer residence.[12]

While von Bernstorff was nominally the head of the secret intelligence network, it was really Albert who held the most influence in the group. "In all matters of policy," a German agent later told U.S. investigators, "it is stated that Dr. Albert ranked Bernstorff, Von Papen and Boy-Ed by many points. They all had to go to him. There was no plot or scheme which was unknown to him. As a result, literally nothing of import went on without Albert's approval or at least his knowledge." Albert's power came from his control of the purse strings. He had been given $27 million from the German government to dispense for a range of activities, including propaganda, espionage, and sabotage. He would raise millions of dollars more through the successful issues of short-term German treasury notes floated through a Wall Street investment firm.[13]

Although Albert, who was born in 1874, used the title "Dr." before his name, there is no evidence that he completed or even started doctoral studies at any university in Germany or elsewhere. He passed the bar exam in 1901 and served in a variety of legal roles in the German Department of the Interior. He rose through the ranks and was promoted to privy counselor in 1911. Albert was a reserved and detail-oriented manager and once in America "became familiar with the exacting ways to fund a secret army." He opened bank accounts throughout the country, transferred money constantly, and laundered the secret funds through legitimate businesses owned by German Americans. Albert was thus able to distribute "a fortune of nearly untraceable funds." He was perfect for the job. "He knew finance, the economy of industry, the finesse of diplomacy and the odd, yet scientific twists of the inventor's mind," author John Price Jones wrote in 1917. He was also a good liar. Even Flynn was impressed with his talent for avoiding the truth:

> One of the most remarkable characteristics of this rather remarkable man was his uncanny ability to remember to-day the details of an intricate untruth he told you two weeks ago. There were times that he lied, knowing that you knew he lied, but knowing also that you couldn't prove it. Two weeks later, even three and four weeks later, he would repeat that obvious untruth in detail, leaving you more or less baffled. Likewise it left you with a sort of respect for the mind that carrying a thousand and one schemes and plans, could revert to a statement a month old and repeat it almost verbatim.[14]

For the first several months, Albert focused mainly on propaganda activities. The British were clearly winning that battle, with the majority of American newspapers pro-British and anti-German. "British publicity in America," wrote William McAdoo, the secretary of the treasury during this period, "was characterized by an artistic unity and singleness of purpose. The main idea was to create an impression that the Germans were barbarians, and the picture was built up carefully, and by degrees, with all unessentials and contradictions eliminated." Britain controlled the transatlantic cables and enforced strict censorship, enabling them to send only the news they wanted Americans to read. They therefore prevented any news dispatches from Europe that were favorable to Germany from reaching the United States. A British newspaper publisher gushed in 1914 that "we have . . . no better allies in America than the editors of the great papers." One of the newspapers that Albert was funding in an attempt to counter British propaganda and tilt American public opinion in favor of Germany was *The Fatherland*, a weekly pro-German newspaper in English published by a young German American, George Viereck. The cover page of the newspaper proclaimed, "Fair Play for Germany and Austria-Hungary." But its polemic and acerbic nature turned off a lot of people. In one of the issues, Viereck bemoaned the pro-British sentiments of the public, newspapers, and Congress, warning that "we will not permit America to be the pawn of Great Britain." He vowed, "We shall teach you a lesson. We shall go into the arena of politics. We shall try to beat you at your own game."[15]

By early 1915, Germany decided it needed to do more than just propaganda activities in America. It was time to let the secret intelligence network now spring into action, the network that had been set up in the United States in August and had since then been recruiting agents and others. On January 24, 1915, Rudolf Nadolny, the chief of the political section of the German Imperial General Staff, requested that the Foreign Office send a telegram in code to the German embassy in Washington, authorizing the beginning of a sabotage campaign in the United States. It instructed von Papen, the military attaché, "to find suitable personnel for sabotage in the United States and Canada" and stated that "in the United States, sabotage can cover all kinds of factories for military supplies." The German sabotage campaign was not limited to only factories, however, but also included ships and other vessels carrying munitions to the Allies.[16]

The attacks on ships began on February 7, when the British freighter SS *Grindon Hall* caught fire in the Norfolk, Virginia, harbor. A little more than a week later, the Italian steamer *Regina d'Italia* burst into flames at a pier in Jersey City, New Jersey. Its destination Naples, the steamer was carrying oil, kerosene, and cotton. Then, on February 29, a "cigar bomb" was found hidden in a bag of sugar on the British freighter SS *Knutsford* in New York Harbor. Another Italian steamer, the SS *San Guglielmo*, was the target of the sabotage campaign when it sailed for Naples from New York with six thousand bales of cotton on March 16, only to catch fire when it arrived at its destination on April 11, burning the entire cargo. There were many other cases of the sabotage of ships from the United States destined for Allied ports in the early months of 1915.[17]

The sabotage campaign continued through the winter and into the spring. But von Papen expressed frustration about attacking munitions factories. "Sabotage against factories over here is making little progress," he wrote in a secret telegram to Berlin on March 17, "since all factories are guarded by hundreds of secret agents and all German-American and Irish workers have been fired." Nevertheless, there were many cases of suspicious incidents at plants producing supplies for the Allies. One of these occurred in January, when a steel mill belonging to the John A. Roebling's Sons Company in Trenton, New Jersey, burned to the ground. The company had been manufacturing antisubmarine netting and artillery chains.[18]

To assist in the sabotage operations, Germany sent a top naval intelligence officer, Captain Franz von Rintelen, to the United States in April along with several teams of saboteurs. Von Rintelen entered the United States under an alias and with a false Swiss passport. He kept busy for several months, planning sabotage attacks on shipping and factories. He also incited labor unrest in order to tie up the docks and delay shipments of supplies to the Allies. Von Rintelen arranged for dock workers to be paid to go on strike, resulting in a series of strikes in ports throughout the country. But during the summer, he was arrested in England while traveling back to Germany and interned there as a prisoner of war. He was extradited to the United States in 1917 and served a prison term in the U.S. penitentiary in Atlanta until his release in 1920.[19]

Another saboteur who came to the United States in April was Lieutenant Robert Fay. His mission was to place time bombs on the rudders of munitions ships sailing from New York to Europe. The plan was to have the bombs explode within an hour or so after the ships left the harbor. If things worked perfectly, Fay expected the ships to sink. But if not, then at least the rudders would be destroyed and possibly the propeller screws, leaving the munitions ships stranded in the ocean.[20]

Working with several other conspirators, Fay went about constructing the bombs in his brother-in-law's garage in Weehawken, New Jersey. Both the Secret Service and the NYPD bomb squad eventually learned of this, and Fay was arrested in October before he could place any of the bombs on the ships. A search of the garage uncovered several completed bombs, twenty-five sticks of dynamite, four hundred and fifty pounds of chlorate of potash, four hundred percussion caps, and two hundred bomb cylinders.[21]

The Secret Service had some fun with the media when discussing the Fay case. It turned out that Fay believed in astrology and had at one time consulted an Egyptian astrologer who told him, among other things, that "there is about you a certain ingeniousness" and that he had "considerable mechanical ability which [he] should develop." The astrologer also told him that "your most fortunate months are February and October" and his "most fortunate days are Sunday and Thursday." The astrologer was right about Fay being smart and having technical skills but dead wrong about his lucky days and months. A Secret Service agent pointed out to reporters that Fay was arrested on a Sunday and arraigned the following Thursday, both days falling in the month of October.[22]

At the same time that Germany was launching a sabotage campaign in the United States, it was also unleashing unrestricted submarine warfare in the Atlantic Ocean. On May 7, a German U-boat sank the British passenger ship *Lusitania* off the coast of Ireland on its return voyage from New York to Liverpool, killing one thousand one hundred and ninety-eight people, including one hundred and twenty-eight Americans. A week before the torpedoing of the ship, which was also carrying a cargo of rifle ammunition and shells, an advertisement appeared in the *New York Times* warning Americans not to travel on British ships due to the risk of being torpedoed. The warning was signed by the German embassy.[23]

The sinking of the *Lusitania* and the loss of American lives angered the U.S. public and led many to believe that the United States would now declare war on Germany. President Wilson, however, was not yet ready to do that. But Germany was in effect fighting an undeclared war against the United States with its rash of sabotage attacks on ships and factories. And now they'd killed Americans traveling on an ocean liner, with the German embassy apparently having advance knowledge of that attack. Wilson wanted to know everything that the Germans were up to and what they might be planning. He issued an executive order on May 14, instructing Secretary of the Treasury William McAdoo to use the Secret Service to conduct surveillance of the German and Austrian-Hungarian embassies in Washington.[24]

This was great news for Flynn. He relished the opportunity to now be able to go after the Germans with no restrictions on whom he could target. Prior to Wilson's executive order, the Secret Service was limited in its operations to targeting only clerks, technicians, errand boys, and other low-level personnel in the network. Diplomats had been off-limits, a frustration for Flynn. "Sometimes perhaps," Flynn wrote, "some of us were impatient with the President. Some of us may have been indignant because the administration did not act more forcefully when the numerous unfriendly acts of Germany were perpetrated." Immediately after the executive order was issued, Flynn had his agents rent an apartment near the German and Austrian-Hungarian embassies and hook up wires connecting every telephone in the embassies with telephones in the apartment. When a phone receiver was lifted in one of the embassies, a light would flash in the Secret Service apartment, and when a phone rang in one of the embassies, one would also ring in the apartment. Four stenographers, who were also expert linguists, worked in relay teams around the clock, transcribing all the conversations.[25]

Flynn knew, however, as did McAdoo, that the center of German espionage and sabotage activities in the United States was New York City. He therefore formed an eleven-man counterespionage unit headquartered on the top floor of the U.S. Custom House in Lower Manhattan. He put his most trusted aide, Frank Burke, in charge of it. Short and stocky, the bespectacled Burke had been with Flynn since the early days in New York, when they were tracking down the Morello–Lupo gang. Prior to that, he was the chief of police in Tampa, Florida, where he helped protect U.S. troops en route to Cuba during the Spanish-American War of 1898. Burke was "shrewd, bold, and fearless, and completely dedicated to his job." The counterespionage unit spent countless hours following German diplomats and others around New York, hoping to find evidence linking them to the sabotage campaign. They were sometimes joined by members of the NYPD bomb squad under the direction of Captain Thomas Tunney, who was conducting his own investigation into the fires and bombings of ships and factories that were occurring in the New York area.[26]

While the Secret Service's special unit was tracking German agents, Flynn was asked by McAdoo to look into another matter. A German-owned wireless station in Sayville, Long Island, was suspected of sending secret messages to another station in Nauen, Germany, regarding the movements of neutral ships departing from the East Coast. These messages would then be retransmitted to the German submarines. But the government had no solid evidence that the Sayville station was actually sending such messages.[27]

Flynn needed a way to determine if and how the apparently harmless Morse code messages, which first had to be approved by U.S. government censors before they were sent out, contained hidden information. He met with L. R. Krumm, the chief radio inspector for the Port of New York, who told him that there was an amateur radio operator who had invented a device that could make phonographic records from wireless transmissions using wax cylinders. This would allow analysts to compare the censored messages that they had approved for submission with those that were sent out and recorded on the wax cylinders. By having the two sets of messages, analysts could determine if there were any subtle variations or other irregularities between the two, variations that government operators who were listening in real time to the transmissions would not have been able to detect. Among the variations that could represent secret words or phrases were sounds too faint to hear when listening in real time but amplified by the recordings, pauses in the Morse code transmissions, slight lengthenings of the spaces between the dots and dashes, and so forth. Recordings of high-speed transmissions could also be played at a slower pace for deciphering.[28]

Krumm arranged for Flynn to meet the amateur radio operator, Charles Apgar, who had made wireless telegraphy his hobby for the past several years. Flynn was impressed with Apgar and his invention and immediately put him on the Secret Service payroll, telling him to "get busy" and start making recordings of the Sayville station transmissions for a two-week period. "Needless to state," Apgar recalled, "it was some pleasure at least to aid in taking the 'Say' out of Sayville." Each night beginning on June 7 and ending on June 21, Apgar made recordings and transcribed them the next morning. He then delivered each recording and transcript to Flynn when the chief was in New York or sent it to him when he was in Washington. (This allowed for an almost immediate comparison with the censored messages that had been sent.) "That not a single message was missed and hundreds were recorded is evidence that every instrument and device of my home set did its duty fully and promptly," Apgar wrote, "which is to me, of course, very gratifying." Apgar's recordings provided enough data for government analysts to determine that Sayville was indeed sending coded messages to Germany. The government seized the site on July 9 and turned it over to U.S. naval officers to operate.[29]

Meanwhile, the counterespionage unit was spending the summer tailing German diplomats and anybody else associated with them. One of their targets was Franz von Papen, the military attaché who directed many subversive activities in the United States and once derisively referred to U.S. law enforcement and intelligence agents as "these American fools" in a letter he wrote to his wife. Von Papen was trained in evasion techniques by Paul Koenig, who headed the Hamburg-American steamship line's corporate security office, where much of the spying and sabotage work was coordinated. For example, von Papen would lead Secret Service agents or police detectives who were following him into a Macy's or Gimbels department store and then change elevators at every floor on the way to the top and do the same on the way down. He would then leave the store using another exit.[30]

One person Flynn's agents had under surveillance who either never received training in evasion techniques or, if so, didn't follow it was George Viereck, the publisher of *The Fatherland*, the pro-German newspaper. Although the Secret Service had no direct evidence at the time that Viereck was linked to the spy and sabotage network, they figured that people who were part of that network might visit or associate with him, thereby providing further leads for their investigations. Little did they know when they first started how important following Viereck around Manhattan would ultimately prove to be.[31]

More Than Just a Briefcase

Frank Burke, head of the counterespionage unit that Flynn had assembled, was about to leave his office to attend to personal matters when the phone rang at half past two in the afternoon on July 24, 1915. On the other end of the line was W. H. Houghton, one of the members of the unit. He told Burke that he had followed Viereck to the Hamburg-American Building at 45 Broadway and seen him enter the structure. Burke wondered what Viereck was doing there. "In spite of my desire to take the afternoon off," Burke would later write, "I told Houghton that I would join him." It didn't take long for Burke to arrive, and the two agents hung around the entrance to the building, waiting for Viereck to exit to see where he might go next.[32]

At three o'clock, Viereck came out of the building with another man, somebody the agents didn't recognize. The person looked "conspicuously German." Viereck and the other man walked to the Rector Street station and boarded a Sixth Avenue elevated train bound for Harlem. Like Viereck, the stranger was not taking evasive action. Burke and Houghton thus had no trouble following them onto the same train. Viereck and his companion sat together on one side of the cross-seats in the center of the car. Houghton took the cross-seat directly opposite them, while Burke took the seat behind Viereck and the stranger. As he sat there, Burke tried to figure out who exactly Viereck's companion might be. The German man was carrying a large, heavily stuffed briefcase, and Viereck was being very polite and deferential to him. That—and the stranger's refined appearance—made Burke think that the man must be somebody of rank and importance in German circles.[33]

Burke also remembered that when he passed the stranger on his way to his seat, he'd noticed several oblique scars on one side of his face.

Then it hit him. He recalled that a U.S. customs attorney had told him six weeks earlier about a man named "Dr. Albert" who was about fifty years old, six foot one, and one hundred and ninety pounds, all of which matched the stranger. The customs attorney had also told Burke that Albert had saber scars on his face and "was the most important representative of the German government in the United States."[34]

When the train stopped at the 23rd Street station, Viereck got off but not Albert. Houghton followed Viereck, while Burke remained focused on Albert, whose briefcase lay on his seat between his body and the window side of the car. A young woman entered the train and took the seat that Viereck had just vacated. Albert began reading and didn't notice when the train reached 50th Street. He lived at the German Club on 59th Street and Central Park, requiring him to exit the Harlem-bound train at 50th Street and take a shuttle train that ran between 50th and 58th streets. Just as the train was about to leave the station, Albert realized that this was his stop, and he jumped from his seat, yelling at the guard to wait and keep the door open for him. He rushed out of the train to the platform and apparently did not hear the young woman shout out to him that he had left his briefcase on the seat. But he soon realized his mistake and tried to get back onto the train. Burke would later explain what happened next:

> When I saw that he had left his brief-case, I decided in a fraction of a second to get it. I told the girl that the brief-case belonged to me; I picked it up and started for the front door. Dr. Albert was then trying to get back in the car through the rear door. I could see, from the corner of my eye, that he was having some difficulty. A very fat woman was planted in the door; she was evidently asking something of the guard, while Dr. Albert tried to push by her.
>
> I suppose the young lady told the Doctor that some one had taken his brief-case when he finally got in the car, as I saw him come pouring out in a hurry. He seemed greatly disturbed. I had reached the platform by that time. There were enough passengers alighting from the train to give me a little cover. The Doctor was between me and the stairs, and I did not dare to start for the street at that moment. I went to the wall of the station, and pretended to light a cigar, striking one match after

another, and blowing them out, with the brief-case against the wall, partly covered by my coat.

After hastily glancing at the people on the platform, Dr. Albert rushed down the stairs. No train was in sight, and to remain on the platform if he returned, I knew would be disastrous, so I followed him, feeling I had more room on the ground than on the platform. When I reached the street, the Doctor was some distance out in the street where he could get a better view of pedestrians, with panic written on his face. Almost instantly he discovered me with the bag and dashed in my direction.[35]

The chase was now on, a German official desperately trying to run down a Secret Service agent in the streets of New York. Burke saw a rapidly moving Sixth Avenue surface car traveling uptown and jumped onto the running board near the conductor. Albert was franticly trying to catch up. Burke told the conductor that the man running toward the car was crazy and had just created a scene on the elevated train. The conductor could see that the man indeed looked distressed and was shouting and shaking his fist. The conductor didn't want him to cause any trouble on his car, so he told the motorman to keep going and not make the next stop.[36]

Burke got off at Eighth Avenue and 53rd Street, clutching the brief-case and dying to know what was inside. But he didn't want to waste a second getting away from Albert. So he boarded another surface car, this time one running downtown. When the car stopped after only a few blocks for what Burke thought was too long a time, he got off and went to a drugstore to telephone Flynn. The chief told him to stay put and that he'd be there right away. Flynn drove to the drugstore in his car, and the two men then went back to the office to examine the bag. Many of the contents were in German, which neither man could read. But a quick glance at the documents, letters, and other materials in the bag neverthe-less satisfied Burke that this was an important find and that "I had done a good Saturday's work."[37]

In the meantime, a dejected Albert went to the German Club and told von Papen and Boy-Ed (the military and naval attachés, respectively) what had just happened. The three men discussed various theories as to who stole the briefcase, figuring that the man Albert chased was either a common thief or a British agent. In an example of wishful thinking, they placed an ad in a newspaper offering a reward in case the man was indeed just a thief who, after opening the briefcase, wasn't interested in a bunch of German documents. The following classified ad appeared in the *New York Evening Telegram* a few days later: "Lost:–On Saturday, on 3.30 Harlem Elevated train, at 50th St. station, brown leather bag, containing documents. Deliver to G.H. Hoffman, 5 East 47th St., against $20 dollar reward." Hoffman was Albert's secretary.[38]

That the organization Albert was running had tens of millions of dollars at its disposal and only offered a $20 reward for the return of such a valuable briefcase is astonishing. It is also bewildering that Albert, as was his custom, took the briefcase home with him every day on the elevated train, risking it being lost or stolen rather than locking up its contents in a safe in his office. Flynn, after looking inside the briefcase with Burke on Saturday, telegraphed Secretary of the Treasury McAdoo, who was at his summer home in North Haven, Maine. He told his boss that he had to see him about an urgent matter. McAdoo told him to come up to North Haven, which Flynn did the next day, bringing the briefcase with him.[39]

McAdoo and Flynn, with the apparent assistance of others who knew German and could translate the materials, spent the day carefully going through the documents. What they discovered startled them. Albert's correspondence and reports showed that the German government was attempting to control and influence American public opinion by buying newspapers, creating news services, and subsidizing pro-German publications. *The Fatherland*'s publisher, George Viereck, for example, was on their payroll for approximately $1,500 a month. The briefcase's contents also revealed that the Germans, working with certain labor leaders, had incited strikes among longshoremen, munitions workers in factories, and employees at other plants producing goods that were of strategic value for the Allies. Additionally, they were cornering the supply of liquid chlorine, used for poison gas, in order to prevent it from being sent to the Allies and were attempting to acquire the Wright Airplane Company and its patents to use them to Germany's advantage.[40]

From Albert's papers, McAdoo and Flynn also learned that the Germans were the secret owners of the Bridgeport Projectile Company in Bridgeport, Connecticut, a plant that supposedly sold munitions to Britain, France, and Russia. But it was just a false-front company with a factory that took large orders for artillery shells and gunpowder from the Allies without any intention of making the deliveries. The idea was to divert orders away from legitimate U.S. munitions firms. In addition, the Germans planned to organize a movement to prevent exports of cotton to Britain and make it appear like a spontaneous effort among cotton growers in the South.[41]

While many of the items in Albert's briefcase were proof that Germany was violating U.S. neutrality and operating a propaganda, espionage, and sabotage network in the country, one item in particular must have made McAdoo and Flynn roll their eyes. There were plans prepared by Albert for a land and seaborne attack on New York City, the first step in a German military occupation of the United States. According to the plans, eighty-five thousand German soldiers would land on the New Jersey coast with the protection of the German navy. It was anticipated that there would be no American fleet in the area strong enough to offer any resistance to the invasion. Albert had statistics that indicated it was necessary to resupply New York City with food every five days. Therefore, the invading forces could cut the city off from the rest of the country within twenty-four hours and starve its residents and officials into submission. Then, "with 75% of the wealth of the entire country concentrated in New York in the enemy's hands, the occupation would cripple all effective resistance. The first invaders were to be reinforced soon after by another force, and the United States could be defeated within a reasonable length of time."[42]

McAdoo consulted with President Wilson, who was his father-in-law; Wilson's top aide, Colonel Edward House; and Secretary of State Robert Lansing regarding what to do about the contents of the briefcase. The United States was in a bind because announcing that it had evidence of German intrigue would mean revealing how it obtained such documents. Wilson did not want to admit that a U.S. Secret Service agent had stolen a briefcase belonging to a German diplomat, something that could cause an uproar in diplomatic circles around the world and possibly even lead to war with Germany. But Wilson wanted to alert the American public about German intrigue and also let the Germans and anybody else helping them know that the United States was aware of what they were doing, thereby making it difficult for them to continue their activities. It was decided that the best option was for the administration to leak some of the documents to the press.[43]

The *World*, a popular New York newspaper, was chosen to receive the documents. McAdoo met in total secrecy in a New York hotel room with Frank Cobb, the editorial manager of the *World*. Cobb was ecstatic to be the recipient of the briefcase's contents, envisioning sensational headlines that would undoubtedly catch the public's eye and increase the newspaper's circulation. McAdoo had one condition for Cobb, though. He was not to tell anybody, including his colleagues, how he came into possession of the documents. "He promised to observe this injunction," McAdoo wrote, "and he did."[44]

On August 15, New Yorkers were startled to read the story of German intrigue in America on page one in the Sunday edition of the *World*. It was under the banner headline "How Germany Has Worked in U.S. to Shape Opinion, Block the Allies and Get Munitions for Herself, Told in Secret Agents' Letters." The *World* continued to print exposés about the German network in two more editions of its paper that week. Newspapers around the country also reported on the *World*'s findings. An editorial in the *New York Evening Globe*, "Insult to the American People," stated that Germany's actions were an insult "as much as if she [Germany] had deliberately fired at our flag." The *Brooklyn Eagle* wrote, "The documents published by the New York World prefer such a serious indictment against agents of the German government that actions should be at once taken in Washington."[45]

It wasn't until December, however, that the State Department finally took action based on the Albert documents and on the files that Flynn and the Secret Service had compiled regarding German secret agents in the United States. Both Franz von Papen and Karl Boy-Ed were declared personae non gratae and ordered to leave the United States. Inexplicably, Albert was allowed to remain in the country despite McAdoo wanting him expelled. No action was taken against Ambassador Bernstorff either, even though he, along with Albert, was a major player in the spy and sabotage network.[46]

While the *World* did not reveal its source for the story about German intrigue, other newspapers strongly hinted that it was the Secret Service that was responsible for one of the biggest finds in U.S. counterespionage history. On August 18, three days after the *World*'s story first appeared, several newspapers ran the same piece provided by the International News Service, which disclosed that "positive proof of German efforts to promote strikes in industries involved in the shipment of war munitions from American ports is in possession of the United States secret service." The newspapers further noted that "a special squad of secret service men, picked for the duty, has been at work on the alleged violation of the United States neutrality laws for the past four months. William J. Flynn, chief of the secret service, is personally directing the efforts of this squad."[47]

Burke's identity as the agent who stole the briefcase was kept secret until 1931, when McAdoo wrote his memoirs and included in his book a firsthand account by Burke of his adventures on the elevated train that Saturday afternoon in July 1915. Until then, there had been many different theories regarding who took Albert's briefcase. One was that a young man had stolen it and, after looking at its contents, realized that this could be a good news story. He then took it to the *World* and got paid $10,000. Another theory was that a *World* reporter had shadowed Albert on the train and grabbed it while Albert was sleeping.[48]

The Germans, however, eventually became convinced that it was a British agent who snatched the briefcase. "Unfortunately they stole a fat portfolio from our good friend, Dr. Albert, in the elevated," von Papen wrote in a letter to his wife. "The English secret service of course." Burke, for his part, had been content to keep his key role in the briefcase affair unknown outside U.S. government circles, which led to some amusing incidents. Burke shared one of these in McAdoo's book: "A man named Pilinas entertained myself and John Meehan one day, to our great but silent merriment, with a long account of how he himself had abstracted the Doctor's brief-case. He had formerly been in the British Secret Service. I don't know about his qualifications as a detective, but he was certainly a fine liar."[49]

The expulsions of von Papen and Boy-Ed and the publication of the documents in Albert's briefcase did not end German intrigue in America. One of their biggest operations took place on July 30, 1916, when German agents set off an explosion at the loading terminals on Black Tom Island in New York Harbor, where nearly seventy freight cars loaded with 2 million pounds of munitions were set to be shipped to Europe and a nearby barge contained one hundred thousand pounds of dynamite. A group of saboteurs placed explosives on the barge and freight cars, which created a fire, causing the entire barge with the dynamite to blow up. The explosion rocked nearby neighborhoods and was the equivalent of an earthquake measuring up to 5.5 on the Richter scale. The death toll was minimal, with five people losing their lives, but the property damage was extensive, totaling approximately $20 million.[50]

As it became apparent that the United States could not maintain its neutrality stance much longer, a series of "Preparedness Day" parades were held across the country. These were aimed at showing support for the expansion of the U.S. armed forces, the increased production of armaments, and the planning for a possible military draft. Even President Wilson, who still wanted to keep America out of World War I, marched in one of these parades. Then, on January 31, 1917, the Germans announced that they were resuming unrestricted submarine warfare, a policy whereby their U-boats would torpedo any neutral or belligerent ships without warning in designated zones around Great Britain, France, Italy, and the eastern Mediterranean. "This was practically ordering the United States off the Atlantic," wrote McAdoo. "Our entire commerce with Europe was concentrated either within the proscribed zone or our ships destined for neutral countries had to pass through that zone." The United States broke diplomatic relations with Germany soon after that announcement.[51]

The final straw that led the United States into the war was British intelligence decoding a secret telegram sent from Arthur Zimmerman, the German foreign secretary, to Heinrich von Eckardt, the German ambassador to Mexico, instructing him to begin negotiations to form a military partnership with Mexico. The Zimmerman Telegram, as it would become known, proposed to Mexico an "alliance on the following basis: make war together, make peace together, generous financial support and an understanding on our part that Mexico is to reconquer the lost territory in Texas, New Mexico, and Arizona." The telegram also instructed Eckardt to suggest to the president of Mexico that he invite Japan to join the military pact against the United States. At this point, President Wilson had no choice but to appear before Congress on April 2 and ask for a declaration of war against Germany. The Senate voted in favor of war on April 4, and the House of Representatives did the same two days later.[52]

Flynn and the Secret Service fully expected that they would continue to take the lead in hunting down German spies and saboteurs for the duration of the war. However, they were shut out by the Department of Justice's Bureau of Investigation (BI, the forerunner of the FBI), the army's Military Intelligence Division, and the Office of Naval Intelligence, all of which monopolized domestic counterintelligence after the United States entered the war. The biggest rival to the Secret Service in terms of counterespionage, however, turned out to be the BI. The two agencies hadn't cooperated during the prewar period. The best Flynn could say of his relationship with BI Chief A. Bruce Bielaski was that they at least "had agreed between them that they would not cross each other in the course of any official investigations insofar as neutrality matters were concerned." Bielaski didn't think much of Flynn, writing later that Flynn had "a good deal of a fat head, but with good intentions for the most part."[53]

The day before the United States declared war, Bielaski was asked by the Senate Appropriations Committee whether the BI was the agency that protected the government against spies or if that was the work of the Treasury Department's Secret Service. Bielaski answered that his group had that responsibility. President Wilson confirmed this when, after declaring war, he issued a proclamation assigning several wartime investigative matters, including alien enemy control, to the Department of Justice. Treasury Secretary McAdoo fought back, proposing that a new agency be created and named the "Bureau of Intelligence," which would coordinate all government intelligence activity. Naturally, he argued that such an agency be placed in the Treasury Department, thereby increasing the power and influence of the Secret Service. This effort failed, and the BI continued to assume the leadership role in counterintelligence during the war years.[54]

All this bureaucratic wrangling between Treasury and Justice didn't stop Flynn from ordering his men to carry on with their pursuit of German spies and saboteurs in America. However, he went too far in one of his investigations. William Bayard Hale was a former *New York Times* reporter and most recently the chief Berlin correspondent for the International News Service, founded by William Randolph Hearst. Hale was of German ancestry and expressed pro-German views in the stories he filed from Berlin. He returned to New York once the United States entered the war. Flynn was suspicious of Hale's loyalties and apparently had one of his agents use intimidation and threats against Hale and his family. Hale complained in November 1917 to President Wilson, who had once employed him as an unofficial emissary to Mexico. Wilson referred the complaint to the Justice Department, which gave BI Chief Bielaski another opportunity to attack the Secret Service. Bielaski produced a report for the president that concluded that the Secret Service investigation of Hale "was not only without . . . the authority of law but in defiance of the act of Congress limiting activities of that service."[55]

At this point, Flynn had had enough. It was déjà vu for him, just like his experience at the NYPD, when he resigned as deputy commissioner because he believed he couldn't do his job there anymore due to interference from others. Now he felt the same way, that his usefulness to the Secret Service was compromised "by lack of support and actual interference on the part of officials at Washington." Those officials were clearly Bielaski and his boss, Attorney General Thomas Watt Gregory. He sent his letter of resignation to McAdoo in November, but the treasury secretary asked Flynn to reconsider. The official reason given for Flynn's resignation, which was to take effect at the end of the year, was that his physician had advised him that "he was badly in need of a rest." Flynn elaborated on that cover story, telling reporters that he had been at work without a vacation since assuming leadership of the Secret Service in 1912 and that once the United States entered the war, "his duties had been particularly arduous."[56]

Nobody really believed that the man whose name was synonymous with the Secret Service would quit the agency he loved in the middle of a war simply because he needed a rest. Shortly after his resignation, he gave an extensive interview to a reporter in which, without stating that he'd resigned due to problems he had with the BI, he let it be known that there were problems with the way the government was handling intelligence matters. "From my experience in the many branches of work where the secret service performs," he said, "I am convinced that for the period of the war at least there should be a unification of all the intelligence activities of the country." He pointed out that investigators were "often running into each other and the result is confusion and general loss of efficiency."[57]

Flynn revealed to the reporter, John W. Harrington, that it was indeed the Secret Service, not British agents, that seized Heinrich Albert's briefcase on the train. He said that he regretted that he could not give credit by name to the agent who stole the briefcase "for obvious reasons." He did say that although he (Flynn) was no longer with the Secret Service, they had allowed him to keep a souvenir: Dr. Albert's leather briefcase. It's not known where in his home he put the briefcase. A good idea would have been to build a large model elevated train car and place the briefcase on a seat, something to remind him of the most spectacular exploit of his Secret Service years.[58]

Flynn continued to sound the alarm about German agents in the country. He urged all Americans to be vigilant, "to keep their eyes open for suspicious actions or people." He estimated in an interview in April 1918 that there were two hundred and fifty thousand German spies in America, "and one of them may be working next to you, waiting on you. A seeming good friend, yet he or she is the most dangerous viper we have in the United States. . . . I again repeat as my best advice, based on my observance of the German espionage system, 'Beware of Spies.' What you know keep to yourself."[59]

But Flynn wasn't content with just talking and writing about the German threat. He wanted people to see firsthand how German spies and saboteurs operated. What better way to do this, he figured, than to make a movie and have one of the silent film era's biggest stars be the hero who saves the day for America.

THE EAGLE'S EYE

"What else could I do?" King Baggot asked laughingly as he signed a contract in December 1917 to star in *The Eagle's Eye*, a twenty-part patriotic serial based on Flynn's and the Secret Service's exploits against the Germans. "I've been a personal friend of Chief Flynn for years. My greatest admiration has always been for the secret service. Some way the name always had held a magic something for me." Baggot's agreeing to appear in the movie was big news since he had retired from the film industry a year before due to illness. The tall, handsome Baggot was known as "King of the Movies" and was an international star, appearing in scores of films and always playing the leading role.[60]

The Eagle's Eye was written by Flynn and his staff and adapted for the screen by Courtney Ryley Cooper, a scenarist and fiction writer who later authored a book with Flynn using the same title. The film and the book tell the story of the fictitious "Criminology Club," whose president, Harrison Grant, played by Baggot, works with Flynn's Secret Service team (including a female agent named Dixie Mason, who becomes Grant's love interest) to expose German spies and saboteurs in America. Flynn played himself in the film, which uses the real-life names of the Germans that the Secret Service battled, including Count Johann Heinrich von Bernstorff, Franz von Papen, Karl Boy-Ed, Franz von Rintelen, and, of course, the famous Dr. Heinrich Albert. Great care was taken by the producers to select actors who bore a resemblance to the Germans they would be portraying. The government also provided the filmmakers with photographs to help ensure authenticity for the movie. Adding to the realism of the film, the scene of Albert losing his briefcase was shot on the same Sixth Avenue elevated train where the actual event happened. For another scene, Flynn had arranged with the Secret Service to borrow one of the bomb cases that Robert Fay used to make the time bombs that he was going to place on the rudders of munitions ships.[61]

The film was produced by the Wharton brothers, Ted and Leo, who were the most popular and sensational serial filmmakers of their day. They utilized technological and scientific innovations in their movies, which were characterized by topical themes and advanced special effects. The first episode, "The Hidden Death," featured the German submarine attack on the passenger ship *Lusitania*. It was filmed on Cayuga Lake, near the Wharton Studio in Ithaca, New York. Rowboats were constructed to resemble the submarine and the *Lusitania*. A preview audience of city officials, judicial representatives, clergymen, and military and naval officers was mesmerized by the scene depicting the sinking of the ship. As one film critic wrote, "The destruction of the Lusitania and the excellent picturization of that ghastly affair, held everyone breathless, for one seemed to actually be on that ill-fated vessel, and, as the torpedo approached it, one involuntarily shuddered with fear." The critic, who previewed three episodes of the serial, praised Flynn for bringing the story to the silent screen and thereby explaining "the reasons for America entering the war, as it is based upon Flynn's private knowledge of German's [*sic*] notorious spy system in this country, the secret service methods, of course, being fictionized, but nevertheless, thrilling and entertaining." The reviewer predicted a huge success:

> This picture will create a positive sensation, for it abounds with everything that [could] possibly be utilized in a screen drama to thrill and enthrall the spectator, and its worth, from a patriotic standpoint, has not yet been approached by any other production.
>
> For pep, ginger, excellent photography, thrills, excitement and patriotism galore The Eagle's Eye starts a new era in the silent drama.[62]

Buoyed by this and other positive reviews, the Whartons launched a nationwide publicity campaign, including taking out full-page color advertisements in the trade papers with bold graphics emphasizing the patriotic theme of the movie. The ads noted that the film was "by William J. Flynn, Chief of the United States Secret Service" and that it was "a production that commands national interest." At the top of the advertisements was a picture of the American bald eagle, with Flynn's face peering out from the eagle's eye. Exhibitors were excited about the film and promoted it in creative ways. For example, William O'Hare, the manager of a movie theater in Des Moines, Iowa, built a model submarine, fifty-two feet long and fifteen feet wide, and placed it on a motor truck along with a real torpedo he'd borrowed from the Des Moines Naval Recruiting Station. He then drove around the city prior to the premiere of the first episode. Accompanying him were sailors who explained to the crowds that gathered around the truck how submarines actually worked. All of this helped ensure a huge turnout for the movie.[63]

Ultimately, though, *The Eagle's Eye* was a colossal failure at the box office. According to one film historian, this "was due in part to the influenza epidemic that was sweeping the country, creating, among other concerns, a steep decline in attendance at movie houses nationwide." While some theaters began showing the weekly episodes in the spring of 1918, when the first mild wave of the influenza struck America, other theaters were still showing it in the fall, when the deadly second wave hit and brought life to a standstill in many parts of the country. Furthermore, World War I ended with the signing of the Armistice between Germany and the Allies on November 11, 1918, causing people to lose interest in war-related movies, books, and other materials. The combination of the pandemic and the Armistice "cut its [the film's] career short . . . [and] caused the cancellation of nearly a half million dollars' worth of contracts." The film's poor box office results were a severe blow to the Whartons, who had invested money in expanding their studio for the production of the film and had also spent funds for the nationwide publicity campaign. The brothers had been facing financial difficulties even before production of *The Eagle's Eye* began, and the movie's failure put them deeper in debt. They soon had to close their studio.[64]

Flynn wasn't in great financial shape either, having been out of work since the end of December 1917. He kept busy by publishing stories in newspapers based on *The Eagle's Eye*'s different episodes. The stories and the movie ensured that the public didn't forget about him and the critical role he played in combating German espionage and sabotage in the years before the United States entered the war. But he longed to serve the country again in an official capacity. That opportunity came in September 1918, when Secretary of the Treasury McAdoo, who earlier had been given the additional responsibility of running the U.S. Railroad Administration (USRA) by President Wilson, appointed Flynn to be the organization's chief detective. Flynn's title was a lengthy one: chief of the Secret Service and Police Section of the United States Railroad Administration.[65]

Flynn was put in charge of twenty thousand railway policemen stationed throughout the country, making it the largest police unit in the world. His job was to protect the entire railroad system from freight car thieves. It was a difficult task, as there were two hundred and fifty thousand miles of trackage. All types of items were being stolen from trains, including liquor, cigarettes, clothing, shoes, tires, and so forth. From April 1, 1918, until April 1, 1919, there were nearly sixteen thousand arrests made for freight robberies, with about six thousand being railroad employees. The insider threat bothered Flynn. "We are working hard to impress on the railroad employe [*sic*] that he should protect the company's property, not steal it," Flynn said in an interview. "In some cases the employe [*sic*] has worked hand-in-hand with the professional freight car thieves."[66]

While Flynn was grateful to McAdoo for bringing him back to government service, the railroad job was destined to only be a temporary one. Flynn was used to high-profile positions—like chief of the Secret Service and deputy commissioner of the NYPD—so being the head of a police force, even the largest in the world, in an agency that very few people had ever heard about was not fulfilling. Flynn stayed with the USRA until the spring of 1919, when a new opportunity arose. It would turn out, however, to be the most difficult job of his long career.

CHAPTER FIVE

The Red Scare

"I INTEND TO PUT MR. WILLIAM J. FLYNN IN THE PLACE OF DIRECTOR of the Bureau of Investigation," Attorney General A. Mitchell Palmer told Congress at an appropriations hearing in June 1919. "Flynn is an anarchist chaser. He is the greatest anarchist expert in the United States. He knows all the men of that class. He can pretty nearly call them by name, and we propose to have them well in hand." It didn't matter to Palmer that Flynn's reputation had been built on dealing specifically not with anarchists but rather with counterfeiters, the Mafia, and German spies. He needed a high-profile, highly regarded detective to be in charge of a new war against a new enemy, and Flynn fit the bill.[1]

It is ironic, of course, that Flynn became the head of the agency that had given him so much trouble and interference when he was chief of the Secret Service. A. Bruce Bielaski, whom he knocked heads with during the investigations into German espionage and other activities in America during World War I, was now out of government and practicing private law. Flynn gave no hint to reporters of any sense of satisfaction in taking over Bielaski's former job or excitement about being back in the game in a high-level, prominent position. In fact, he made it seem like he'd reluctantly accepted the job. "I have tried hard to go home to New York and rest but it seems that some duty always beckons me back here [to Washington, D.C.]," he told reporters. The press, not surprisingly, received Flynn's new appointment with enthusiasm. "Flynn to Direct Search for Reds," the *New York Times* ran as its headline, reminding its readers that "Flynn has a worldwide reputation as a detective who never gives up, and he demonstrated his ability and tenacity many times as head of the Secret Service."[2]

Flynn took the reins of the BI at a time of unprecedented violence in America. Palmer himself had been the target of two terrorist attacks, including a bombing that occurred on the front steps of his home. It would be Flynn's job to use the skills he'd honed over many years of detective work to find the perpetrators of these and other attacks and organize America's first war against terrorism. His antagonists were one of the most creative, innovative, and dangerous terrorist groups the world had ever known.

THE GALLEANISTS

Luigi Galleani and William Flynn had a lot in common. Both were towering figures, each with a commanding presence. Both men loved to write, and they built loyal followings among those who came in contact with them. Both also knew how to use the media to their advantage. But that is where the similarities ended. Galleani was educated in European universities, Flynn in the streets of New York. Galleani worked to bring about an anarchist revolution in America. Flynn was dedicated to preventing it and ridding the country of all who practiced anarchist doctrines. It made for a classic battle of wits between the two men and their formidable organizations.[3]

Flynn would later write of Galleani that he was one of the most difficult individuals the U.S. government ever had to deal with "because he was the brainiest." He was a gifted writer and speaker, a charismatic figure who won a loyal following among many Italian immigrants who were experiencing discrimination, low wages, and long working hours (for those able to find jobs) instead of the better life they'd hoped for when they came to America. Those who heard Galleani speak described him as a "forceful orator," a "most effective debater," and the "soul of the movement." One anarchist recalled that "you hung on every word when he spoke," while another said that "he spoke directly to my heart." Still others said that "he expressed what I wanted to say but couldn't because I didn't have the words" and that "you heard Galleani speak and you were ready to shoot the first policeman you saw."

The anarchist leader was born on August 12, 1861, in Vercelli, a city in the Piedmont region of northern Italy. He grew up in a middle-class family with his father, an elementary school teacher, pressuring him to study law at the University of Turin. Galleani didn't see himself as a lawyer and never graduated, instead becoming an outspoken militant who denounced government and capitalism. He was also rebelling against his father, who he described as the "son of a solider who had the cult of authority in his blood." Galleani wrote articles for democratic, socialist, and anarchist publications and was also active in the Italian labor movement, leading a number of strikes. In 1889, he fled Italy to avoid arrest, settling in Paris, where he soon ran into further trouble. He was imprisoned there for several months and then expelled in 1890 for taking part in a May Day celebration. (May 1 is a date that annually honors working-class solidarity around the world and has sometimes been marked by violent demonstrations.)

Getting expelled from countries became a familiar way of life for Galleani, who, after moving to Switzerland, was soon forced to leave that country too after the Swiss government labeled him a dangerous agitator. He returned to Italy, where he delivered spellbinding speeches throughout the country calling for the creation of a society with no restrictions at all. A police report stated that he was "a very ardent advocate of that anti-social existence in which each person has a law of their own." Galleani would later describe anarchism as "the struggle for a condition of society where the only link among individuals is solidarity, basically the solidarity of material and moral interests, which leads to the elimination of vicious daily competitions between individuals and peoples."

In June 1894, Galleani was convicted of conspiracy to commit crimes "against the administration of justice, or public trust, or public safety" and was sentenced to three years of imprisonment. Then, at the end of his term, he was sent to the remote volcanic island of Pantelleria, located sixty miles south of Sicily and forty miles east of Tunisia, to serve two more years under police supervision. This policy was known as *domicilio coatto*, or internal exile. Being sent to Pantelleria was considered one of the harshest punishments one could receive. Many anarchists and other agitators were sent there after completing their prison sentences in mainland Italy. At the time, the island, which today is a popular tourist spot with five-star luxury hotels, was sparsely populated, poor, and isolated.

Although he was nearing the end of his penal colony sentence, Galleani decided to escape Pantelleria by boat in February 1900. He landed in Tunis, then went to Malta and eventually Egypt. In 1901, he was offered the editor's job at the leading anarchist periodical in America at the time, *La Questione Sociale* (The social question), in Paterson, New Jersey. He had a family now to support—his partner Maria Rallo, whom he met in Pantelleria; her two children; and a child they had together. (The couple would eventually have three more children.) The editor's job seemed a good way for him to provide for his family and continue to espouse his anarchist ideas.

He arrived in Paterson in October 1901. By late the next spring, he was again on the run, having been indicted for inciting to riot and atrocious assault during a silk workers' strike in Paterson. He fled to Montreal, where he lived for several months before sneaking back across the border and settling in Barre, Vermont, in early 1903. There, he launched a new anarchist newspaper, *Cronaca Sovversiva* (Subversive chronicle), that became the most widely read anarchist periodical in the United States. The Department of Justice would later label it "the most rabid, seditious and anarchist sheet ever published in this country." Galleani used his newspaper and other writings and speeches to inspire others to engage in "propaganda by deed"—namely, taking violent action in order to achieve the anarchists' goals. He even published a bomb manual in 1905, just like al Qaeda and the Islamic State of Iraq and Syria (ISIS) have done more recently with their online publications.

It wasn't until 1914, however, that the Galleanists began their campaign of terrorism against the government, capitalists, religious institutions, and other perceived enemies. The Galleanists were decentralized, with several autonomous cells scattered around the country. There were only fifty to sixty hard-core members, but Galleani's supporters, who worked in construction, mining, factories, and other manual labor jobs, numbered in the thousands. In July 1914, a Galleanist faction in New York, the Gruppo Gaetano Bresci of East Harlem, also known as the Bresci Group (named after Gaetano Bresci, an anarchist who assassinated King Umberto I of Italy in 1900), was involved in a plot to bomb the estate of industrialist John D. Rockefeller in Tarrytown, New York. However, the bomb that they had built along with other anarchists and stored in a New York City tenement for later use at the Rockefeller estate exploded prematurely, killing three anarchists and another person who lived in the building.

A few months later, the city was rocked by a series of bombings at churches and courthouses. The Bresci Group was believed to be responsible for the violence. Galleani approved of the attacks, writing in *Cronaca Sovversiva* that anarchists should "continue the good war, the war that knows neither fear nor scruples, neither pity nor truce." One of his followers, Nestor Dondoglio, using the alias Jean Crones, took that advice to heart and attempted to poison George Mundelein, the newly appointed archbishop of Chicago, who was the guest of honor at a reception in February 1916. Dondoglio was working as a chef at the University Club in Chicago, where the banquet dinner was being held. He put arsenic in the soup prepared for the more than two hundred distinguished guests. Mundelein, however, did not eat the soup. The guests who did, approximately a hundred others, became violently ill, clutching their stomachs and falling to the ground. Luckily for them, Dondoglio had miscalculated and put too much arsenic in the soup, causing the diners to vomit it up, thereby preventing the poison from taking its full effect. Dondoglio did not report for work the next day and, despite a nationwide manhunt, was never caught.

Like Dondoglio, many Galleanists were able to avoid capture. One who wasn't was Gabriella Antolini, a teenage member who was arrested in January 1918 for transporting thirty-six sticks of dynamite by train from Youngstown, Ohio, to Chicago, where another Galleanist would construct the bomb and bring it to Milwaukee. The probable target there was the home of a prosecutor in a case against several anarchists. Antolini was arrested in Chicago with the explosives in her bag. She became a national celebrity, with the media portraying her as the "Dynamite Girl" and fascinated by the story of a beautiful young girl willing to blow up buildings and people. Antolini pleaded guilty to transporting explosives and was sentenced to eighteen months in prison. She was released in January 1920.

Galleani was always careful to distance himself from any direct involvement in the terrorist plots and attacks by his followers. The Galleanists worked in devious ways. "Galleani, for instance, will suggest," Flynn later wrote. "One of his close companions will pass on the suggestion. The idea will pass hither and yon until eventually a particularly wild man or woman will touch off the bomb or ignite the fire. Trace it back and you become lost in the most complicated labyrinth of indirect statements, evasions and plain lies, and you learn sooner or later you are destined to emerge from the maze at the same spot you entered, having gained nothing."

While the government could not pin any of the violence on Galleani, they could target his newspaper. *Cronaca Sovversiva* was banned from the mails in 1917 under the Espionage Act, which, among other things, gave the postmaster general the right to deny the mails to printed matter that urged treason, insurrection, or forcible resistance to federal laws. In July 1918, the government shut down the newspaper entirely, which had managed to survive by being distributed by railway transport and private means. Then, in October 1918, Congress passed the Anarchist Exclusion Act, which excluded and expelled from America "aliens who are members of the anarchistic or similar classes." To make sure that the Galleanists would be among those targeted for deportation, the Department of Labor issued a memorandum to guide the Bureau of Immigration when dealing with members of the group. It specified that "in the cases of Italian anarchists, evidence of their continued subscription to the *Cronaca Sovversiva*, the leading anarchist newspaper in the United States . . . shall be considered good grounds for deportation on the charge of advocating and teaching anarchy in the United States."

The Galleanists, naturally, didn't take kindly to this. After a deportation order was issued for Galleani in January 1919, his followers decided to strike back. They distributed a flyer throughout New England, *Go-Head!* It was signed by the "American Anarchists." It warned of dire consequences if Galleani and other anarchists were deported: "You have shown no pity to us! We will do likewise. And deport us! *We will dynamite you!* Either deport us or free all!" [emphasis in the original].

True to their word, the Galleanists came up with an ingenious plan for revenge. They decided to turn the tables on the government that had once banned *Cronaca Sovversiva* from the mails and instead use the U.S. postal system to deliver something other than newspapers—namely, thirty identical package bombs addressed to prominent individuals across the country. Their list of targets was an impressive one, ranging from cabinet officers and U.S. senators and representatives to governors, mayors, judges, district attorneys, and industrialists. Among those targeted for assassination with the package bombs were Attorney General Palmer; Richard Enright, police commissioner of New York City; Kenesaw Mountain Landis, U.S. district judge in Chicago; Anthony Caminetti, commissioner general of immigration; William Wilson, secretary of labor; Ole Hanson, mayor of Seattle; John Hylan, mayor of New York City; Lee Overman, senator from North Carolina; and J. P. Morgan and John D. Rockefeller, both well-known capitalists.

Never before had any group attempted to send so many bombs at the same time through the mail. The Galleanists intended for all the bombs to arrive at their destinations on May 1 (May Day). If they arrived on different days, then some of the targeted individuals would not open their packages since they would have been alerted to the danger likely from news accounts of the earlier bombs. The postal authorities would also be on the lookout for package bombs being sent through the mail.

While the idea to send multiple package bombs across the country was innovative, even more so was the way the Galleanists made the bombs and wrapped the packages. To ensure that the recipients would not be suspicious and would open the packages, the group cleverly wrapped them in straw-colored paper and used a notable return address: Gimbel Brothers, a famous New York department store. Each package, which was about the size of a one-pound candy box, had the words "novelty" and "sample" stamped on it in red letters. Underneath the paper wrapping was a green cardboard box, and within the box was a dynamite bomb constructed of a small, black, glass vial of sulfuric acid fastened by brass screws to a cork at the top of a wooden cylinder. The cylinder was polished so it would look like a gift. Opening the lid of the cylinder would force the cork with the screws into the fragile glass vial, breaking it and releasing the acid onto three fulminate-of-mercury percussion caps resting on a stick of dynamite within the cylinder. This would ignite the caps and set off an explosive charge packed with metal slugs at the bottom of the package. It was an ingenious contraption in both design and construction.

When a bomb expert later examined one of several bombs that had never left a New York post office due to insufficient postage, he marveled at the workmanship that had gone into creating the device. "It doesn't resemble any machine I have ever come across," said Owen Eagan, referring to it as an "infernal machine," as bombs were often labeled in those days. "It is the neatest and, from the standpoint of mechanical arrangement, the cleverest I have ever seen. Whoever perfected this thing must have been an expert mechanic and chemist."

The Galleanist plot was only partially successful. The packages that had the proper postage arrived at their destinations on different days, thereby alerting later recipients to the danger in opening a package from Gimbels. But a maid to Thomas Hardwick, a former senator from Georgia, lost both her arms when one of the package bombs exploded in Hardwick's house. The senator's wife was also injured, suffering burns on her face and neck. No other recipients of the package bombs were harmed.

The sending of bombs around the country garnered banner headlines. "Bombs in Mails Show National Terrorist Plot," blared the *Pittsburgh Gazette Times*, while the *Miami Herald* exclaimed, "Widespread Conspiracy of Terrorists to Assassinate Highly Placed Persons Is Unearthed in New York City." The Galleanists succeeded in demonstrating to the government and the nation that they would not take the deportation of their leader or other members of their group without a fight.

Federal, state, and local law enforcement agencies launched a wide-scale investigation into who might be responsible for sending the package bombs. Executives at Gimbels told investigators that their store did not have wrapping paper that in any way resembled what had been used for the package bombs. The wrapping paper and the cardboard paper used for the green boxes were eventually traced to their suppliers, but that too did not result in any meaningful progress in the investigation. A fingerprint analysis of the outer wrappings of the packages, the wooden cylinders, the glass vials containing the sulfuric acid, and the sticks of dynamite also turned up nothing of value for investigators. The same was true of an examination of the bomb components.

There was one important clue, however, that investigators missed. It should have led them straight to the Galleanists. All the people who were sent package bombs had in some way angered the Galleanists, Bolsheviks, International Workers of the World (IWW) militants, and other radicals through their actions, policies, or statements. One name, though, stood out as a person only the Galleanists would know about and want to take revenge against. This was Rayme Finch, a BI agent whom most anarchists and radicals had probably never heard of (his name did not appear often in the newspapers). He had made his career going after the Galleanists. As historian Paul Avrich notes, "Should any doubt remain concerning the plotters, the appearance of Finch on the list must dispel it. Why should a lowly Bureau of Investigation operative be selected as a target? The answer seems clear. It was Finch, during the early weeks of 1918, who had arrested [Giovanni] Scussel [a Galleanist] in Youngstown and dogged [Carlo] Valdinoci [another Galleanist] through the mining camps along the Ohio River. In February 1918, moreover, he had led the raid on *Cronaca Sovversiva* and arrested Raffaele Schiavina [manager of the newspaper]. Transferred to New York, he had continued his pursuit of the Galleanists, arresting Andrea Ciofalo [a Galleanist] in the Bronx. Ciofalo, released on bail, may have been a party to the bomb conspiracy. Like Valdinoci and Schiavina, he bore a special grudge against Agent Finch."

By the end of May, the investigation of the package bomb plot remained stymied. There had been no arrests made in connection with the attacks, and none were on the horizon. The Galleanists had to be happy that nobody from their group had been caught so far but disappointed that so many of their bombs never reached their intended targets. They decided that the next time, rather than rely on the U.S. postal system to deliver their bombs, they would place them themselves right at the victims' homes. On the evening of June 2, 1919, they put their plan into action.

First, a bomb exploded in Washington, D.C., around 11:15 p.m. outside the home of Attorney General Palmer, killing Carlo Valdinoci, whose identity wouldn't be known for some time. Valdinoci had carried the bomb up the steps to the front entrance of the house, and either he tripped, setting off the explosive, or the bomb went off prematurely. Palmer was inside with his wife and daughter, but they were not injured. At about the same time, another bombing occurred, this time in Philadelphia, in the rectory of a church. Nobody was injured in that attack. Then, fifteen minutes later, the home of Mayor Harry Davis in Cleveland was bombed, again with nobody injured. Davis had recently suppressed a May Day celebration and cooperated in the prosecution of two Galleanists.

At this point, there had been three bombings in three different cities, all within fifteen minutes of each other. Then, between 11:35 p.m. and 11:45 p.m., two bombs exploded at different homes in Pittsburgh. There were no injuries. In both these cases, the Galleanists apparently hit the wrong targets because neither home belonged to anyone who had angered radicals. They were, though, near the homes of individuals who had. Meanwhile, in Boston, a bomb went off at the home of Judge Albert F. Hayden shortly before midnight. Hayden had dealt harshly with May Day demonstrators, issuing prison sentences for some of up to eighteen months. No one was injured in that attack. Then, a few minutes after midnight, there was a bombing at the Boston area home of a state representative who had introduced an anti-sedition bill in the Massachusetts legislature. This attack slightly injured the representative's young daughter.

The Galleanists weren't finished yet. At 12:20 a.m., a bomb exploded in Paterson, New Jersey, at the home of a manufacturing association executive who had opposed a forty-four-hour workweek for silk workers. The final bombing occurred in New York City at 12:55 a.m. at the home of Judge Charles C. Nott Jr., who in 1915 had sentenced two Galleanists to prison for attempting to blow up St. Patrick's Cathedral. This bombing resulted in the only casualty from the night of terror. A security guard for several homes on the street was killed.

The public woke up on June 3 to read in their newspapers that during the night, nine bombs had exploded in seven cities within two hours of each other. America had never before experienced this type of terror-

William J. Flynn, 1914. Flynn weighed about three hundred pounds and was once described by a reporter as "large, mountainous almost, up and down as well as circumferentially." He was one of the most famous detectives of his time and nicknamed "the Bulldog" for his tenacity in pursuing leads. LIBRARY OF CONGRESS, HARRIS & EWING COLLECTION, LC-H261-3463

Anne Evelyn Mackey (undated). She emigrated from Ireland to the United States in 1883, and Flynn married her two years later. They had seven children together. One child died after being bitten by an insect while playing in the yard outside the family home. COURTESY OF WILLIAM FLYNN SANDERS

The Flynn family (undated). The family's nanny is seated below Flynn's wife. When Attorney General A. Mitchell Palmer lobbied Congress (in June 1919) for a high salary for Flynn, whom he had just appointed to head the Bureau of Investigation (BI), the forerunner of the Federal Bureau of Investigation (FBI), he told the committee that Flynn "can not take any place [job] for $4,000 a year because, as he told me, he has half a dozen little Flynns" to support.
COURTESY OF WILLIAM FLYNN SANDERS

Flynn's children in front of their house in New York City, circa 1906. From left to right: Elmer, Kathleen, Gerard, Veronica, and William Wallace Flynn Jr. Daughter Jane took the picture.
COURTESY OF WILLIAM FLYNN SANDERS

Jane Flynn Sanders, circa the late 1940s. Flynn's daughter was upset that J. Edgar Hoover was depicted in the media as the first director of the FBI. She believed her father should get the credit since he, as director of the BI, transformed it into a federal investigative agency before Hoover later renamed it the FBI. "My mother [Jane] and father would chase down and force a correction on any newspaper who falsely listed Hoover as the first Director of [the FBI]," William Flynn Sanders, Flynn's grandson, wrote. COURTESY OF WILLIAM FLYNN SANDERS

William Flynn Sanders, 2022. Will, Flynn's grandson, has maintained the family collection of photographs, documents, and other materials related to William J. Flynn. He believes, like his mother did, that his grandfather should get credit for being the first director of the FBI. "All he [Hoover] did was put a different badge on the same organization to create the illusion he was the first [director]. The [FBI] agents should be going to work in the WM J Flynn Bldg [and not the Hoover Building]," he maintains. COURTESY OF WILLIAM FLYNN SANDERS

William Brockway, 1880. Before he joined the Secret Service, Flynn worked as a keeper at the Ludlow Street Jail in New York City from 1895 to 1897. Many counterfeiters were held there, and Flynn hoped he might learn something about the art of counterfeiting from them that could help land him a job with the Secret Service. One of the prisoners was William Brockway, "the oldest, greatest, cleverest counterfeiter of this country." Brockway took a liking to the young Flynn and told him all about his life in crime. Flynn later wrote, "Here I was, Bill Flynn of Forty-First Street, the confidant of the biggest counterfeiter in the country— possibly the world!" LIBRARY OF CONGRESS, WILLIAM KENNOCH COLLECTION OF U.S. SECRET SERVICE PHOTOGRAPHS, LC-DIG-PPMSCA-80921

Flynn as a Secret Service agent with President Theodore Roosevelt at the Law Building dedication at the University of Chicago in April 1903. Flynn is looking toward the camera, and Roosevelt is in an embellished commencement gown, third from the left, at the top center of the photo. UNITED STATES SECRET SERVICE

The Secret Service provided security for Russian and Japanese delegations at a peace conference in Portsmouth, New Hampshire, in 1905. The conference was aimed at ending the Russo-Japanese War. Here, Flynn (far left, in a light-colored hat) is with Serge Witte (third from left), who was head of the Russian delegation, as Witte and his staff take a Sunday morning walk. (Witte looks like he's checking a cell phone back in 1905!) LIBRARY OF CONGRESS, LC-DIG-PPMSCA-08830

Giuseppe Morello, 1900. Known as the "Clutch Hand" because of his deformed right hand, Morello was the godfather of the first Mafia family in New York and was responsible for murders, extortion, kidnappings, and counterfeiting. Flynn pursued him and other Mafia members for almost a decade, eventually arresting Morello and his associates in 1909 for running a counterfeiting operation. The arrests resulted in long prison terms for Morello and several other members of the crime family. U.S. NATIONAL ARCHIVES

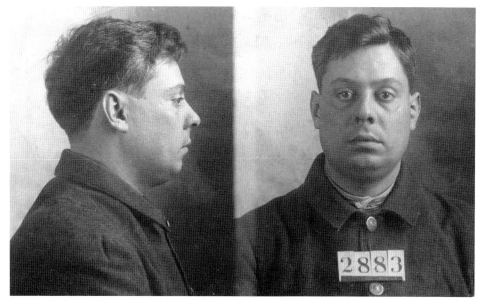

Ignazio Lupo, 1910. Known as "Lupo the Wolf," he was Morello's most trusted associate and also received a long prison sentence for counterfeiting. "I give you my word," Flynn wrote, "Lupo needed only to touch you to give you the feeling that you had been poisoned."
U.S. NATIONAL ARCHIVES AT ATLANTA

Mulberry Street, Little Italy, circa 1900–1910. The Morello–Lupo gang preyed on fellow Italian immigrants living in the Italian section of New York City during the early 1900s. LIBRARY OF CONGRESS, DETROIT PUBLISHING COMPANY COLLECTION, LC-DIG-DET-4A27271

New York Police Department (NYPD) Detective Joseph Petrosino (left) escorting Tommaso Petto ("Petto the Ox," second from left), 1903. Petto was an enforcer for the Morello–Lupo gang. Petrosino was a famous New York City detective who, like Flynn, pursued the Mafia during the early 1900s. LIBRARY OF CONGRESS, *NEW YORK WORLD-TELEGRAM & SUN* NEWSPAPER PHOTO-GRAPH COLLECTION, LC-USZ62-137644

Funeral procession for Petrosino, 1909. Petrosino traveled to Sicily in 1909 on a secret mission to gather information about the Mafia and other Italian criminals who might have emigrated to New York. He was assassinated in Palermo in March. The Morello–Lupo gang was believed to have orchestrated the killing with their contacts in Sicily. Petrosino died a hero and was given one of the largest funerals in New York City history. LIBRARY OF CONGRESS, BAIN COLLECTION, LC-DIG-GGBAIN-03255

Flynn served as a deputy commissioner of the NYPD from October 1910 to April 1911. He was recruited for the position by Mayor William J. Gaynor, shown here throwing a baseball at a World Series game in 1912 at the Polo Grounds in New York. Flynn attempted to reform the Detective Bureau but faced opposition from within the department. On resigning, he called it "a thankless job." LIBRARY OF CONGRESS, BAIN COLLECTION, LC-DIG-GGBAIN-10851

Flynn became chief of the Secret Service in 1912 and held that position until 1917. In this photo, he is standing (left) with Assistant Chief William H. Moran in front of other Secret Service personnel on the steps of the Treasury Department, circa 1913–1917. LIBRARY OF CONGRESS, HARRIS & EWING COLLECTION, LC-DIG-HEC-20490

Dr. Heinrich Friedrich Albert (undated). Albert was the commercial attaché for the German embassy in the United States in the years preceding American entry into World War I. On a New York City subway train in 1915, he inadvertently left behind a briefcase containing documents about a sophisticated German propaganda, espionage, and sabotage network in the United States. He had been followed onto the train by one of Flynn's men, who retrieved the briefcase. LIBRARY OF CONGRESS, BAIN COLLECTION, LC-DIG-GGBAIN-36650

Franz von Papen, circa 1910–1915. Von Papen was the military attaché at the German embassy and directed many of the subversive activities in the United States. LIBRARY OF CONGRESS, BAIN COLLECTION, LC-DIG-GGBAIN-20672

Frank Burke, 1935. Burke was the Secret Service agent who seized Dr. Albert's briefcase after Albert left it on a subway train in 1915. "When I saw that he had left his brief-case," Burke wrote, "I decided in a fraction of a second to get it." Burke, who was "shrewd, bold, and fearless, and completely dedicated to his job," was Flynn's most trusted aide both at the Secret Service and later at the BI when Flynn became director there. LIBRARY OF CONGRESS, HARRIS & EWING COLLECTION, LC-DIG-HEC-39493

Flynn's and the Secret Service's exploits against German spies and saboteurs built up his legend and caught the attention of the movie industry. A twenty-part silent movie serial about his adventures, *The Eagle's Eye*, was made in 1918. King Baggot, an international film star, played a fictional character patterned after Flynn. In this advertisement for the movie, Flynn can be seen peering out from the eye of the eagle.
EXHIBITOR'S TRADE REVIEW

Flynn was president of an organization named "Real Men of America." The group had only fourteen members, all prominent individuals from New York who had performed patriotic and effective service for the country during World War I and afterward. It was a secretive organization that held no public meetings. The group discussed among themselves the current state of affairs in the nation and what each of them could contribute to uncovering plots or any type of activity harmful to the United States. In this photo, the group is holding its annual dinner in New York in 1920. Flynn is seated underneath the U.S. flag. COURTESY OF WILLIAM FLYNN SANDERS

Luigi Galleani, circa 1912. Galleani was the charismatic leader of a group of militant Italian anarchists active in the United States at the beginning of the twentieth century. His group, the Galleanists, was responsible for several terrorist attacks in the country. Flynn described him as "one of the most difficult individuals the United States Secret Service has ever had to deal with because he was the brainiest." INTERNATIONAL INSTITUTE OF SOCIAL HISTORY, AMSTERDAM

Emma Goldman seated on a street-car, 1917. Goldman was a famous Russian-born anarchist in the United States. Also seated is fellow anarchist Alexander Berkman, wearing a white hat and glasses. Goldman, Berkman, and hundreds of other anarchists were deported to Russia in December 1919 when Flynn was director of the BI.
LIBRARY OF CONGRESS, BAIN COLLECTION, LC-DIG-PPMSC-00139

Attorney General A. Mitchell Palmer with his daughter in front of his home in Washington, D.C., 1920. A year earlier, Palmer's home was bombed, one of nine bombings that occurred in seven cities on the evening of June 2, 1919. The bombings led to the Palmer Raids, a series of raids across the United States that resulted in illegal roundups, detentions, and deportations of alien radicals. LIBRARY OF CONGRESS, NATIONAL PHOTO COMPANY COLLECTION, LC-DIG-NPCC-01199

J. Edgar Hoover, 1924. Hoover was in charge of the Radical Division (later renamed the General Intelligence Division) of the BI, where he organized and directed the Palmer Raids. Hoover became director of the bureau in 1924. The BI's name was changed to the Division of Intelligence in 1933 and then to the FBI in 1935. LIBRARY OF CONGRESS, NATIONAL PHOTO COMPANY COLLECTION, LC-USZ62-92411

On September 16, 1920, the worst act of domestic terrorism in U.S. history until the 1995 Oklahoma City bombing occurred when a bomb hidden in a horse-drawn wagon exploded on Wall Street, killing thirty-eight people and injuring hundreds of others. Flynn, as director of the BI, was not able to solve the case (nor was anybody else). Mario Buda, a Galleanist, is considered the likely suspect. LIBRARY OF CONGRESS, *NEW YORK WORLD-TELEGRAM & SUN* NEWSPAPER PHOTOGRAPH COLLECTION, LC-USZ62-132521

The Wall Street bomb was equipped with a timer and composed of one hundred pounds of explosives and five hundred pounds of heavy, cast-iron slugs that were hurled in all directions. This photo shows some of the slugs. LIBRARY OF CONGRESS, UNDERWOOD & UNDERWOOD, LC-USZ62-111322

William J. Burns, like Flynn, was one of the most famous detectives in America. This photo was taken in August 1921 after he became director of the BI. He and Flynn didn't like each other, and Burns continually interfered with Flynn's investigation of the Wall Street bombing when Flynn was BI director. Burns's career was marked by several scandals, and he was forced to resign in 1924. LIBRARY OF CONGRESS, NATIONAL PHOTO COMPANY COLLECTION, LC-DIG-NPCC-04843

William J. Flynn Detective Agency, Inc.

Established by

Former Chief, United States Secret Service
Deputy Police Commissioner, New York City
Director, Bureau of Investigation,
U. S. Department of Justice
Director, United States Railroad Administration.

*Personnel trained by Chief Flynn and
with individual experience in Government and State Branches of Detection.*

REPRESENTATIVES THROUGHOUT THE WORLD

1457 Broadway, New York City   Night Phone: Larchmont 1626

Day Phones:
WIsconsin
7-0537, 7-3136

Flynn opened a private detective agency in 1921. It was not successful because he entrusted a lot of the work to his daughter Veronica and son Elmer, whom he made partners in the firm. Both alcoholics, they overspent and drove clients away due to their erratic behavior. COURTESY OF WILLIAM FLYNN SANDERS

One of Flynn's clients was a Hollywood movie studio that hired his agency to spy on silent film legend Rudolph Valentino, who was in a contract dispute with the studio. LIBRARY OF CONGRESS, LC-USZ62-90327

In 1924, Flynn launched a detective magazine, *Flynn's*. The magazine published both fiction and true crime stories as well as a series of reminiscences written by Flynn about his life and career. In one of the first issues, Flynn wrote, "It is my keenest desire that the readers of FLYNN'S will find in the reading something of the thrill and the pleasure that have been mine in the living. Then I shall not have written in vain." RED STAR NEWS COMPANY

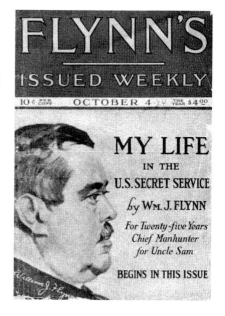

One of the writers published in *Flynn's* was the famous mystery writer Agatha Christie, who early in her career (1925) wrote the piece "Traitor Hands" for the magazine. She later retitled it "Witness for the Prosecution." It became a hit Broadway play and an Oscar-nominated movie. This is an advertisement for the play. LIBRARY OF CONGRESS, LC-DIG-PPMSCA-12370

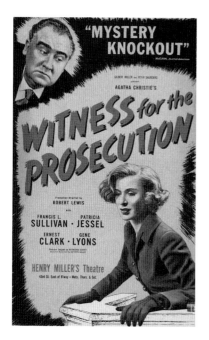

William J. Flynn (undated). Flynn died in 1928 of heart disease at the age of sixty. "There developed a mighty legend around William J. Flynn," the *New York Herald Tribune* wrote upon his death. "His activities against counterfeiters, smugglers, diplomatic enemies, bombers, [and] wartime food hoarders, brought a halo around his name and the words Secret Service." COURTESY OF WILLIAM FLYNN SANDERS ism. The attacks shocked and angered the country. One newspaper ran the headline "Reign of Terror Starts," while another blared, "Bombing Brigade Very Busy: Effort to Kill Att'y-General Palmer: Terror Reign in Many Cities." Most people assumed that some group of "Reds" was responsible for the attacks. Judge Hayden, who was one of the targets of the bombings, said, "We have got to defeat Bolshevists; we have got to deport them. They should not be allowed in this country. They should all be deported at once." Another target, Mayor Davis, promised that all measures would be taken to "rid Cleveland of this red terror."

America was now in the midst of the "Red Scare," a period of public frenzy encouraged by the government, Congress, media, and law enforcement agencies. Fears of a Bolshevik revolution spreading to the United States, continued labor strife, and now major acts of terrorism all added to the public's support of any and all measures against "the Reds." As historian Paul Avrich writes, "Wartime hatred of Germans transformed itself into peacetime horror of radicals, especially alien radicals. If only the menace of un-Americanism could be eliminated, it was widely felt, the nation would be cleansed, its difficulties and tensions mitigated."

WAR ON TERROR

It was this environment that William Flynn stepped into when he took charge of the BI. To say that expectations were high that he would obtain results would be an understatement. In addition to Palmer's gloating that he was "the greatest anarchist expert in the United States," newspapers around the country showered Flynn with effusive praise. The *Washington Evening Star* wrote on June 4 that Flynn "is to have a free hand in organizing and waging the war against the 'reds,' and that practically his entire instructions may be summed up in the words, 'end anarchy in the United States.'" A few months later, the *Pasadena Post* wrote, "In due time, and that not very distant, the government expects not only to have the largest organization of its kind in the world in its bureau of investigation, but a great body of men so competent and experienced in the art of running down criminals that it will furnish an unprecedented bulwark of strength and protection for the government against every element that attempts to direct its unlawful operations against the United States." Another newspaper boasted, "William J. Flynn, the great detective, former chief of the U.S. Secret Service, is in charge of the bureau of investigation. All this foreshadows results, so that it ought not to be very long before conspirators are traced to their lair and the leaders apprehended."[4]

Flynn wasted no time in organizing America's first war on terrorism. Although he was not formally installed as BI director until the end of June, he nevertheless ran things from the start. He was given authority "to 'borrow' any man anywhere in the country if he needs him." Flynn assigned practically every agent in the BI to the task of identifying and capturing those responsible for the bombings. All U.S. federal agencies, including the Secret Service, the Bureau of Mines, and the Post Office, were instructed to cooperate with Flynn, who also established contacts with local police departments throughout the country.[5]

Flynn's organizational plan was aimed not just at capturing those responsible for the bombings but also at preventing additional attacks. The fact that the June 2 bombers struck so many different cities and the earlier package bombs were intended for targets from coast to coast meant that investigating and countering terrorism required a national approach. "Flynn faced a new geography of terror and acted within an entirely new national landscape of counterterrorist activity," scholar Brent Roberts writes. "Geographically, because terrorists could strike anywhere, the fight against them had to be highly mobile, flexible, and able to relocate whenever needed in response to late-breaking developments. . . . Unlike many crimes, which could be centered on a single locality, the new counterterrorism did not have the luxury of geographical fixity." Flynn had an additional objective in mind in reorganizing the BI. He wanted to establish the bureau as "the nation's preeminent federal detective force" not just in matters of terrorism but also in dealing with radicalism and all types of revolutionary threats.[6]

The challenges facing Flynn in the investigations into the June 2 bombings were immense. The bombing at the house of the attorney general of the United States naturally became a high-profile inquiry, covered daily by the media and followed by the public. But Flynn had several other bombings in different cities to deal with. He told reporters a few days after the attacks that the investigations were going well: "There are a hundred leads to be traced out and these we are now following carefully. I am not shooting wild. We are making progress, but I cannot say when any definite action will be taken."[7]

It was clear from the beginning of the investigations that the perpetrators of all the June 2 attacks were connected in some way. This was due to the discovery of identical flyers at the bomb sites. Titled *Plain Words*, the flyer warned of more violence to come:

> The powers that be make no secret of their will to stop here in America, the world-wide spread of revolution. The powers that be must reckon that they will have to accept the fight they have provoked.
>
> . . . The challenge is an old one, oh "democratic" lords of the autocratic republic. We have been dreaming of freedom, we have talked of liberty, we have aspired to a better world, and you jailed us, you clubbed us, you deported us, you murdered us whenever you could.
>
> Now that the great war, waged to replenish your purses and build a piedistal [*sic*] to your saints, is over, nothing better can you do to protect your stolen millions, and your usurped fame, than to direct all the power of the murderous institutions you created for your exclusive defence, against the working multitudes resing [*sic*] to a more human conception of life.
>
> . . . Do not expect us to sit down and pray and cry. We accept your challenge and mean to stick to our war duties. We know that all you do is for your defence as a class; we know also that the proletariat has the same right to protect it self [*sic*], since their press has been suffocated, their mouths muzzled, we mean to speak for them the voices of dynamite, through the mouth of guns.
>
> . . . We are not many, perhaps more than you dream of, though but are all determined to fight to the last, till a man remains buried in your bastiles, till a hostage of the working class is left to the tortures of your police system, and will never rest till your fall is complete, and the laboring masses have taken possession of all that rightly belongs to them.
>
> There will have to be bloodshed; we will not dodge; there will have to be murder: we will kill, because it is necessary; there will have to be destruction; we will destroy to rid the world of your tyrannical institutions.

We are ready to do anything and everything to suppres [*sic*] the capitalist class just as you are doing anything and everything to suppress the proletarian revolution.

...Just wait and resign to your fate, since privilege and riches have turned your heads.

Long live social revolution! down with tyranny.

THE ANARCHIST FIGHTERS[8]

An analysis of the *Plain Words* text by the Military Intelligence Division of the U.S. War Department soon after the bombings concluded that it was probably Italians who had authored the flyer based on various words and phrases that were used. One clue was the word *piedistal*, similar to the Italian word *piedistallo*. Another clue was the word *usurped*, which was used more often in Italian than in English. Adding to the likelihood that it was Italians responsible for the attacks was the discovery of an Italian–English dictionary at the scene of the Palmer bombing. And a large segment of the terrorist's scalp, which authorities did not yet know belonged to the Galleanist Carlo Valdinoci, was recovered, analyzed, and found to contain dark and bushy hair. A French hairdresser examined it and determined that the man was an Italian in his twenties.[9]

There was plenty of other evidence recovered in the area near Palmer's house. This included two handguns; two hats; a tan, sandal-type shoe with a rubber heel; shreds of a black pinstripe suit; a blue polka-dot bow tie; and a piece of a shirt collar with the laundry mark "K.B." All of this evidence and more would be investigated for months afterward. Flynn's agents were eventually able to identify Valdinoci as a suspect in the bombing. He had black hair, wore sandals, and was associated with the Galleanists. But more important, a BI informant reported in January 1920 that an anarchist had told him that Valdinoci was the person killed in the Palmer bombing. When the informant asked the anarchist for more information, he was told that Valdinoci had been missing since the date of the bombing. In June 1920, Palmer placed in the *Congressional Record* a report from the General Intelligence Division (better known as the Radical Division) noting that Valdinoci was probably the man blown up at Palmer's house. The BI later removed any doubt about the identity of the bomber and stated emphatically in November 1922 that it was indeed Carlo Valdinoci, Galleani's trusted aide.[10]

Early on the investigations, the BI suspected that the Galleanists were involved in all of the June 2 bombings. On June 19, the Boston BI office wrote, "It is the unanimous opinion of various officials who have come into touch with Galleani and his affiliations that any acts by the Italian anarchists of this country are known to Galleani." The same office declared on October 3 that "in all probability the Galleani Group are responsible for the June 2nd outrages." And in May 1920, the New Jersey BI office concluded, "It is established beyond a reasonable doubt that the bomb plot of June 2nd were conceived and directed by Luigi Galleani and were exploded on the day that he was deported from this country. Naturally persons or his followers who remained in this country were selected to do the deeds and it would appear that he appealed to the more ignorant of his followers, who desired to become martyrs to the cause."[11] (Galleani was deported on June 24, not June 2.)

As the investigations continued during the summer of 1919, a new player entered the picture. J. Edgar Hoover was named by Palmer to head the recently created Radical Division of the Justice Department and given the title special assistant to the attorney general. It was a meteoric rise in power for the young Hoover. Only twenty-four years old, he had gained a reputation for meticulous work and had a talent for bureaucratic administration, first as a cataloger at the Library of Congress and then as a top analyst with the Alien Enemy Bureau of the Department of Justice, where his responsibilities included surveillance of radicals during World War I. A law school graduate, he was now put in charge of peacetime surveillance of the "Reds," a label that for the government, media, and the public meant Bolsheviks, communists, socialists, anarchists, and IWW militants.[12]

Under Hoover's direction, the Radical Division became the fastest-growing unit in the Justice Department. In its first year of operation, Hoover oversaw the creation of an extensive file system with more than two hundred thousand names of radical agitators. Any person, group, or publication connected with radical activity in any way became part of the file. It was "an unprecedented experiment in peacetime political surveillance." Hoover was also co-opting the investigation of the June 2 bombings from Flynn, with all reports and letters dealing with the attacks coming across his desk. "Even when addressed to Flynn," notes historian Paul Avrich, "they were labeled 'Attention Mr. Hoover,' and afterwards marked 'Noted J.E.H.'"[13]

It was Hoover, not Palmer or Flynn, who organized and directed what became known in the media as the "Palmer Raids," a series of actions aimed at arresting and deporting alien radicals. These raids "really should be called the Hoover Raids," writes historian Adam Hochschild, "because it was Palmer's determined deputy . . . whose Radical Division had drawn up the lists and orchestrated the close coordination with local police departments." The first of these raids occurred on the evening of November 7, 1919, when BI agents raided the offices of the Union of Russian Workers, an anarchist organization consisting mainly of Russian immigrants, in cities across the country. That date had been chosen because it was the second anniversary of the Bolshevik revolution, and Hoover knew that supporters of the revolution would be celebrating in their local meeting places. More than a thousand people were arrested in the raids, which the media reported "were made at the direction of A. Mitchell Palmer, Attorney General, with the co-operation of Anthony Caminetti, commissioner of immigration." This helped lead to the public and media perception that Palmer was the driving force behind the raids. Palmer did nothing to change that perception, as he hoped it would help him win the 1920 Democratic nomination for president. Then, on December 21, two hundred and forty-nine aliens, including one hundred and ninety-six members of the Union of Russian Workers, were deported to Russia. Hoover had arranged for the loan of an army ship, the *Buford*, for the occasion. Hoover gloated about the mission of the *Buford*, telling reporters, "The Department of Justice is not through yet, by any means. Other 'Soviet Arks' will sail for Europe just as often as it is necessary to rid the country of dangerous radicals."[14]

Among the deportees were two of the most famous radicals in the country, Emma Goldman and Alexander Berkman. Both were born in Russia and met as young adults in a coffee shop in New York in 1889. They became lifelong friends, comrades, and, for a brief time, lovers.

Berkman spent fourteen years in prison for the attempted assassination of industrialist Henry Clay Frick in Pittsburgh in 1892 and on his release reunited with Goldman and worked together with her on a variety of radical causes. Both were viewed by the public and government officials as "menacing symbols of revolution and chaos." Goldman, whom Hoover called "the Red Queen of Anarchy," was the more celebrated radical of the pair, having become an international figure through her writings and lectures. She was "keenly intelligent, powerfully persuasive, [and] she promoted her ideas with restless coast-to-coast tours, defying critics, police officers, journalists, and bureaucrats with equal ferocity."[15]

Hoover made sure he was at Ellis Island to view Goldman, Berkman, and the other deportees climb aboard a barge that would take them a short distance to the *Buford* for the long journey to Russia. Joining Hoover on the dock that cold, wintry morning were other government agents and officials, including Flynn and Caminetti. Berkman decided to direct his last angry words to Flynn before leaving the country. Perhaps it was because Flynn was the most famous of the group and one whom Berkman had no trouble recognizing. "I'm coming back to America," he hissed at Flynn, "and I'm going to get you."[16]

It wasn't long after the *Buford* set sail that the second and much larger phase of the Palmer Raids was put in motion. The targets this time were members of the Communist Party of America and the Communist Labor Party. Beginning on January 2, 1920, and continuing for several days, BI agents and local police in thirty-three major cities across the country rounded up between six thousand and ten thousand people. (The exact number has never been known.) Many were arrested without warrants. The authorities "entered bowling alleys, pool halls, cafés, club rooms, and even homes, and seized everyone in sight. Families were separated, prisoners were held incommunicado and deprived of the right to legal counsel." While all this was going on, Hoover was keeping abreast of developments. He "worked around the clock, answering the ringing telephones and reading the urgent telegrams as his squads checked in from across the country."[17]

Palmer was elated with the results of the raids, claiming that the efforts had "halted the advance of 'red radicalism' in the United States" and that "a second, third, and fourth Soviet Ark" would soon be leaving America. As it turned out, however, there would be no more "Soviet Arks" sailing away. Most of the deportation cases that Hoover's Radical Division had prepared as a result of the Palmer Raids were dismissed by Acting Secretary of Labor Louis F. Post. (The Department of Labor was in charge of the Bureau of Immigration, which was the government agency that held deportation hearings.) Post found in many cases that those arrested had been denied proper counsel and that the evidence gathered against them had often been illegally obtained and did not justify deportation.[18]

Although Flynn had praised the Palmer Raids, stating that they "mark the beginning of the decline of organized, rapid revolutionarism [sic] throughout the country," he knew they were not going to help him find the culprits of the June 2 bombings. The Palmer Raids were aimed at Bolsheviks and communists and not Italian anarchists, who the BI had already determined were responsible for the bombings. But Flynn received some good news in February 1920, when a raid of an anarchist group in Paterson, New Jersey, led to the discovery of a batch of pink papers that the group had once used for their newspaper. The papers were similar to those used for the Plain Words flyers found at the sites of the bombings. Although the Paterson anarchist group wasn't under suspicion for the bombings, the owner of the print shop where their newspaper had been prepared told the BI agents that the same type of paper was used by Roberto Elia, a Galleanist, who worked at a print shop in Brooklyn, New York. This was confirmed by one of the anarchists arrested in the Paterson raid who knew many of the Galleanists. In exchange for not being deported, Ludovico Caminita cooperated with the BI and gave the bureau several other names of Galleanists he suspected were involved in the attacks. This included Nicola Recchi, who Caminita said constructed the bombs at Galleani's house in Massachusetts. Recchi, however, was never found. But after months of being frustrated in his search for the June 2 culprits, things were finally looking up for Flynn.[19]

BI agents and an NYPD detective went to Elia's shop and found a quantity of anarchist literature and pink papers resembling those used for the Plain Words leaflets. A search of his apartment uncovered a revolver for which he did not have a permit. Elia was arrested by the police detective on the gun charge, and after pleading guilty to unlawful possession of a firearm, he was given a suspended sentence and turned over to the BI, as they had a warrant for his deportation. Instead of being taken to Ellis Island for a deportation hearing, though, he was brought on March 8 to the BI offices on the fourteenth floor of a building on Park Row in Lower Manhattan. BI agents also brought Andrea Salsedo, Elia's coworker and another close associate of Galleani, to the same building after arresting him in East Harlem. Both men would be held there for almost two months.[20]

The detention of Elia and Salsedo was Flynn's big chance to break the June 2 bombing case wide open. Perhaps realizing the mistake the government had made in deporting Galleani so soon after the bombings instead of keeping him in the country, where he could continuously be interrogated and perhaps eventually reveal the identities of everyone involved in the conspiracy, Flynn did not bring Elia and Salsedo to Ellis Island. He wanted to keep them under tight watch and extract as much information as possible from the two suspects. He was also hoping to keep their detention secret from other Galleanists who, fearing that their identities and roles in the bombings might be revealed by Elia and Salsedo, would either try to flee the United States or go underground before they too could be arrested.[21]

The detention did not remain secret for long. Both men's families and friends learned about their situation and apparently hired a lawyer, Narciso Donato, whose offices were in the same Park Row building. Donato was present for all of his clients' interrogations except for the first night they were held. Salsedo's wife (Elia was single) was allowed to visit once a week. The men were given a furnished room in the office suite and provided a deck of playing cards and some books. They were also taken to a nearby restaurant for their meals and allowed to walk daily up to two miles under escort by BI agents. Flynn was trying to do all he could to keep them happy (or at least content) so as to facilitate their cooperation in the investigation of the bombing. He might also have been hoping to eventually get them to agree to spy on their colleagues. He had given them early on the choice of staying at the BI offices or being released, on which they would immediately be arrested by the police, charged with violation of the New York State sedition law, and taken either to jail or to Ellis Island for deportation hearings. It was an easy decision for the two men to make since the living conditions and privileges they were given in the Park Row building were much better than those that they could expect in jail or at the detention center on Ellis Island.[22]

There was, however, apparently some rough treatment of Salsedo on the first night of his confinement. Elia said he appeared the next day with red marks on his cheeks and temples and told him that BI agents had repeatedly struck him in the face with a bloodstained sandal (presumably the one found at the scene of the Palmer bombing). Salsedo said they asked him whose blood was on the sandal. The BI denied this and stated that Salsedo did not bear any signs of a beating. Both men, however, confessed on March 11 to printing *Plain Words* when questioned by Flynn in the presence of their lawyer, Donato. They stated that Nicola Recchi, the Galleanist who Caminita said constructed the bombs, had brought them the *Plain Words* manuscript to print seven hundred leaflets. Recchi then returned a few days later to retrieve the leaflets and the original manuscript.[23]

Elia and Salsedo cooperated with Flynn and the BI in the weeks that followed, pointing out several Galleanists and other anarchists in photographs that were shown to them for identification. Elia was holding up adequately in detention. But Salsedo was having a much harder time. He became increasingly depressed after he confessed to Flynn. By cooperating with the BI, "he had violated the anarchist code of honor, whose chief article forbade giving information to the authorities. Even worse, he had informed on his comrades, a cardinal sin in the anarchist lexicon, the most hateful offense a Galleanist could commit." He was afraid of reprisals from his comrades.[24]

His wife, Maria, became alarmed during her visits. "He was always nervous and worried when I saw him," she stated. Elia too was concerned about the mental state of his comrade. Sharing the room with him at the BI offices, he could hear him groan all night and complain of stomach pains and headaches. "He showed signs of an unbalancing mind," Elia would later say. Salsedo also showed signs of paranoia, telling Elia that the BI had tampered with their playing cards by placing some type of spying device in the cards. He said he thought they were recording their conversations and had agents watching their every move in their room from the Woolworth Building across the street.[25]

When his lawyer, Donato, visited him on May 1, Salsedo "was in a state of near collapse," his eyes bulging and his speech incoherent. The next evening, he walked for a while with Elia in the hallway of the BI offices, his mental condition still the same. He then went to bed at nine o'clock. Elia remained outside, talking with some of the agents, until he returned to his room at eleven. When he switched on the light, Salsedo asked him to turn it off, complaining again about a headache and how a cigarette that Elia had earlier given him made him feel worse. As Elia tried to sleep, he heard Salsedo groaning. At some point, Elia was finally able to fall asleep, still worried about his troubled friend.[26]

The end of Salsedo's tormented life came at 4:20 a.m., when he quietly rose from his bed so as not to awaken Elia and walked to the window. After climbing on a chair, he jumped out, plunging fourteen stories to his death. A policeman in the street was nearly struck by the falling body. After questioning a porter in the building, he was told to inquire at the BI offices upstairs. The officer told the agents there what happened, and they then rushed into Elia and Salsedo's room to find to their horror that Salsedo's bed was empty and the window open. The agents went downstairs and saw Salsedo dead on the sidewalk.[27]

The death of Salsedo touched off a whirlwind of accusations and conspiracy theories. Salsedo's friends and family told the media that he had been beaten while in detention and possibly thrown out the window by the agents. One of his fellow Galleanists, Emilio Coda, claimed that Palmer and Flynn had made sure that Salsedo was "'suicided' by falling from the fourteenth floor, remaining a mass of unrecognizable flesh and bones on the sidewalk below." Louis Post, the labor secretary who had dismissed many of the Palmer Raid deportation cases, labeled what happened in the Park Row building "the Salsedo homicide." Bartolomeo Vanzetti, a Galleanist who along with another Galleanist, Nicola Sacco, would be executed in 1927 for robbery-murders that took place in South

Braintree, Massachusetts, in April 1920, wrote, "I don't believe Salsedo committed suicide. I believe he was murdered by the Federal police in New York. If he committed suicide it was because they drove him to it."[28]

The most virulent prose against the bureau came from across the sea in Italy, where Galleani, having revived *Cronaca Sovversiva*, his banned anarchist periodical in America, under a new name (*A stormo!* [To the flock!]) and smuggled issues of the paper into the United States, launched an attack against Flynn. "It is no more to be denied," he wrote, "Andrea Salsedo . . . did not commit suicide. He was killed by the cruel agents of Flynn, of Palmer, of Woodrow Wilson. Nor did he denounce his accomplices, as the abominable federal gang has the pretensions to assert, and with this gang all those who are as cowardly and abject as they. . . . The filthy mouth of William J. Flynn launched the hypothesis of the suicide, insinuating that Andrea Salsedo had killed himself to escape the revenge of the comrades betrayed by him. . . . [But it was] the agents of Flynn [who] threw him out the window on the 14 Floor."[29]

When Salsedo's suicide was reported in the newspapers, there was no criticism levied by the papers against Flynn and his men for holding Salsedo and Elia in the BI offices for almost two months. Quite the contrary, there was praise for the government having finally made some arrests for the June 2 attacks. The *New York Times* went as far as to claim that the case was now solved: "When Andrea Salsedo, Sicilian anarchist, jumped fourteen stories to his death at dawn yesterday in Park Row his suicide disclosed that Government operatives, working day and night for months had solved the mystery of the attempt to kill Attorney General Palmer and prominent men in seven cities last June, and that the principals in an anarchist plot against the Government and officials, fugitives abroad, were being sought by the secret police of five countries."[30]

But the case was seriously compromised. Those Galleanists who had not learned earlier through leaks and other means that Elia and Salsedo were being held now knew for sure that they had been and that they themselves were in danger of being arrested. The newspaper reports of Salsedo's death made it clear that both men had been cooperating with the authorities. Plans for a massive roundup of Galleanists were thus dashed, as most of them went underground or fled the country. Hoover's

Radical Division prepared a report on the bombings that all but raised the white flag concerning the investigations:

> It has now been ascertained that while Elia and Salsedo were staying at the Park Row Building, and probably through the efforts of [Carlo] Tresca [a leading anarchist], a large number of anarchists have been leaving the country as stowaways, sailors, and under false passports and in other manners have disappeared. The names of many of these are known to the department. [Nicola] Recchi [a Galleanist] has disappeared and according to the latest reports is supposed to be in Mexico. Galliani [*sic*], before mentioned, is in Italy, where he is engaged as one of the leaders in the impending revolution in that country. Other members of the group are in Italy and other parts of Europe. Others have scattered and are working in out of the way places in the United States.
>
> The net results of the investigations of the bomb plot of June 2, therefore, are that every physical clue has been run out to the last possible extreme, resulting in the discovery of the man that printed the circular Plain Words, the probable discovery of the man who was killed at the house of the Attorney General, the inference that the plot originated with members of the Galliani [*sic*] group, and that the perpetrators of the crime have succeeded in leaving the country, with the possible exception of one or two, and that the principal source of information is now closed by virtue of the suicide of Salsedo.[31]

Hoover's report provided some optimism by stating, "Nevertheless, there are several avenues of information yet to be explored and hold out fairly substantial hopes that ultimately the plot will be solved." But there would be no more arrests of Galleanists for the June 2 bombings. It was a bitter disappointment for all concerned, particularly Flynn, who "had made preparations to seize the Galleanisti in a round of triumphal arrests" before Salsedo's suicide.[32]

The death of a key government witness against the Galleanists wasn't the only bad news for the BI. Warnings from the government in the days leading up to May 1 about potentially violent May Day demonstrations throughout the country by radical organizations never materialized. Combined with a growing public backlash to the illegal measures used during the Palmer Raids (the National Popular Government League, a group consisting of twelve prominent lawyers and professors, including future Supreme Court Justice Felix Frankfurter, issued a scathing report in May outlining the illegalities of the raids), the era of the Red Scare was coming to an end. Congressional appropriations for the Department of Justice were cut in July, and many BI agents were let go.[33]

The backlash to the raids doomed Palmer's chances for the 1920 Democratic presidential nomination. He withdrew his name from consideration after failing to win the nomination after thirty-eight ballots at the national convention in San Francisco in July. Meanwhile, Flynn's reputation as "the greatest anarchist expert in the United States," as Palmer had once described him, also took a hit, as he had failed to round up all the Galleanists involved in the package bomb plot and the June 2 bombings and was also associated with the Palmer raids. There were rumors that both Palmer and Flynn would resign. Neither did, but Frank Burke, the Secret Service agent who had seized the briefcase from Heinrich Albert on the Sixth Avenue elevated train in 1915 and who Flynn had appointed as the number two person in the BI after he became director, submitted his resignation, effective August 1.[34]

The only person to emerge from the Red Scare period unscathed was Hoover. For years afterward, he denied any role in the Palmer Raids. An FBI monograph written in 1969 and approved by Hoover attempted to whitewash his role by placing the blame for the raids on Flynn: "The Palmer raids under Attorney General A. Mitchell Palmer in 1919 and 1920 involved excesses in arrest procedures that were directed by William J. Flynn, then head of the Bureau of Investigation. Mr. Hoover, then in charge of the General Intelligence Division of the Bureau, had no control over the Bureau's field work."[35]

Palmer never quite recovered politically from the stigma of the raids and "returned to Washington a beaten man" after the convention in San Francisco. He would be removed from office the following March, when the new president, Warren G. Harding, appointed Harry M. Daugherty to the role of attorney general. Palmer would to the end defend the raids, telling a Senate Judiciary Committee investigative hearing about the abuses in January 1921 that "I apologize for nothing. I glory in it. I point with pride and enthusiasm to the results of that work. . . . [If my agents] were a little rough and unkind, or short and curt, with these alien agitators . . . I think it might well be overlooked in the general good to the country which has come from it."[36]

Unlike Palmer, Flynn was anything but a beaten man during the summer of 1920. Although he was connected with the Palmer Raids, as noted above, he was still beloved by the media and the public. His name wasn't in the news as frequently as it had been during the investigations into the bombings, but he still generated a lot of favorable publicity. Most of it was due to a series of short stories that he had written based on his experiences with the Secret Service that were adapted into movies. The films, with such titles as *The Silkless Banknote*, *The Five Dollar Plate*, and *Chang and the Law*, drew record attendance that summer in theaters. They were promoted as "facts not fiction" and as being based on "the remarkable career of William J. Flynn." One newspaper also reprinted his 1909 article about the barrel murder and how he battled Mafia leaders Giuseppe Morello and Ignazio Lupo.[37]

Soon, however, the media would once again report on Flynn's current exploits and not his past ones. In September, he was put in charge of investigating what at that time was the worst terrorist attack ever to occur in America. It would be another chance for the Bulldog to prove he was capable of bringing to justice those who were intent on wreaking havoc on the United States.[38]

CHAPTER SIX

Last Hurrah

"THERE ARE ABOUT 25 DEAD AND ABOUT 200 HURT AND SOME ARE VERY badly hurt," Charles Scully, head of the BI's Radical Division in New York, wrote in a memorandum during the evening of September 16, 1920. Hours earlier, an explosion rocked Wall Street, sending the city into a frenzy. Scully was right about the number injured but wrong about the number dead. The death toll would eventually rise to thirty-eight. Contrary to popular belief, the people who worked on Wall Street were not all rich bankers, brokers, and financiers. Many were young men and women who'd found jobs there as clerks, stenographers, errand boys, and other positions. They were the majority of those who lost their lives on that tragic day.[1]

It was a typical Thursday in the Financial District, with the streets crowded around noontime as workers filed out of their offices to go to lunch. Ella Parry, a twenty-two-year-old stenographer at a company whose office was near the J. P. Morgan and Company Building on Wall Street, had just left her desk and was washing her hands when the explosion occurred. "It was the most awful sound I had ever heard and I was terror stricken," she said. The window glass and the ceiling of her building fell all around her: "Where I had just been sitting was covered with heavy plaster. I did not wait to get my hat, but with others rushed into the street." Her coworkers "were screaming in terror and I was among them. When we got to the door policemen were there and they made us stay back. I looked down into the street and saw the reason."[2]

It was something that would haunt her for the rest of her life:

There were not less than a dozen dead persons on the sidewalk in front of our building and the Sub-Treasury. Some of them had their faces almost completely blown off, and their clothing had either been blown from their bodies or burned off. Some of them had their legs blown off, and oh! It was awful. The police threw sheets over the bodies as fast as they could get them and when they had the bodies covered they let us out of the building.

The street was then filled with hysterical and screaming girls, and the police did their best to quiet them. There was at least half a foot of glass on the street and sidewalk.

I have never seen such sights. The front of Morgan's was blown out and the interior was an awful looking wreck. In front of Morgan's office was a burning automobile, the flames jumping high.

Windows on every side had been smashed and the buildings them-selves looked like wrecks, the front of them having been torn out. . . . Ambulances seemed to come from everywhere, and all the emergency wagons in the city seemed to be there while the fire engines and trucks came in from all sides.

When I turned my back on the scenes, the bodies of men were still burning and the doorways were filled with screaming girls. Some of them seemed too frightened to leave their buildings, but others ran through the police lines, they didn't seem to know what they were doing.[3]

The young girl was still shaking after telling her story to a reporter and was unable to write her own name. She and most people didn't know it at the time, but the carnage on Wall Street was caused by a bomb that had been placed in a horse and wagon parked in front of the U.S. Assay Office, right next to the Sub-Treasury Building and across the street from the Morgan headquarters at Broad and Wall streets. The bells from nearby Trinity Church were still ringing out the noon hour when the bomb, equipped with a timer and composed of one hundred pounds of explosives and five hundred pounds of heavy, cast-iron slugs, exploded. The cast-iron slugs were hurled in all directions. People ran in panic, but when they saw the scores of victims lying in the street, many of them tried to help.[4]

The stories of heroism that day by ordinary citizens are remarkable. Ignoring the possibility of more bombs going off in the area or being injured by the glass that was still raining down from the buildings, New Yorkers by the thousands joined the first responders—emergency workers, police, firefighters, doctors, nurses, and other professionals—in attending to the injured. Among the first to provide aid were young women from offices in the area who rushed into the street before the arrival of ambulances and surgeons and tore their clothing to make bandages to dress the wounds of the victims. A seventeen-year-old office boy who had been knocked down and cut by the blast got up and commandeered an abandoned automobile so he could take victims to one of the nearby hospitals. He made four trips, transporting more than thirty of the injured to the hospital. Other survivors carried victims on their shoulders to hospitals in the area, which soon resembled field hospitals in a war zone, overcrowded with victims either dead or dying, as well as the lucky ones who, with treatment, would survive.[5]

In the meantime, a volunteer Red Cross worker canvased all the hospitals during the afternoon and made a list of the dead and wounded who had been taken there. She then gave the list to a policeman stationed outside the Morgan Building. He used it to inform relatives of people working in the Financial District whether their loved ones had been injured or killed in the blast.[6]

Among the victims were twenty-five-year-old twin sisters Amelia and Esther Huger, who'd been meeting up for lunch in front of the Assay Office when the blast went off. On hearing the news that they were seriously injured, their mother frantically rushed from her home in the Bronx to Volunteer Hospital in Manhattan. Doctors there told her that her daughters had suffered severe burns and lacerations and were not expected to live. "The girls just went to work," their mother cried out, "and here they are at the point of death." Amelia died a little more than a week later, while Esther survived. Lying next to them in hospital cots were another pair of young twin sisters, Margaret and Charity Bishop, who were eighteen years old. They too were severely burned and cut in the explosion. Their mother was told that there was little hope for

Margaret's recovery. The young girl did indeed die, but Charity survived, although she was physically scarred for the rest of her life.[7]

Two of the victims had survived the horrors of war only to meet their deaths on the streets of New York. Both Bernard Kennedy and T. Montgomery Osprey were young veterans of the Great War, as World War I was known at the time. Kennedy had been gassed and wounded by shrapnel in the knee while serving with the American Expeditionary Forces (AEF) in France, while Osprey, also with the AEF, had been wounded in the right arm and eye by shrapnel at Beaucourt. Osprey spent a long time recuperating in a hospital after returning home in December 1918. When he was finally released, his right arm was still paralyzed. Both men, who worked as clerks for the same brokerage firm, were killed as they were walking together near the Morgan Building when the bomb exploded.[8]

Another young man who lost his life was Charles Hanrahan, who was celebrating his seventeenth birthday. He worked as a messenger for a Broad Street brokerage house, and September 16 was to be his last day of work before a vacation. His family had prepared a frosted cake with seventeen candles for him to enjoy after work. Instead, his father was called to the morgue and collapsed after identifying the body.[9]

With large crowds milling around Wall Street—forty thousand people had converged on the area to view the damage and inquire about the safety of their friends and loved ones—the Treasury Department called for army troops to be sent to guard the Sub-Treasury and Assay Office. More than $900 million in gold bullion and coin was in the process of being transferred that day from the Sub-Treasury vaults to the new Assay Office. The transfer was being made via a wooden chute set up across the alley between the two buildings. A conveyor belt moved boxes of gold bars, each worth $6,500, into the Assay Office. The troops arrived and stood guard with fixed bayonets and light Browning automatic rifles for several hours. After things calmed down, they left, and the police took their place in front of the buildings. A Secret Service agent at the scene telephoned his office and reported that while the front of the Assay building was damaged, the Sub-Treasury was not affected by the explosion. He said that the gold in both buildings was intact and that the vaults were sealed and locked. A statue of George Washington on the steps of the Sub-Treasury also survived the attack with no damage, offering a symbolic image for those who wanted to take something, anything, positive away from the day's tragic events.[10]

During the night, one hundred and fifty detectives and policemen patrolled the Financial District, guarding buildings, keeping the public away, and looking out for anybody or anything that seemed suspicious. Joining them with a different task was "a full 'battalion' of sweepers, repairmen, street cleaners, stonemasons, and mechanics" hired by the banks and exchanges to prepare Wall Street for business the next day. When people returned to work on September 17, they were greeted with hand-lettered signs in the doorways of buildings that read, "Business as Usual." Corporate America was determined to demonstrate to everybody that terrorism would never bring down capitalism. As one newspaper noted, "The nation's money mart resumed operations just as if the explosion which spread death and destruction at the corner of Broad and Wall streets yesterday had never occurred."[11]

Whereas the business community wanted everyone to put the tragedy behind them, investigators naturally had to put it front and center. The cleanup crews didn't do them any favors by inadvertently destroying and contaminating potentially valuable physical evidence in their haste to get rid of all the debris from the bombing. The investigation would prove to be one of the most challenging and frustrating efforts in U.S. history.[12]

SORTING OUT THE CLUES

William Flynn was in Washington when word reached him about the bombing. Attorney General Palmer immediately put him in charge of the federal investigation, which involved about five thousand government detectives connected to the Department of Justice, Treasury Department, Post Office, and Bureau of Immigration. Palmer ordered all agents to send their reports to Flynn and arranged for a special train to bring him to New York. Flynn wouldn't arrive at Penn Station until later that evening. In his absence, Scully and George Lamb, the BI's New York division superintendent, led the investigation at the bomb site. Several dozen BI agents were on the scene within ten minutes of the explosion, as was the entire New York force of the Secret Service. Joining them on Wall Street were members of the NYPD bomb squad along with Police Commissioner Richard Enright and Mayor John Hylan.[13]

It was wishful thinking on Palmer's part that he could have Flynn or anybody control the bureaucratic rivalry sure to arise in the wake of the bombing. Solving the case would be a major coup for any agency or individual. In addition to the police and Secret Service, the New York City Fire Department also launched its own investigation to trace the explosives. Travelers Indemnity, which was the insurer for Morgan and Company, conducted an investigation to determine whether there was any liability in the bombing. A grand jury later in September opened an investigation aimed at finding the perpetrator(s) of the crime. And Military Intelligence was also involved, given the strategic importance of Wall Street.[14]

Palmer said congressional cuts to the Justice Department's budget were the reason the attack occurred in the first place, which he labeled part of a major plot to overthrow the capitalist system. The budgetary cuts, he claimed, had forced him to reduce his operational staff by one-third, resulting in his department not being able "to keep in as close touch with ultra-radicals as we were some six months ago or keep as well informed on what is taking place or about to take place." Palmer viewed the bombing as vindication and justification for the Red Scare campaign that he and the Justice Department had pursued and hoped this latest attack would result in support for another round of deportations of alien anarchists.[15]

Of all the different investigators that would become involved in the case, there was one that Flynn knew would make life hard for him. William J. Burns was as famous as Flynn, if not more so. The two men didn't like each other, even though they had much in common. They were both Irish and stubborn and loved media attention. They willingly granted interviews to reporters, wrote stories about their exploits, and delved into the movie business. They also even worked together for a brief time at the Secret Service. But whereas Flynn was more concerned with serving his country in government positions than making money in the private sector, Burns was the opposite. He had an entrepreneurial spirit and became a confidante of the rich and powerful. And while Flynn was never tainted by any type of scandal, Burns, who was six years older, dealt with scandals throughout his career.[16]

Burns was a short and stocky man with a broad belly and large jowls. His red hair, thick moustache, and fondness for three-piece suits (probably due to being the son of a tailor) made him stand out wherever he went. He was born on October 19, 1861, in Baltimore and wanted to pursue an acting career. His father, Michael, was opposed to that, believing it would be better for his son to have a steady job. He therefore urged him to become a lawyer or a bookkeeper. William dutifully completed his high school studies and enrolled in a business college. He then began working for his father, which he hoped would just be temporary until he found something better. In the meantime, his father, who had moved the family to Columbus, Ohio, in 1873, became involved in local politics. Several years later, he was elected the city's police commissioner, which was a part-time job. William couldn't wait to go to the police station each day after finishing his bookkeeping duties and watch the detectives at work. He listened to their stories, and they even let him work the streets as an unofficial detective. He knew then that his future career would be in law enforcement.[17]

Burns continued to work for the Columbus police and also for the local prosecutor after his father's one-term position as commissioner ended. In 1889, he joined the Secret Service, eight years before Flynn did. He succeeded in breaking up several counterfeit rings, including that of the famous Bill Brockway, who, as noted in chapter 1, would later enthrall Flynn with stories of his counterfeiting adventures while Flynn was a keeper at the Ludlow Street Jail in New York. In 1903, Burns was loaned to the Department of the Interior to work with a special prosecutor on land fraud cases in Oregon and California. Burns's investigations helped lead to more than thirty individuals, including a former U.S. senator, being sent to jail. Burns continued to work with the same prosecutor on a new case, one of corruption in San Francisco's municipal government. The investigations resulted in highly publicized graft trials in 1906 and 1907 that gave Burns more national exposure.[18]

By 1909, Burns felt he had built up enough national recognition to leave the Secret Service and establish his own private detective agency.

This would give him the opportunity to earn more than the $7-per-day wages that he received from the Secret Service. The Burns National Detective Agency (the name was later changed to the Burns International Detective Agency after he added offices in Montreal, Toronto, and London) would soon grow to be one of the most famous detective agencies in the world. Helping it along would be a bombing in Los Angeles that would make Burns and his agency household names.[19]

People living in Los Angeles, as is true for most people in California, are used to earthquakes. It is one of the risks of living on the West Coast. When residents were awakened by a thunderous sound at 1:17 a.m. on October 1, 1910, many thought at first it was yet another earthquake, even though their homes weren't shaking. When they ran into the streets to see what had happened, instead of collapsed or damaged buildings nearby, they saw the sky over Los Angeles reddened as flames burst upward from the Los Angeles Times Building on First Street and Broadway in the downtown area.[20]

There had been a long period of union/management disputes and strikes at the *Times* prior to the explosion, which was caused by a time bomb containing sixteen sticks of dynamite that had been placed inside a suitcase and left in an alley next to the building. That area was known as Ink Alley because of the barrels of ink that were stored there. When the bomb exploded, it ignited the printers' ink, causing a massive fire. Twenty-one nonunion workers were killed—most from burns and suffocation—and an estimated $500,000 in damages resulted. Two other bombs were discovered that same day, one at the home of *Times* publisher Harrison Gray Otis and another at the home of the secretary of the antiunion Merchants and Manufacturers' Association. Police removed the bomb at Otis's home to an open area and detonated it safely, while the second bomb failed to explode due to a weak battery.[21]

The bombing generated headlines across the country. It was the worst act of domestic terrorism at that time, only to be surpassed ten years later by the Wall Street bombing. Both the city of Los Angeles and Otis, who blamed organized labor for the attack, hired Burns to track down the culprits. Burns was elated, knowing that "the publicity would be both gratifying personally and enormously beneficial to business." His investigation led him to John B. McNamara, the secretary-treasurer of the International Association of Bridge and Structural Iron Workers, and James McNamara, John's younger brother. With the aid of the police, he arrested James in Detroit in April 1911 and shortly after that apprehended John in Indianapolis. The McNamara brothers were then taken by train to Los Angeles to face charges for the *Times* bombing.[22]

Organized labor rallied to their defense, claiming it was a frame-up by Otis and big business to destroy labor. Clarence Darrow, one of the most famous lawyers in America, was hired to defend them. But they eventually confessed to the crime to avoid the death penalty, James admitting to placing the suitcase bomb next to the *Times* building and John to being an accessary to the attack. James was sentenced to life imprisonment, while John was sentenced to fifteen years. Their confessions were a big blow to the labor movement but a boon to Burns's career. His "reputation as a foe of dynamiters would bring lucrative contracts for years to come." It also made Burns "Flynn's only true rival on a national scale."[23]

But it wasn't all smooth sailing for Burns following his success with the McNamara case. In 1916, he almost lost his New York State private detective license after being found guilty of wiretapping the offices of a legal firm on behalf of one of his clients, J. P. Morgan and Company. He was fined $100, but his conviction was reversed on appeal. The case, however, led to hearings on whether Burns's New York State private detective license should be renewed. Burns was able to survive this challenge.[24]

By the time of the Wall Street bombing, though, Burns had lost a lot of his luster. He "had never quite replicated his McNamara success." Just as Flynn needed the bombing to prove to everyone that he was the great detective who could solve major cases, so too did Burns, who "was extremely excited over the Wall Street bombing." He needed it to get back in the limelight and generate the praise and acclaim that he had grown accustomed to. Investigating the bombing could also mean more lucrative contracts for his private detective agency.[25]

While Flynn was racing from Washington to New York on a special train, Burns was already holding court with reporters at the scene of the bombing. His offices were in the Woolworth Building, just a few blocks from the Financial District. He was thus able to go to Broad and Wall streets soon after he heard the explosion. When reporters, who easily recognized the famous Burns, asked him what he was doing there, he replied that he was working for Morgan and Company, something the bank never confirmed. He also said that "the police will have the case cleared up within ten days."[26]

Burns made this bold prediction based on only a cursory examination of the area. There had been speculation that the explosion was due to an accident involving a wagon or truck carrying dynamite. Burns quickly dismissed that theory. "We have evidence to prove it was the work of time-lock bombs," he told reporters. Burns also said that he had sent out warnings about a month earlier to his clients that an attack like this was likely to occur.[27]

Flynn also claimed that he wasn't surprised by the bombing. "The bureau has had twenty special agents around that section for weeks in expectation of such an outrage as this," he said before leaving Washington for New York. But he wasn't ready yet to officially state that it was a bomb that caused the destruction, even though he was pretty sure it was. After arriving in New York later that evening, he telephoned BI headquarters to inform them that it could not definitively be determined whether the explosion was due to a bomb or an accident. But he said that "the fact that iron slugs were found at the point of explosion and in the vicinity would indicate that it is a bomb." With reporters the next day, Flynn left no doubt as to what caused the explosion. "You can settle your mind on this point," he said, "that it was a bomb which exploded. The wagon destroyed in front of the U.S. Assay Office carried the bomb, and the driver of it was four blocks away from the scene when the explosion occurred."[28]

Investigators had already checked out the businesses that the victims of the bombing were involved with and were able to determine that none of them owned or operated the horse-drawn wagon that exploded. That meant that whoever set off the bomb had gotten away. But just like Burns, Flynn was optimistic that the perpetrators would be found. "We'll get them," he told the press. From the start, he was convinced that it was the Galleanists who were behind the attack. A newsman reported that

Flynn claimed "the plot was conceived and consummated by the same group of Italian terrorists who planned and executed the June 2, 1919, outrages." The reporter wrote that "it is to the Galleiani [*sic*] group . . . that the Department of Justice officials are looking for a solution of this latest outrage." Flynn said that it was just bad luck that prevented him from catching the perpetrators of the previous bombings: "We solved the mystery of the June 2, 1919 bombs, but were frustrated in bringing the criminals to justice when Salsedo jumped from our offices to the street below and killed himself. That tipped our hand and the crowd got away." He promised things would be different this time.[29]

According to Flynn, the terrorists were not trying to kill anyone in particular, including J. P. Morgan, even though the bombing occurred right across the street from the Morgan bank. "You might add as an expression of my personal opinion," Flynn told reporters, "that the bomb was not directed at Mr. Morgan, any member of the Morgan firm, or any other individual. It was planted in the financial heart of America as a defiance against the American people and the American Government. That is my opinion."[30]

Flynn was under enormous pressure to solve the case. The New York Chamber of Commerce labeled the bombing an "act of war." The *New York Times* wrote in an editorial that the perpetrators "will be hunted down in their lairs like wild animals. Every device and stratagem of detection will be put in operation against them." Newspapers across the country reported daily on the progress (or lack of it) in the investigations. And once again, just like with the June 2 bombings, expectations were high that Flynn would be the right man for the job. "Chief William Flynn, the famous 'Big Bill' hurried to New York to assume personally the task of the unraveling of the mystery," the *Los Angeles Times* reported. Another newspaper ran a story about the bombing under the heading "William J. Flynn Will Run Down Conspirators." And the *New York Daily News* wrote, "William J. Flynn, chief of the Bureau of Investigation of the Department of Justice—big, fat, friendly, conservative and yet generous with information ('a whale of a man' . . .)—will within twenty-four hours, it is believed, hold in the toil of the law those responsible for the Wall street disaster."[31]

In New York, Flynn conferred with executives from J. P. Morgan and Company, whose building suffered more than $2 million in damages. J. P. Morgan himself was in England at the time. Flynn then met in his office with his assistants and various witnesses to the explosion until three in the morning. The task of interviewing witnesses, which BI agents and other investigators had started doing shortly after the explosion, would continue for weeks ahead. As is often true when there are multiple witnesses to a crime, there were varying accounts. A sample of twenty-one witnesses did, however, reveal some points of agreement. Most of them said that the wagon was parked in front of or near the U.S. Assay Office and that it was old and dilapidated, its paint worn off. The color of the body of the wagon was dark or dirty gray, while the wheels were dark red. The horse, a dark bay, was aged, thin, and in poor condition, its front knees badly sprung. The witnesses could not, however, provide sufficient information about the most important clue the investigators were after: a description of the driver.[32]

Investigators also could not determine exactly how long the wagon was parked in the street before the explosion. One witness said he saw a delivery wagon driving toward the Assay Office about one minute before the explosion occurred. Flynn believed the driver abandoned the wagon on Wall Street after setting the timer for the bomb a few minutes ahead. Another witness, however, said he saw a wagon parked unattended outside the Assay Office for at least an hour. If true, then it meant an old, beat-up wagon with a sickly looking horse had been parked in the heart of Wall Street without arousing suspicion about its presence there. The *Wall Street Journal* criticized city officials for not policing the Financial District, which might have prevented the attack.[33]

Since the horse suspected of drawing the bomb-laden wagon to Wall Street had been killed, investigators set out to determine whether any stables were missing a horse, either one that had been stolen or one that was never returned after being used on September 16. They hoped this might lead to the perpetrator. The NYPD assigned thousands of its men to canvas all the stables in the city, while George Lamb, the BI division superintendent for New York, instructed his agents to focus mainly on Italian stables. But there were no reports of any stables missing a horse and wagon.[34]

Photostat copies were also made of two horseshoes with specific markings that were found outside Trinity Church near the bomb site. These were shown to approximately four thousand blacksmiths along the Eastern Seaboard. One of them, Gaetano DeGrazio, whose shop was in the Little Italy section of Manhattan, recognized them and told agents he had made the shoes and shod the horse the day before the bombing for a man he described as Sicilian. Flynn arranged for DeGrazio to view hundreds of photos of anarchists with the hope that he might be able to identify his customer. To make sure, however, that DeGrazio wasn't in some way connected to the bombing, Flynn had a BI confidential informant, code name "P-137," watch his shop in case any suspicious people visited or in the eventuality that DeGrazio tried to get in touch with anybody who could be of interest to the bureau. The informant reported that he observed nothing of importance during his surveillances.[35]

While DeGrazio was viewing the photographs, investigators were busy on many different fronts. One involved trying to locate the person or persons who had bought a set of rubber letter stamps that were used to make propaganda leaflets found in a mailbox (without any envelopes or addresses) just a few blocks from Broad and Wall streets on the day of the explosion. These leaflets, which Flynn described as "a challenge to the American Government," were similar in message to those that were discovered at all the sites of the June 2, 1919, bombings. There were also misspellings in the leaflets, like the earlier ones. Rubber-stamped in red ink on white paper, the Wall Street leaflets warned of additional attacks: "Remember, we will not tolerate any longer. Free the political prisoners, or it will be sure death for all of you." They were signed "American Anarchist Fighters." This signature convinced Flynn that the same group of Italian anarchists (the Galleanists) had composed both sets of leaflets. "You can see," he said, "they have simply added American to their title now." (The flyers found at the sites of the June 2 bombings were signed "The Anarchist Fighters.") "The similarity of the circulars makes available all our knowledge of the gang who committed the outrages last year," Flynn also said.[36]

Investigators learned that the R. H. Manufacturing Company of Springfield, Massachusetts, had produced the set of rubber stamps used to create the leaflets. This discovery was made because the word "for" in the leaflet ("death for all of you") had a distinct style found only in "The Easy Sign Maker #0" rubber letter set that the company manufactured. More than two thousand retail stores were visited by agents in the New York area to see to whom they might have sold such sets. No results were obtained from this part of the investigation. The same was true for stores visited in other cities throughout the East and Midwest.[37]

Immediately after the bombing, several witnesses claimed to have seen a DuPont Powder Company vehicle (some said wagon, others said truck) in the area with the word "Explosives" painted on its side. Before he died from his injuries, one person told a doctor at a hospital that he had been standing on the steps of the Sub-Treasury Building when a red wagon marked "Dupont-explosives" with a red flag came around Wall Street and hit a curb, setting off the explosion. His account and those of other witnesses led to the initial theories that an accident, not a bomb, had caused the carnage. However, the discovery of cast-iron slugs on the ground and in several buildings disputed that, as Flynn would later note, since such slugs could be used as shrapnel in a bomb. Nevertheless, investigators still checked out the businesses in the New York vicinity that handled explosives and found that all their vehicles and wagons were accounted for. Statements from the officials of these companies also indicated that no explosives were delivered by them in or near Wall Street on the day of the explosion.[38]

But investigators were puzzled as to the type of explosive used. Was it dynamite, TNT, blasting gelatin, or something else? "Many chemists have ventured opinions concerning the character of the explosive used, and to date no two agree," Scully wrote in a memorandum for Flynn on October 18, summarizing progress in the case up to that point. Flynn had his agents check out many places throughout the country that sold or carried various types of explosives, but nothing was gained from this phase of the investigation. To this day, the type of explosive used in one of the worst bombings in U.S. history has never been determined.[39]

Scully had some more bad news for Flynn in his October 18 memorandum. Despite investigations of more than two thousand known Italian anarchists living in the New York area, none of them could be linked to the Wall Street bombing. An investigation of various radical groups in the area, including the Union of Russian Workers, the Wobblies, communists, and others, was also conducted to no avail. "It would appear that none of the aforementioned organizations had any hand in the matter," Scully wrote, "and that the explosion was the work of either Italian Anarchists or Italian Terrorists."[40]

Flynn was asked by reporters about a week after the bombing why there hadn't yet been any arrests. He replied that because of congressional cuts to the Department of Justice's budget, he didn't have enough agents at the present time. He told the reporters that they should ask NYPD Commissioner Richard Enright why there hadn't been any arrests thus far, implying it was the police's fault. This enraged Enright, who said, "The police have investigated every clew that offered any hope at all and they have been working hard and unceasingly. They have left nothing undone that should have been done." He added, "I am not concerned with anything Mr. Flynn may say." Coming to the police's defense was Burns, who agreed with Enright that the police were doing all they could and said, in his opinion, that the police would eventually solve the case, not the federal government.[41]

In the frenzy to find the culprits, there were a number of individuals who were falsely accused of being involved with the bombing. One was a young Polish miner, Florean Zelenko, who had spoken about the Wall Street bombing with a person on a train from Cincinnati to Pittsburgh in early October. The traveling companion became suspicious and informed police about the conversation, saying he also thought that Zelenko was carrying dynamite with him. When police searched Zelenko's hotel room in Pittsburgh, they found seven sticks of dynamite and arrested him. His arrest and possible link to the Wall Street attack became national news.[42]

It turned out, however, that Zelenko was an itinerant miner who, like other miners, was often required to buy the dynamite, fuses, and percussion caps needed for his work from mine operators. He was simply carrying the unused sticks of dynamite with him on the train from a previous job. When BI agents searched his former residence in Brooklyn, New York, they found some radical literature but nothing of a significant nature. They also looked at Zelenko's activities prior to the bombing and were convinced that he had no connections to any radical movements. BI agents who interviewed him in Pittsburgh reported that they found Zelenko "to be truthful in every way." Although no charges were brought against him for the bombing, he was still convicted in federal court in Pittsburgh for interstate transportation of explosives. But given the notoriety Zelenko had to endure, with the nationwide publicity linking him to the Wall Street bombing, the judge showed compassion and sentenced him to only one day in prison.[43]

Another suspect in the early days of the investigation was a mentally ill former tennis star, Edwin Fischer, who had written to friends working on Wall Street to stay away from that area on September 15. He also told Thomas Delahunty, a caretaker at a tennis court, "Tom, I want to tell you a secret. We are going to blow up Wall Street on the 15th. We got them where we want them." Even though he had the wrong date by one day, his letters and statement got the attention of the BI, which had received a tip about Fischer from a phone call the night of the bombing. Fischer was in Toronto and was brought to New York for interrogation. But after questioning him extensively, the police and the BI released Fischer and sent him to the psychiatric ward at Bellevue Hospital in New York City after concluding that he had no prior knowledge of the explosion and that he believed he had received telepathic messages from God regarding the attack.[44]

As would be expected after a major crime, Flynn and BI offices around the country were bombarded with letters, phone calls, and visits by people who claimed to have knowledge about the bombing or to know people who did. Most of these accusations would then have to be investigated, often wasting the valuable time and resources of the bureau. Sometimes, an accusation was based on just a comment a person made to somebody else. In one case, a drummer in a band playing in a hotel told agents he had had a conversation with a waiter at the hotel who said the night before the bombing that "in a short time J. P. Morgan and other capitalists would 'got [sic] theirs.'" The waiter was brought to the New York BI office and interrogated, but apparently no valuable information was obtained.[45]

In another case, a man from Indianapolis, Elbert Leib, wrote to Flynn after reading a story about the bombing in his local newspaper.

The story quoted a vendor who sold chocolates on Wall Street as claiming that the driver of a horse-drawn wagon shouted at him to get out of the way shortly before the explosion occurred. The vendor described the driver as having a Scottish accent and a dark complexion. He said he was unshaven and probably thirty-five or forty years old. Leib told Flynn that this description matched that of a labor leader in Buffalo he once knew. "Of course the possibility is remote," Leib admitted, "but never the less it exists just the same." Then, after writing a long, detailed account of the labor leader's life and activities, Leib apologized for taking up the director's time: "Now, Mr. Flynn, it is possible that I am bothering a very busy man, with something that you may consider of no importance." Flynn nevertheless wrote back, thanking him for his letter "with its very interesting detail. Perhaps it would be helpful and will be further developed." It is not known if there was indeed any follow-up investigation.[46]

Many people who came forward with information about the bombing were undoubtedly motivated by the possibility of cashing in on the rewards that had been offered for the case. The city of New York offered a $10,000 reward for information leading to the conviction of the perpetrator or perpetrators and $500 for the identity of the owner of the horse-drawn wagon. An insurance company also offered a $10,000 reward. Not to be outdone, William Burns offered his own reward, a staggering $50,000. There was only one catch: any information had to be given to the William J. Burns International Detective Agency exclusively. It was a shrewd move by Burns, ensuring that he, not Flynn or the police, would be the one receiving the information that could possibly solve the case. He could then bask in the glory of public adoration for bringing the perpetrator(s) to justice.[47]

Meanwhile, Flynn alerted his agents to be on the lookout for any interference by Burns in their investigation of the bombing. In October, he received a letter from William Hazen, the former chief of the Secret Service who was now the BI's special agent in charge of the Connecticut district, informing him that an Italian working for the Burns agency had come to his office inquiring as to where the anarchists in Hartford held meetings. Hazen told the visitor that he did not know where they met and that there was only one small group of anarchists in the area. The

Burns detective said that had to be the Galleanists. He also told Hazen's stenographer while waiting to meet with Hazen that he had already been to the police department to gather information about Italian anarchists in Hartford. This indicated, Hazen wrote, "that Burns is operating in this District in rather a crude manner looking for the GALLINI [*sic*] group. I treated this Italian indifferently, because I did not want to have him report that we were in any way anxious about his movements."[48]

RUNNING OUT OF TIME

Flynn didn't have any success locating the remaining members of the Galleanists who were still in the United States. But as the weeks and months passed by with no progress in the investigation, Flynn decided on a long shot. He would send one of his informants undercover to Italy to try to track down Luigi Galleani and elicit information from him about the bombing. This was ironic, of course, because had the government not deported Galleani in 1919, they wouldn't have had to look for him overseas.[49]

The task of finding Galleani fell to Salvatore Clemente, the former counterfeiter Flynn used when he was with the Secret Service to infiltrate the Morello–Lupo gang in New York and later the Galleanists in Vermont and Massachusetts. Clemente, posing as an anarchist from Paterson, New Jersey, was given the code name "Mull" and set sail for Italy, his home country, at the end of December 1920. When he arrived in Rome, an American diplomat gave him photos of Galleani and other Italian anarchists. He then went to Milan and met up with a Galleanist he knew from America, Antonio Mazzini, who confirmed that the person who carried the bomb up the steps of Attorney General Palmer's home on June 2, 1919, and was killed when it went off was Carlo Valdinoci. Mazzini said that Galleani had tears in his eyes when he learned of Valdinoci's death.[50]

Mazzini informed Clemente that Galleani was nowhere to be found in Italy, having fled the country to avoid arrest by the Italian authorities after resuming the printing of his newspaper, *Cronaca Sovversiva*, in Turin. Clemente was able to locate Galleani's sister Carolina in Vercelli, who also told him that her brother "had to leave the country." Having not achieved his mission, a disappointed Clemente returned to the United States in March 1921.[51]

By that time, Flynn was feeling increased pressure for not yet solving the Wall Street bombing. Many people wondered if it would ever be solved. And there were media reports that Flynn would soon be replaced as director of the BI by none other than William Burns. A new president had taken office, and he appointed a new attorney general, and neither of those developments boded well for Flynn. President Warren Harding, who won the 1920 presidential election, was inaugurated in March 1921 and replaced Attorney General Palmer with his campaign manager—and a friend from Ohio—Harry Daugherty. Daugherty was close friends with Burns, so rumors naturally flew that Flynn's days as BI director were numbered.[52]

But Flynn, a lifelong Republican, had support from influential party members, and since both Harding and Daugherty were Republicans, he was able to keep his job, at least for now. He soon dodged another bullet when it appeared that Burns would be named to head a new organization that would combine Flynn's BI, the Treasury Department's Secret Service, and other federal police and investigative agencies into one government body. This reorganization, however, never materialized.[53]

Flynn, meanwhile, was working on what he hoped would be the big break in the case. Early in January, he began circulating to chiefs of police and postmasters in eastern cities a composite drawing of who he suspected was the driver of the horse-drawn wagon that exploded on Wall Street. Gaetano DeGrazio, the blacksmith who shod the horse's shoes, identified two photographs from the hundreds of anarchists he was shown, claiming they somewhat resembled the driver who brought the horse to his shop. It was, however, as historian Beverly Gage points out, only "educated guesswork." DeGrazio worked with a commercial artist combining the two photos to make a composite drawing, suggesting changes to various features along the way. The wash drawings were then photographed and circulated to the select audience. Included with the photograph was a physical description of the driver as being "apparently Italian, 28 or 30 years; 5 feet 6 inches; medium build; broad shoulders; dark hair; dark complexion; small dark mustache, which at the date of the explosion represented about two week's growth. He wore a gold cap, pulled down over his forehead, and khaki shirt turned in at the neck, as indicated in photograph." The communication to the police chiefs and postmasters was supposed to be confidential, but the *New York Herald* got hold of one and published it on March 31. Other newspapers then reported on the story. "I have no knowledge as to how or where the newspaper obtained the circular and photograph," Flynn wrote in a memo to Daugherty in April.[54]

Flynn informed Daugherty that he had received many replies regarding the circular he sent out (he did not mention whether any information came from the newspaper publishing the material) and that all of the replies "have been or are under investigation." One of the leads involved a person named Vincenzo Leggio, but the bureau soon learned that Leggio had moved to Italy in the spring of 1920. There were no reports that he had ever returned. But when police in Scranton, Pennsylvania, arrested an Italian anarchist named Tito Ligi for draft evasion, they found what they said were sash weights identical to the shrapnel used in the Wall Street bomb in the back room of a restaurant where Ligi once worked. Flynn now thought that he had finally gotten his man, given the similarity in the last names, and that Ligi was actually Vincenzo Leggio.[55]

Even though the so-called sash weights turned out to be irregular blocks of iron and steel that Italians in the city used for playing a game, Flynn still summoned to the BI offices in New York a number of people who had previously stated that they had seen the driver of the bomb-laden wagon. These witnesses were shown twenty-five photos, Ligi among them. Two of the witnesses (Thomas Smith, a former New York Fire Department lieutenant, and James Nally, a stockbroker's clerk) picked out Ligi's photo "as that of a man closely resembling the driver." But when the photograph was shown to DeGrazio, the blacksmith, he said Ligi was not the man who came to his shop the day before the bombing. Nevertheless, Flynn arranged for Smith and Nally, as well as a few other witnesses, to travel to Scranton to identify Ligi in a police lineup.[56]

Only Smith was able to make the identification. The other witnesses did not recognize Ligi. Smith, however, now claimed that Ligi was not the driver of the wagon but rather a person he saw talking to the actual driver about a half hour before the explosion. New York police detectives had little faith in Smith's account, claiming he was nowhere near Wall Street at that time on September 16. The case against Ligi soon fell apart, with Flynn admitting publicly that the BI had no evidence connecting Ligi to the bombing. But Ligi was still sentenced to one year in prison for draft evasion.[57]

By now, Flynn was like a boxer, far behind in points going into the last round against his opponent. Only a knockout would win the bout for him. With Burns waiting in the wings, Flynn likely knew he needed to solve the case soon to keep his job. Even that, though, might not have been enough given Burns's close friendship with Daugherty. His last hope came around the same time that Ligi went to prison. A man named Giuseppe De Filippis was arrested in early May in Bayonne, New Jersey, because of his alleged resemblance to the composite drawing of the wagon driver. Witnesses were once again brought in, this time to the Bayonne jail, to identify him as the driver. Once again, inexplicably, Smith was among the witnesses. He now identified De Filippis as the driver, as did two other witnesses. But once again, the case fell apart, as there was no other evidence against De Filippis, who was not an anarchist. He claimed that he was at a Bayonne railroad siding on September 16, hoping to be hired to haul California grapes that were being unloaded there from a refrigerated car. Several witnesses confirmed his story.[58]

Flynn remained in his job for most of the summer. But the ax fell on August 18, when Daugherty announced that Burns would be the new BI director. He told reporters that Flynn had not yet resigned but that he had been notified of Burns's appointment. Daugherty had sent Flynn a telegram to his New York office informing him of the decision while Flynn was on vacation in Saratoga. A different version of how Flynn was dismissed was presented by one of his close friends who had Washington connections. According to Richard Butler, Flynn received news of the firing in a most humiliating way:

> It was a damn shame the way the government treated Chief Flynn, letting him out without proper notice and without a pension after all his years of faithful service. In the last days of the Wilson administration,

I was in Washington, trying to get a pardon for a young man through Joe Tumulty, secretary to President Wilson, who was so ill he couldn't sign a paper. I tipped Flynn off then that he was to go, having heard this from a friend of John Weeks, who became Secretary of War. Flynn wouldn't believe it, and said I was an alarmist. A few months after Harry Daugherty became Attorney-General under President Harding, he gave a letter to William J. Burns, who handed it to Flynn. I saw the letter, and it read like this: On and after this date, Mr. Burns will assume entire charge of the office. Take your orders from him. "So this is the game, is it?" Chief Flynn said to Burns. Flynn's heart was broken. He would have been willing to resign if given thirty days' notice, but he hated to be rushed out without a minute's notice. To add insult to injury, Daugherty offered to let Flynn remain as Burns' assistant. Of course, the Chief indignantly declined that offer.[59]

Many in the media also viewed Flynn's dismissal as unfair and the result of Burns's close relationships with Daugherty and President Harding. The latter three all had Ohio roots. One newspaper editorial wrote, "Mr. Flynn loses his official head because he didn't 'pal' up with the Marion [Ohio] bunch in past years. . . . It is becoming evident that men of great ability are not desired in the government service unless they are friends of someone from Marion. . . . The ruthless booting of Flynn from office may deter other men of great ability from seeking to give their services to Mr. Harding's—or rather Mr. Daugherty's—government unless they can produce the Marion 'good fellow' passport." And it wasn't just Flynn who got booted from government service after Burns took over. The new director appointed George Brennan as head of the BI's New York office, and Brennan summarily dismissed eight agents who were friends and supporters of Flynn, including Flynn's prospective son-in-law.[60]

Flynn returned from his vacation to supervise the removal of government filing cabinets from his New York office. He had nothing to say to reporters regarding his dismissal and Burns's appointment. His only comments were that he planned to resume his vacation in upstate New York, where he had been recovering from a bout of hay fever. It is not known if he was paying attention to what Burns was doing or saying in his new position, which often seemed to be a dig at how Flynn had run the bureau. In commenting on the establishment of a new detective school for BI agents, Burns said, "We are going to teach our men to get results. Slipshod investigation, making discoveries only by chance, is going to stop. And men who cannot be taught to be effective will be dropped." He further promised that "we are going to give this country a detective service of which its citizens can be proud as the English are of Scotland Yard."[61]

As Flynn continued his vacation, he probably wondered about one thing: would his nemesis succeed where he had not in solving the Wall Street bombing? For Burns, it wasn't necessarily going back to square one in the investigation. He had been unofficially investigating it for his Burns International Detective Agency since the day of the explosion. Now, though, he had the full force of the U.S. government to assist in trying to find the culprits. One of his first steps as director was to request reports from all the field offices on their progress to date in the case. After reviewing them, he was convinced that Flynn had been wrong in focusing most of his efforts on trying to find the Galleanists, even though, as noted earlier, he too had tried to find them in New England in October 1920. Burns believed that Russian-based communists, not Italian anarchists, were behind the bombing.[62]

This was a belief he had held for a long time. Soon after the bombing, Burns issued a statement claiming that the attack was committed by adherents of the Third International of Moscow, an association of communist parties around the world that was controlled by Russia. The NYPD and district attorney's office said they had found no evidence supporting that assertion and stated that if Burns had such information, he should bring it before a grand jury. There is no indication Burns ever did that.[63]

Meanwhile, in March 1921, when he was still conducting his own private investigation of the bombing, Burns gave nearly $3,000 to an informant, William Linde (also known as Wolfe Lindenfeld), and sent him to Europe and Russia to find the driver of the wagon and anybody else involved in the attack. But Burns lost contact with Linde, who cut off all communications soon after leaving the United States. After he became BI director in August, Burns sent one of his agents, Sylvester

Cosgrove, overseas to look for Linde. Cosgrove and another agent Burns had sent earlier were able to find him in Warsaw in November. With the help of the Polish authorities, who had also been looking for Linde because he had been reported to them (by unknown sources) as "a very dangerous man," Linde was arrested in December 1921 and held in a Polish jail.[64]

Linde then reportedly produced a ten-thousand-word "confession" that four or five communists had been paid $30,000 by the Third International to commit the Wall Street bombing with the aim of killing J. P. Morgan. Burns told reporters that Linde had originally been sent overseas by his private detective agency to gather information leading to the arrests of those involved in the bombing. After not receiving any reports from him, Burns said he sent Cosgrove to Europe to find out why. Burns emphasized that Linde was not a suspect in the attack but that he knew all about it. "There is no question in the world," Burns boasted, "that we [now] have the proper solution of this mystery."[65]

There was only one problem: Linde had made up the whole story about communist involvement in the bombing. He was known to friends and others as "a fantasist and probably a swindler to boot," yet Burns had placed great stock and confidence in him. When Linde's fabrications became publicly known, Burns's reputation took a hit. He became "the butt of jokes and gleeful jabs." Burns finally admitted after interrogating Linde that his informant had no reliable information about the Wall Street bombing.[66]

Burns held onto his job for few more years but was eventually forced out in May 1924 after a major scandal involving spying on a U.S. senator. Burns had used BI agents to try to gather evidence of criminal activity on the part of Senator Burton K. Wheeler from Montana after the senator called for Congress to investigate abuses in the Justice Department. Attorney General Daugherty was also forced to resign for his involvement in the scandal.[67]

Burns left office, just like Flynn, without having solved the Wall Street bombing. J. Edgar Hoover took over for Burns in 1924 when he was only twenty-nine years old. He would remain director of the BI and then the FBI until his death in 1972. (The BI's name was changed to the Division of Intelligence in 1933 and then to the FBI in 1935.) He too couldn't solve the bombing, but it wasn't his priority like it had been for his two predecessors. Hoover focused more on Prohibition and antitrust campaigns after he was appointed BI chief. Hoover was a survivor. In contrast to Flynn and Burns before him, as well as Palmer, he was not going to let himself get swallowed up following one false lead after another and in the process possibly lose his job for a case that was already fading from public discussion. While he never totally abandoned the investigation, nothing of significance was ever uncovered in the ensuing years. The last time the FBI looked into the bombing was in 1944, and once again, no results were obtained. In a summarizing memo to headquarters that year, the New York office repeated the contention made just a month after the attack by Agent Scully—namely, that "Italian Anarchists or Italian Terrorists" were responsible for the bombing.[68]

By 1959, the case had become such ancient history that an FBI agent in an internal memo wanted to know if the entire file could be destroyed since it was taking up valuable storage space. A decision was made then to keep the file. Another request to destroy the file was made ten years later, but again the decision was made to keep it. In a handwritten response to the memo, the reviewing supervisor, Herbert A. Grubert, explained why: "Exhibit consists of original notes, photographs and documents regarding the 1920 Wall Street Explosion which resulted in the deaths of scores of people. The case has never been solved. While there is little chance of exhibit having future evidentiary value it is felt that it would have certain historical value." All scholars, reporters, and people interested in history owe a debt to Agent Grubert (and the reviewing supervisor before him) for saving this valuable file.[69]

Who, then, committed the Wall Street bombing? Renowned historian Paul Avrich makes the compelling argument that it was a lone wolf Galleanist, Mario Buda. Buda was one of the most militant members of the Galleanists and their expert bomb maker. He was the one the group turned to whenever they needed somebody to construct and set off bombs. He was involved in many (if not all) of the Galleanist plots and attacks. With most of the Galleanists either being deported or eluding the authorities and escaping to Italy by the summer of 1920, Buda was left to carry on the struggle alone.[70]

It became a personal struggle after fellow Galleanists Nicola Sacco and Bartolomeo Vanzetti were indicted on September 11, 1920, for two murders that occurred in South Braintree, Massachusetts, in April. (Both would be executed in 1927.) "Sacco and Vanzetti were the best friends I had in America," Buda would later say in an interview in Italy. According to Avrich, their indictments propelled Buda to initiate a retaliatory strike. He was in Portsmouth, New Hampshire, when he heard the news. He traveled to Boston and then to New York, where he acquired an old horse and wagon and placed a bomb equipped with a timer and filled with heavy, cast-iron slugs into the vehicle. He then drove it to the corner of Broad and Wall streets, "the symbolic center of American capitalism." There, after parking it in front of the U.S. Assay Office and across the street from the J. P. Morgan and Company headquarters, he climbed down from his seat and walked away. A few weeks later, he sailed for Italy and never returned to the United States. "It was his final act of reprisal in America," Avrich writes. "The biggest of them all, it had gone off without a hitch." His name never came up in the lengthy investigations into the bombing.[71]

Avrich acknowledges that no irrefutable evidence links Buda to the bombing: "That Buda was the Wall Street bomber cannot be proved; documentary evidence is lacking. But it fits with what we know of him and his movements. I have it, moreover, from a reliable source and believe it to be true." Avrich's source was likely Charles Poggi, an Italian-born New York waiter who, along with his father, Giovanni, was friends with Buda. Avrich interviewed Poggi in 1987. "Buda was a real militant, capable of anything," Poggi told Avrich. "In 1933, I drove to New York with Buda's nephew, Frank Maffi. We stayed with friends on Sixty-Second Street. Frank said, 'Let's drive downtown and see my uncle's bomb,' and he took me to Wall Street where the big explosion took place in September 1920, just before Buda sailed for Italy. You could still see the holes in the Morgan building across the street." Poggi met up with Buda when he visited Italy in 1955 but never asked him about the bombing. Many historians, journalists, and others agree with Avrich's conclusion that Buda was likely responsible for the attack on Wall Street.[72]

The failure to solve the Wall Street bombing was clearly a major disappointment for Flynn. "The labor we put into this," he said sadly to a reporter in 1922. "The wasted labor, probably!" he added. He had been correct in pointing to the Galleanists as responsible but just never identified Buda as the perpetrator. As he resumed his vacation after being so unceremoniously dumped by Attorney General Daugherty, he probably wasn't too worried about what he would do next. After all, he had survived all the career bumps in his life, returning to the Secret Service as its top person when his brief stint with the NYPD didn't work out and then becoming director of the BI after leaving the Secret Service. Surely, he must have thought, somebody will soon be calling to hire the great detective. It probably never occurred to him that that call might never come.[73]

CHAPTER SEVEN

Longing for the Old Days

SHORTLY AFTER RETURNING TO NEW YORK CITY FROM HIS VACATION, Flynn decided to try his hand at what a lot of famous detectives had done—namely, form a private detective agency. That would at least keep him busy and presumably enable him to earn some money for his large family until his next important government or law enforcement job came along. There might also have been a bit of Flynn's competitive nature coming into play when he was deciding on this move since it would pit him against the Burns International Detective Agency, which was still operating while Burns was the BI director.

Flynn, however, had no illusions that his new agency could reach the level attained by Burns's outfit, which had been in business since 1909 and had built up a worldwide clientele. But he loved detective work, even though he would be doing it for the first time in his career as a private citizen. The William J. Flynn Detective Agency was launched on October 2, 1921, with offices in Manhattan. He hired a loyal staff of former Secret Service agents, all of whom had worked for him in the past. "We will handle general detection work and also corporation work," Flynn told reporters, "but will not enter the labor field or furnish strike breakers." This was a dig at Burns, "who had built much of his business and reputation on 'getting the goods' on unions and the labor Left." One of Burns's most famous exploits, as noted in chapter 6, was tracking down and arresting the McNamara brothers, who were wanted for the bombing of the Los Angeles Times Building during a labor strike in 1910. Burns's detectives also "specialized in infiltrating unions and breaking strikes for the employers."[1]

Among the "general detection work" Flynn's agency engaged in was something he had never been asked to do before: spy on a movie star at the request of the actor's film company. Rudolph Valentino, a silent-film heartthrob and one of the most famous actors of his time, became embroiled in a scandal when he married Natacha Rambova, a costume designer, in May 1922 before his divorce to his first wife, actress Jean Acker, was finalized. Valentino had been granted an interlocutory divorce decree two months earlier, but under California law, he was required to wait a year before marrying again. He was arrested and tried for bigamy, but the judge dismissed the case. His second marriage was annulled, and Valentino planned to marry Rambova again (which he did in 1923) after his divorce to Acker became official. In the meantime, he and Rambova were prohibited from living together, or he might again face criminal charges.[2]

It is here where Flynn entered the picture. Valentino claimed that his studio, Famous Players-Lasky Corporation, with whom he was involved in a contract dispute, had hired a detective from Flynn's agency to get evidence that he was indeed living with Rambova and use that information as blackmail to keep him from leaving the studio for another company. He said that the detective had snooped around the estate of Rambova's parents in the Adirondacks when he went there to visit Rambova. "The only object Famous Players-Lasky Corporation could have for sending a detective to Foxlair Camp [the estate]," Valentino said, "was to attempt to secure or claim that they had secured evidence of my adultery at Foxlair Camp, this being a crime under the New York State laws, and then by threats and persuasion to secure my continued employment by the company." Valentino first learned that Flynn's agency was spying on him when a man went to the Waldorf Astoria in New York, where Valentino had previously stayed, and asked a hotel worker questions about the actor. The man identified himself as a Flynn detective.[3]

Another of Flynn's assignments must have seemed ironic to him. After years of safeguarding the lives of presidents while at the Secret Service, Flynn was now asked to provide a detective to serve as a bodyguard for a horse! He could take solace, however, in the fact that it wasn't just any horse but one that was the favorite to win the 1922 Kentucky Derby and was worth about $500,000. Benjamin Block, a New York stockbroker and the owner of the unbeaten Morvich, wanted to make sure nothing happened to his prized possession before the race. He therefore employed a detective from Flynn's agency to be the racehorse's bodyguard day and night. Everything went smoothly, including the twenty-nine-hour train ride from New York to Louisville. Large crowds greeted the train when it arrived and followed Morvich and his entourage to his stall at Churchill Downs. The crowd "was as big as one sees at an average circus parade." Morvich won the derby by one and a half lengths but never won another race afterward.[4]

It wasn't, of course, just movie stars and racehorses that Flynn's agency was busy with. Some of the cases reminded him of the old days when he was chasing criminals. Edward de Ulzeren, president of the Cuban Sugar Refining Company, hired Flynn's firm in October 1922 to investigate the blowing up of the company's office safe and the stealing of cash and bonds. What Flynn's men uncovered was a clever scheme that had been going on for years by two brothers who worked as porters for various offices on Wall Street. The brothers would make duplicate keys for the offices they were responsible for, quit their jobs, and then return in the evening with the duplicate keys to steal the goods. Sometimes, they forced desks open in the hope of finding a combination to a safe or at least valuable documents hidden inside. Other times, they had already discovered combinations through their jobs. It was not until the Cuban Sugar Refining Company theft, in which the brothers blew open the safe, that Flynn's operatives were brought in on the case and, with the help of the NYPD, were able to arrest the brothers and a third man who was part of the crime spree. The gang had stolen more than $100,000 during their years of operation.[5]

RELIVING THE PAST
While Flynn was building up his detective agency, he wanted to make sure he would not be forgotten by the public. Therefore, beginning on January 22, 1922, and continuing for ten successive weeks, he arranged

for the *New York Herald* to publish one story each week about his most exciting escapades while in the government. "'My Ten Biggest Man-hunts'—told by Chief W. J. Flynn" was the headline, along with a blown-up image of Flynn peering out at the reader. "Thrilling Adventures with International Criminals of All Grades, from Mere Assassins to Those Who Played for World Power, Given to the Public for the First Time" boasted the *Herald*. To remind readers of who Flynn was, the editors wrote this glowing profile:

> Among modern detectives the outstanding figure for many years has been William J. Flynn. Few men in the world have had so much to do with crime and criminals, plot and counterplot, as has this big, silent, mysterious figure who for so long was the chief of the United States "Secret Service." His field was not that of a city or State—but the whole world.[6]

The first of the installments deals with one of Flynn's greatest triumphs: the uncovering of German intrigue in the United States prior to America's entry into World War I. This involved the seizing of Dr. Heinrich Albert's briefcase containing the incriminating evidence on an elevated train in New York City, although Flynn did not discuss that famous caper. Rather, he simply wrote that the papers were found in Albert's rooms and offices while he was under surveillance by the Secret Service.[7]

The next installment in the series is about a lone-wolf counterfeiter, Henry Russell Wilken, who "was a clever boy and a nice one" but one who created banknote paper so well that even the manufacturers of the notes for the government and experts in the Treasury Department thought it was genuine. Wilken eluded the Secret Service and police for four years beginning in 1910. He was finally caught when he used a bogus $10 bill to buy a fountain pen but never tried out the pen, as most customers would, to see how it wrote. He simply took the change, which was of course in real money, from the clerk and dropped the pen into his coat pocket as though he didn't care at all about his purchase. The suspicious clerk took the bill to two banks. One said it was genuine, but the other said it was not. Then, along with a policeman, they were able to track down Wilken, who was arrested. Flynn admired the skill of the young man who taught himself the complicated business of counterfeiting. "You couldn't help liking the fellow," Flynn wrote.[8]

Some of the other stories in the series detail his pursuit of the Morello–Lupo gang in New York, the uncovering of the plot by Captain George B. Boynton to finance a revolution in Venezuela with counterfeit money, and Flynn's experiences with the anarchist leader Luigi Galleani, "one of the most difficult individuals the United States Secret Service has ever had to deal with because he was the brainiest." In the story about Galleani, Flynn wrote that it was Galleani and his followers who were responsible for the Wall Street bombing.[9]

In his final story for the *Herald*, Flynn recounted one of his earliest adventures that resulted in his own arrest. It all started in 1900, when he went after a gang of counterfeiters in the hills and woods of Warren County in western Pennsylvania. Among the group was Johnny Henderson, a criminal known as "Nitro Johnny." Henderson was an expert with explosives, having worked as an oil well shooter before becoming a counterfeiter. His job had been to drop nitroglycerin or dynamite into a drilled hole as the finishing touch to producing the oil gusher. He taunted the Secret Service by leaving notes claiming that he carried nitroglycerin with him all the time and that he would blow himself up along with any law enforcement person who came near him.[10]

Flynn and a group of agents raided a camp where Henderson was living but were only able to arrest a few minor figures. Henderson and two other counterfeiters that the Secret Service was after, George Black and his wife, had gotten away. Flynn then learned that Black owned a farm nearby and that Henderson was a frequent visitor. He and a deputy sheriff went there and searched the farmhouse, but Henderson was nowhere to be found. Flynn became engaged in a scuffle with Black's wife, who was a rather large woman, when he tried to arrest her. She swung at his jaw with a "forearm [that] suggested the middle-aged blacksmith." He finally subdued her and, with the help of the deputy, arrested her and her husband.[11]

Flynn returned to Pittsburgh, where one day he had a surprise visitor at his office. "I'm a constable up in Warren and here's a warrant for you," the man said. When Flynn asked what the warrant was for, the constable replied, "For assault and battery upon the person of Mrs. George Black and unlawful entry and trespass upon the premises of George Black." Another Secret Service agent who had been with Flynn in Warren was also arrested for searching a different place without a warrant. After posting bail, the two agents resumed their work, awaiting word from headquarters in Washington regarding any repercussions stemming from this situation.[12]

It turned out the Secret Service was happy about the arrests of their agents. "For a long while," Flynn wrote, "we had longed for a test case such as this promised to be. There had been some trouble between local and Federal authorities about the right of Secret Service men to search and arrest without procuring warrants therefor. The Department of Justice considered the case and on December 24 ... [the other Secret Service agent] and I were ordered to proceed forthwith to Warren and stand trial on the charges." They did so, and the judge ruled that they had been justified in their searches and in the methods used.[13]

Flynn titled his last story "The Man the Government Couldn't Catch." He could have used that title to describe several other counterfeiters, anarchists, spies, and terrorists that the government went after during his years of service but could never quite capture. His final words in the article are telling of the frustration the Bulldog felt as he looked back on his career and his successes and failures:

> I have come to the end of this series of reminiscences. I have tried not to be tautological, although the sameness in a Secret Service man's work makes a certain amount of reiteration unavoidable. One case is much like another in so far as methods of the detective go. I dare to hope I have implanted, in however small a degree, the idea that a detective is no more nor less than an average human being trying to protect society from the criminal.
>
> He is no miracle worker. The Father Browns, the Sherlock Holmeses of fiction are neither more nor less than just that—detectives of fiction. We are mere policemen using our experience and cultivated intuition to best advantage. It is so easy to sneer at a policeman's failure that a majority of folks do it. But the next time results are not forthcoming as rapidly as you would care to have them try to put yourself in the place of the detectives on the job.

And consider that probably there are obstacles in their way of which you know nothing.

Forgive me for poor preaching.[14]

Despite Flynn urging the public not to compare real-life detectives with the miracle-worker fictional detectives, he created one himself for a series of stories he published serially in a popular weekly magazine. *The Adventures of Peabody Smith* ran in *Argosy-Allstory Weekly* from October 1922 until January 1923. Never one to be modest, Flynn left no doubt who the hero detective resembles. Peabody Smith, Flynn wrote, is "the famous investigator, late of the United States Secret Service and now retired after years of fine service." And just like Flynn, Smith is a patient man who likes to smoke cigars. But unlike Flynn, and perhaps this was Flynn's way of saying he wished some things had turned out differently in his career, Peabody Smith always solves his cases.[15]

The publisher of *Argosy-Allstory Weekly*, Frank A. Munsey, joined forces with Flynn in September 1924 to launch a new detective fiction magazine, simply named *Flynn's*. The Bulldog was listed as the editor, although it is not clear how much editing Flynn actually did for the many different stories that were published in the magazine. But his name was the drawing card, and with great fanfare, the magazine published a series of reminiscences by Flynn about his life and career, some of which had previously appeared in various forms in newspapers. "My Life in the U.S. Secret Service, by Wm. J. Flynn, for Twenty-Five Years Chief Manhunter for Uncle Sam" was the banner headline chosen for the cover of an early issue of the magazine, along with a drawing of his face. There would be no mention of his experiences at the BI. For Flynn, the Secret Service represented his glory years, and that is what he wrote about. It was almost as if his time as BI director didn't exist.[16]

In the introduction to the series of articles about his career with the Secret Service, Flynn expressed his excitement about telling his story:

In the twenty-five years since I entered the Secret Service of the United States I have dealt with all kinds of offenses against law, and I have known most of the great lawbreakers of that period. As I have gone over the records and the files in the preparation of these articles, my memory has reconstructed the past until it seems almost as though I were reliving those busy days.

It is my keenest desire that the readers of *Flynn's* will find in the reading something of the thrill and the pleasure that have been mine in the living. Then I shall not have written in vain.[17]

Flynn's was a huge success and ran under different names (*Flynn's Weekly, Flynn's Weekly Detective Fiction with the Thrill of Truth*, and *Detective Fiction Weekly with Thrilling True Stories*) for more than two decades. The magazine published both fiction and true crime stories. It encouraged writers of all types to submit their stories. "William J. Flynn is keen to see the work of new writers," an advertisement in a trade newspaper stated. "Flynn's is creating an entirely new field for manuscripts. Although it is a detective story magazine, Flynn's will use all sorts of mystery stories. We request contributions of true stories, of imaginative fiction and verse of the underworld. It makes no difference whether an author has ever sold before or not. If he has ever imagined and worked out in his head a mystery story we will be interested in seeing it. As long as it is a good story with a punch, in which the mystery is not carelessly revealed too early, the story has just as good [a] chance of success with Flynn's as the work of any writer with a national reputation."[18]

One of those new writers who took up this offer was Agatha Christie, who would become one of the most famous mystery writers in history. Only five years into her publishing career, she penned a piece for *Flynn's* titled "Traitor Hands." She later retitled it "Witness for the Prosecution." It became a hit Broadway play and an Oscar-nominated movie in the 1950s. Another new writer the magazine published was Mignon Eberhart, who went on to write fifty-nine mystery books during her long career.[19]

There is one surprising author in the inaugural issue of *Flynn's*. NYPD Commissioner Richard Enright, with whom Flynn quarreled during the Wall Street bombing investigation, wrote a seven-part thriller, "Vultures of the Dark." A 1924 article in *Time* relayed praise for Enright as a "wholly new writer whose prolific brain can evolve and depict fresh sparkling detective situations." His stories in *Flynn's* received rave reviews, with *Time* also noting the reporting of the *New*

York World: "Almost any reader might be pardoned for thinking the Commissioner had been an author all his life."[20]

In addition to the series of reminiscences he wrote for the magazine, Flynn also had a column, "Headquarters Gossip," that appeared occasionally. Since Flynn was no longer employed at any headquarters, whether that be the NYPD, the Secret Service, or the BI, he wasn't privy to any "gossip." But he described the column as "random memories from a life-time of contact with the kings and princes and lords of crookdom." He sometimes used the column to voice his opinions about various issues, including prison reform. "The records show," he wrote, "that the men, or a goodly number of them, come out [of prison] more steeped in crime than when they went in and with a grudge against society. I instance Sing Sing [the prison in New York], not because it is unique but typical of the type of prison that should be wiped out." He decried the conditions in that prison, writing that "no self-respecting farmer would keep his cattle within its walls. And yet we house human beings in there, expecting that when they finish their terms they will come out reformed. They don't very often." Flynn also called for better treatment of all prisoners: "More care, and a little more humanity, would do more to lessen crime and prevent the making of hardened criminals than anything else."[21]

An innovative feature in *Flynn's* was its "Dictionary of the Underworld." Beginning with "A" and proceeding through the entire alphabet, it provided a "full list and authoritative definitions of words used by crooks and hoboes, grafters and grifters." It was, the magazine boasted, "the product of a decade of intensive scientific study" and aimed at helping readers understand some of the stories that appeared in the magazine. It was also intended for anybody interested in crime and detective work. There are numerous entries for each letter. Under "S," for example, readers learned that "sand" was money or sugar, "scatter" was a saloon or a hiding place for thieves, "scotch" was to die in the electric chair, "scrix" was to betray or squeal, and so forth. Under "O," readers were informed that an "owl" was a night watchman, an "oil bird" was a man about town, and an "old man" was a safe-breaking tool. And under "P," readers learned that a "palatch" was a hangman, a "parlor man" was a safe blower, and a "pelican" was a magistrate.[22]

THE DOWNWARD SPIRAL

As the years passed and there were no apparent offers to return to government service, Flynn realized he might be spending the rest of his life tending to his private detective agency and writing stories. That doesn't sound too bad, except that Flynn was a man who thrived on being where the action was. His name was no longer continually in the news, as it had been throughout his long government career. He was rapidly fading from public memory. He could take solace, however, in knowing that at least there was a very popular detective magazine bearing his name.

But even that was taken away from him in June 1928. Frank Munsey, who'd come up with the idea to launch a magazine named *Flynn's* with Flynn as the editor, died in December 1925. His company continued publishing the magazine but changed the title to *Detective Fiction Weekly* beginning with the June 2, 1928, issue. They announced this change in an insert in the May 26 issue, promising "to make a bigger and better magazine than before"—not exactly a compliment about Flynn's work with the publication. They threw Flynn a bone by explaining that "Mr. Flynn, who is about to make an extensive tour in the interest of enlargement of his international detective agency, will continue to be found among the contributors to *Detective Fiction Weekly*." Flynn never wrote another story for the magazine, and there is no record of his embarking on any "extensive tour" related to his detective agency.[23]

It was the agency, in fact, and the role that two of his children played in the business that contributed to Flynn's downward spiral in 1928. He had entrusted a lot of the work to his children Veronica and Elmer, whom he made partners in the firm. However, as mentioned in this book's introduction, both were alcoholics, as was Flynn's wife, Anne, and they overspent, most of the money going to booze. Their erratic behavior drove clients away and greatly weakened and worried Flynn. He began overeating to cope with the stress. He fell ill during the fall and died of heart disease at the age of sixty on October 14. As author Mike Dash notes, Flynn "died a disappointed man."[24]

One of his sons, William W. Flynn Jr., told reporters that his father had been "about to return to his post in Washington" at the time of his death. That presumably meant Flynn again becoming chief of the Secret Service, as J. Edgar Hoover was firmly entrenched by this time as director of the BI. But there were no rumors during the summer and fall of 1928 about Flynn's possible return to the government, and there was no confirmation in Washington regarding the younger Flynn's statement.[25]

As expected, scores of newspaper obituaries and editorials were published across the country following Flynn's death. The *New York Times* wrote that Flynn "was a quiet, unassuming man" who "won the devotion of all his men." The *Daily Times and Mamaroneck Paragraph* stated that "Chief Flynn's loyalty to his country was never questioned. . . . Now that he is dead we will hear more of his exploits but we will never hear enough to enable us to truly estimate the value of his service to his country." The *Tampa Daily Times* exclaimed that "in 30 years with the secret service he attained a world wide reputation and became an almost legendary figure through his activities against criminals of every degree." And the *Cincinnati Enquirer* wrote, "Chief Flynn was a real detective. His man hunts ended only when the criminal or criminals were caught."[26]

Not all the newspaper editorials, however, were complimentary. The *Des Moines Register* lamented his role with the Secret Service during World War I, writing that he "participated in many of the excesses of the secret service during the war. He was relentless in his pursuit of 'spies,' and this term included at that time all who disagreed with the common denominator of political opinion in America." And the *Brooklyn Daily Eagle* wrote that "functions such as Flynn held for several troublous years do not belong in our ordinary scheme of things."[27]

Flynn's funeral services were attended by a thousand people in Larchmont, New York, where he had lived with his wife for the past four years. Among the attendees were representatives of the Secret Service, the Department of Justice, and the NYPD. Herbert Hoover and New York Governor Al Smith, the two candidates for the 1928 presidential election (Hoover would win), sent telegrams of condolence, as did five hundred other people. Flynn was buried in a family plot in nearby Valhalla.[28]

"When I was only ten years old I longed to be a detective," Flynn once wrote. "I became one. A little later on I hoped that one day I would be a Secret Service man. I became one. But even in my wildest boy-dreams I never dared hope to become chief of the Secret Service. I did, however." The man who started out as a plumber in New York and rose to the highest ranks in the Secret Service and the BI is basically forgotten today. There is no monument or statue of him anywhere to be found. Outside of a small circle of historians and other scholars, he is not known. Yet in many ways, he was as important a figure in American law enforcement in the early twentieth century as anybody else. How, then, should William J. Flynn be remembered?[29]

CHAPTER EIGHT

An Incorruptible Public Servant

HAD FLYNN BEEN ABLE TO READ HIS OWN OBITUARIES, ONE IN PARTICular would have made him cringe but also nod sadly in agreement. The *New York Herald Tribune* wrote that Flynn "had been living a comparatively uneventful life here for the last four years." For the man who had battled counterfeiters, the Mafia, German spies, and terrorists and protected presidents and foreign dignitaries throughout his long government career, living an uneventful life in retirement was indeed quite difficult to accept.[1]

Flynn had always been where the action was. His career at the top of U.S. law enforcement was continually profiled in newspapers and movies, and he became a beloved figure by both the public and those who worked for him. But while his career was characterized by incredible achievements that served the country well, it was also marked by unsolved terrorism cases and his support for the Palmer Raids.

His time with the Secret Service resulted in his greatest accomplishments, first bringing down Giuseppe Morello, the "boss of bosses" of the American Mafia, and his associates and then uncovering a sophisticated propaganda, espionage, and sabotage ring run by German agents prior to U.S. entry into World War I. The success against the Mafia demonstrated to Italian immigrants that those who were preying on them would eventually be held accountable for their crimes of murder, extortion, and kidnapping. And his success against the German agents led one newspaper, as noted earlier, to proclaim that Flynn "probably did more than any one man to rid this country of foreign spies."[2]

Flynn's two years with the BI didn't turn out as well. He could never apprehend and bring to justice those responsible for a series of terrorist attacks, including the Wall Street bombing. He was also associated with the violations of civil liberties stemming from the Palmer Raids, even though J. Edgar Hoover, who ran the Radical Division of the Justice Department, was the driving force behind those raids. When a journalist, George Seldes, wrote in 1941 that "the Palmer raids of 1919, during which 5,000 persons were arrested in one night, were conducted on Hoover's orders," Hoover wrote Seldes back personally: "This statement is untrue. The raids were conducted by the Bureau of Investigation which at that time was under the direction of Mr. William J. Flynn. At that time I was a subordinate official in the Department of Justice assigned as a special assistant to the Attorney General. In connection with these raids, my only assignment was to correlate the evidence to be used in prosecuting the deportation proceedings."[3]

Flynn was not around to defend himself against Hoover's accusations. Flynn, did, however, support the raids, which came at a time of unprecedented turmoil in the United States. America was in crisis in 1919, when Flynn took over the BI. There seemed to be labor strife everywhere, with more than 4 million workers joining picket lines across the country. In Boston, police officers went on strike after being denied the right to unionize. The absence of police in that city during the strike led to a period of violence and unrest, including nine people killed. Race riots also erupted in Chicago, Washington, Detroit, and other cities. In addition, there were two major terrorist attacks unlike any America had seen before. First, there was the sending of package bombs across the country in late April and then the June 2 bombings in seven cities. As historian Beverly Gage writes, "It looked as if American society was tearing itself apart." There was public and congressional support for drastic actions to be taken against "the Reds," particularly alien radicals, who were blamed for the troubles in America.[4]

Flynn reorganized the BI with the aim of making it into "the nation's preeminent federal detective force." By doing so, he set the foundation for what would later become the FBI. Jurisdiction over investigations of bombings and related violent acts had previously been the purview of local or state officials. But no single local or state law enforcement agency would be able to deal with an investigation as complex as the June 2 bombings promised to be, requiring detective work that would span multiple cities in several different states. The reorganized BI would not only investigate the June 2 bombings and launch the nation's first war on terrorism but also conduct a relentless campaign against radicalism and revolutionary dissent.[5]

As Flynn was given the title "director" (previous BI heads were known as "chief"), he was in effect the first director of the FBI since under his leadership, the BI took on an expansive federal investigative role. The BI's official name changed over the years, as noted earlier, first to the Division of Investigation in 1933 and then to the FBI in 1935, when J. Edgar Hoover, who became BI director in 1924, pushed for approval of the change. This became a bone of contention for Flynn's descendants. "My mother [Jane] and father would chase down and force a correction on any newspaper who falsely listed Hoover as the first Director of [the FBI]," William Flynn Sanders, Flynn's grandson, wrote. "All he [Hoover] did was put a different badge on the same organization to create the illusion he was the first one, a shell game and that still pisses me off. The [FBI] agents should be going to work in the WM J Flynn Bldg [and not the Hoover Building]."[6]

Flynn never made much money during his lifetime. When Attorney General Palmer appeared before a House Appropriations Committee in June 1919 asking for more funds for the Department of Justice in the wake of the bombings earlier that month, he lobbied for a high salary for Flynn, whom he had just appointed to head the BI. He told the committee that Flynn "can not take any place [job] for $4,000 a year because, as he told me, he has half a dozen little Flynns, and he has been working for the Government so long that he has not laid anything by, and on that account I have put in this estimate a provision to allow the employment of a director of the Bureau of Investigation at not to exceed $7,500 per year."[7]

Financial rewards never motivated Flynn. Just being a detective was all that he ever wanted to do. And he was a good one. There was never a hint of corruption or scandal associated with him during his lengthy government career. Flynn was a straight shooter who "had no leisure in which to cultivate the pleasant art of conversation." He believed that "unnecessary words . . . are as wasteful and unwise as are unnecessary motions." He never learned or cared for the skills of backroom bargaining and lobbying or other maneuvers that often characterize successful politicians and high-level government officials. His lack of political and financial ambitions insulated him from any potentially corrupting influences. He was, in the words of John E. Wilkie, his predecessor as chief of the Secret Service, "an absolutely honest man."[8]

After Flynn's death, his daughter Veronica inherited the Flynn Detective Agency, as well as some of Flynn's physical characteristics. A reporter described her as "a blonde roly-poly 200-pound lady hawkshaw." She ignored her father's pledge when he started the firm not to become involved in labor disputes or provide strikebreakers to companies. Several unions filed charges against the agency in 1937 for sending heavily armed men to automat restaurants on the eve of a strike to intimidate the workers and prevent a walkout. She also apparently didn't pay her ruffians well enough. During a building service workers' strike in 1936, strikebreakers hired by the agency went on strike themselves! "These strikebreakers of the Flynn Detective Agency are on strike against $9 a day and for fair conditions," their sign read as they joined the service workers at one of the buildings they were picketing.[9]

Flynn's widow, Anne, moved back to Manhattan from Larchmont and became active in the opera world, serving on the board of directors for the Light Opera Guild. She died in April 1937 after a long illness. Her excessive drinking and that of most of Flynn's family "created much heartache" for Flynn. "One [Secret Service] agent told my father the drinking of the family was the death of him and I believe it," wrote Flynn's grandson William, "as my mother [Jane, Flynn's daughter] also had the problem. Wm Flynn Jr [the eldest son] ran off [and] joined the Navy and became a Capt. in the Merchant Marines and freely said he could not stand to see what the drinking of the others was doing to his father. I think he [Flynn] would have lived a lot longer and accomplished even more without this profound burden he worried over."[10]

Flynn still managed to lead a remarkable life, one filled with adventure, excitement, and disappointment. He rose from meager financial means and a limited education to assume positions of power and influence in the U.S. government. "There developed a mighty legend around William J. Flynn," wrote the *New York Herald Tribune* on his death. "His activities against counterfeiters, smugglers, diplomatic enemies, bombers, [and] wartime food hoarders, brought a halo around his name and the words Secret Service."[11]

That halo, however, was more like an albatross for Flynn. Unrealistic expectations followed him everywhere he went. He was not the supersleuth detective portrayed in the media who could solve every crime and protect the nation from all enemies. But Flynn was a man of unquestionable integrity, loyalty, and forthrightness who put serving his country above personal gain. The Bulldog deserves better than to be a forgotten man in history.

Acknowledgments

THERE ARE MANY PEOPLE WHO HELPED MAKE WRITING A BIOGRAPHY OF William J. Flynn a rewarding and exciting journey. First and foremost, William Flynn Sanders was indispensable in providing personal stories, photographs, and other materials about his famous grandfather. Will graciously gave of his time to answer my queries about the "Bulldog." Mike Sampson, archivist and historian at the U.S. Secret Service, was extremely helpful in providing documents and photographs related to Flynn's long career there. Mike's enthusiasm for this project is greatly appreciated. I am grateful as well to Jonathan Fox, historian at the Federal Bureau of Investigation (FBI), for his insights into Flynn's time at the Bureau of Investigation, the forerunner of the FBI. I also want to thank William Andrews and Chris Manders at the New York Police Department for their valuable assistance.

I am indebted to the librarians and archivists who helped immensely with the research that went into this book. These include Jonathan Eaker, Melissa Lindberg, and Josie Walters-Johnston at the Library of Congress; Sarah Bseirani, Elizabeth Burnes, Kaitlyn Crain Enriquez, Nathan Jordan, Tab Lewis, Kelly McAnnaney, and Heather Sulier at the National Archives; Meredith Mann at the Brooke Russell Astor Reading Room for Rare Books and Manuscripts, New York Public Library; Diane Mizrachi at the Charles E. Young Research Library, University of California, Los Angeles; and Ellen Belcher at the Lloyd George Sealy Library Special Collections, John Jay College of Criminal Justice, City University of New York.

My colleague Bennett Ramberg provided valuable feedback and encouragement during our many discussions about this story, as did Phil Rothenberg, Lorron Snell, Martin Balaban, Eric Baldwin, Steven Kafka,

Ted Zwicker, and Mike Dash. I am grateful to all of them. I also want to thank Howard Blum, Bill Bratton, Adam Hochschild, Alex Hortis, Bennett Ramberg, Richard Sandor, and A. T. Smith for reading the manuscript.

The following colleagues, friends, and others helped in many different ways: Annie Abbot, Athena Angelos, Denise Ballew, John Barry, Theresa Hart Barry, Joe Black, Kevin Brownlow, Eddie Chan, Shirley Chan, Ken Chin, Sandy Chin, Joe Cirillo, Gary Citrenbaum, MaryAnne Cliff, David Critchley, Matt Egan, Beverly Gage, Louis Goldman, Steve Greene, Thomas Hunt, Eddie Kamiya, Janet Kamiya, Ken Karmiole, Larry Karp, Rikki Klieman, Ed Kobak, Matt Kovary, Ira Latto, Rosanne Levin, Anthony McGinty, Lewis Merletti, Sue Moran, James O'Keefe, Niko Pfund, Dennis Pluchinsky, Gerald Posner, Margo Raines, David Rapoport, Alice Richter, Howard Rothenberg, Kenneth Ryan, Michael Ryan, Kenneth Ryan, Ken Schmier, Kathy Schreick-Latto, Cindy Forrestal Snell, Douglas Snyder, Shoshana Snyder, Paul Sogol, Travis Sorrows, Richard Spence, Warren Spencer, Gene Sunshine, Bill Teachworth, Kevin Terpstra, Donna Wald, Sue Walther, Munish Walther-Puri, Norm Weiss, and Carole Wood.

Catherine L. Hensley provided superb editing skills for the manuscript and, as usual, was a joy to work with. I would also like to thank everybody at Prometheus Books, especially editor Jake Bonar, for their enthusiasm for a book about William J. Flynn. Jake was a constant source of encouragement and support throughout the research and writing of this book. I am also grateful to production editor Nicole Carty Myers for her excellent work.

My amazing agent, Jill Marsal, championed this book from its very beginning, and I am indebted to her once again for her unwavering support. Nobody could ask for a better agent.

Finally, heartfelt thanks go to Ellen, Richard, Julie, Penya, Jack, Eric, Caleb, Oscar, Elijah, and Justine for being a very special part of my life.

A Note about the Notes

Each source appears in the notes with a full citation on first mention in each chapter and then in an abbreviated form thereafter. The following abbreviations are used for sources from the National Archives and Records Administration, as well as ones obtained through the Freedom of Information Act from the Federal Bureau of Investigation.

BI, FOIA: Bureau of Investigation, Records of the Federal Bureau of Investigation, obtained through the Freedom of Information Act.

RG 65, BS, M1085, Fold3, NARA: Record Group 65, Bureau Section Files (1909–1921), Bureau of Investigation, Records of the Federal Bureau of Investigation, Microfilm Publication Number M1085, Fold3, National Archives and Records Administration, College Park, MD.

RG 65, OG, M1085, Fold3, NARA: Record Group 65, Old German Files (1909–1921), Investigative Case Files of the Bureau of Investigation (1908–1922), Records of the Federal Bureau of Investigation, Microfilm Publication Number M1085, Fold3, National Archives and Records Administration, College Park, MD.

RG 87, DRA, Flynn: Record Group 87, Records of the U.S. Secret Service (1863–1999), Daily Reports of Agents (1875–1937), Reports of William J. Flynn, Chief of the New York Office (1901–1910), National Archives and Records Administration, College Park, MD.

RG 87, DRA, Hazen: Record Group 87, Records of the U.S. Secret Service (1863–1999), Daily Reports of Agents (1875–1937),

Reports of William P. Hazen, Chief of the New York Office (1898–1901), National Archives and Records Administration, College Park, MD.

RG 87, DRA, New York: Record Group 87, Records of the U.S. Secret Service (1863–1999), Daily Reports of Agents (1875–1937), Reports of the New York Office (1920), National Archives and Records Administration, College Park, MD.

RG 87, GC: Record Group 87, Records of the U.S. Secret Service, General Correspondence (1894–1918), 76019-77360, National Archives and Records Administration, College Park, MD.

NOTES

INTRODUCTION

1. Ernest Wittenberg, "The Thrifty Spy on the Sixth Avenue El," *American Heritage*, December 1965, https://www.americanheritage.com/thrifty-spy-sixth-avenue-el.

2. Wittenberg, "The Thrifty Spy."

3. Wittenberg, "The Thrifty Spy." Although Secret Service agents were referred to as "operatives" during the late nineteenth and early twentieth centuries, the term "agent" is used instead in this book since most readers are more familiar with it.

4. Wittenberg, "The Thrifty Spy"; Mike Dash, *The First Family: Terror, Extortion, Revenge, Murder, and the Birth of the American Mafia* (New York: Random House, 2009), 349; "William J. Flynn, Long of Secret Service, Is Dead," *New York Herald Tribune*, October 15, 1928; Charles H. McCormick, *Hopeless Cases: The Hunt for the Red Scare Terrorist Bombers* (Lanham, MD: University Press of America, 2005), 46; "An American Sherlock Holmes," *Philadelphia Inquirer*, October 16, 1928.

5. James B. Morrow, "Counterfeiters; Their Ways Told by New Chief of U.S. Secret Service," *Washington Herald*, January 12, 1913; "Started as Tinsmith," *Boston Globe*, November 18, 1910; William J. Flynn, "My Life in the Secret Service," *Flynn's*, October 4, 1924, 389–90.

6. Morrow, "Counterfeiters"; Dash, *The First Family*, 261–63, 275–76; Thomas Hunt, "Nemesis of Counterfeiters: William J. Flynn," *Informer: The Journal of American Mafia History* 3, no. 2 (April 2010): 50–53.

7. "Started as Tinsmith"; "Life's Detective Yarns Are Dull, Says William J. Flynn," *Rutland Daily Herald* (Rutland, VT), May 26, 1922.

8. Hunt, "Nemesis of Counterfeiters," 53–54; "Flynn Has Quit His Police Job," *New York Times*, April 27, 1911; Dash, *The First Family*, 153–54; "Survey of the World," *The Independent* 70, no. 3257 (May 4, 1911): 922, https://

books.google.com/books?id=IstZAAAAYAAJ&pg=PA922&lpg=PA922&dq
=%22william+j.+flynn%22+%22thankless+job%22&source=bl&ots=VlN6CK9
MyD&sig=ACfU3U1N_2VXQyIKHrs7NdfJiW8WbN7HAg&hl=en&sa=X&
ved=2ahUKEwi92c2e8vnvAhWUCjQIHeU3BSsQ6AEwAXoECAEQAw
#v=onepage&q=%22william%20j.%20flynn%22%20%22thankless%20
job%22&f=false; "Topics of the Day," *The Literary Digest* 42, no. 19 (May 13,
1911): 930–31, https://books.google.com/books?id=n1VFAQAAMAAJ&pg
=PA931&lpg=PA931&dq=%22william+j.+flynn%22+%22thankless
+job%22&source=bl&ots=cotGzzgY88&sig=ACfU3U13sw-3gD0B-9qQ54bx
TMhAh0A78A&hl=en&sa=X&ved=2ahUKEwi92c2e8vnvAhWUCjQI
HeU3BSsQ6AEwBHoECAIQAw#v=onepage&q=%22william%20j.%20
flynn%22%20%22thankless%20job%22&f=false.

9. William Flynn Sanders, e-mail message to author, March 22, 2021; Dash, *The First Family*, 267–68.

10. Barbara Tepa Lupack, *Silent Serial Sensations: The Wharton Brothers and the Magic of Early Cinema* (Ithaca, NY: Cornell University Press, 2020), 207–26.

11. "Clear and Present Danger: A. Mitchell Palmer Goes Hunting for Bolsheviks," *Lapham's Quarterly*, Spring 2014, https://www.laphamsquarterly.org/revolutions/clear-and-present-danger.

12. Paul Avrich, *Sacco and Vanzetti: The Anarchist Background* (Princeton, NJ: Princeton University Press, 1991), 167–68, 175.

13. William Flynn Sanders, e-mail message to author, March 23, 2021; Dash, *The First Family*, 352–53.

14. Dash, *The First Family*, 352.

15. Morrow, "Counterfeiters."

Chapter 1: Learning the Trade

1. William J. Flynn, "My Life in the Secret Service," *Flynn's*, October 4, 1924, 390; William Flynn Sanders, e-mail message to author, April 26, 2021.

2. Flynn, "My Life in the Secret Service," October 4, 1924, 388–89; William Flynn Sanders, e-mail message to author, April 26, 2021; Thomas Hunt, "Nemesis of Counterfeiters: William J. Flynn," *Informer: The Journal of American Mafia History* 3, no. 2 (April 2010): 47. Hunt writes that Flynn's childhood home was an apartment on East 46th Street, not 41st Street as Flynn stated.

3. Flynn, "My Life in the Secret Service," October 4, 1924, 390–92; William Flynn Sanders, e-mail message to author, April 26, 2021.

4. Becky Little, "What Type of Criminal Are You? 19th-Century Doctors Claimed to Know by Your Face," History.com, August 8, 2019, https://www

.history.com/news/born-criminal-theory-criminology; Flynn, "My Life in the Secret Service," October 4, 1924, 392; "Flynn Thinks Little of the Fixed Post," *New York Times*, February 11, 1912. Lombroso argued that criminals have distinct facial features. Reporting on the examination of a deceased criminal, he wrote, "At the sight of that skull, I seemed to see all of a sudden . . . the problem of the nature of the criminal—an atavistic being who reproduces in his person the ferocious instincts of primitive humanity and the inferior animals. Thus were explained anatomically the enormous jaws, high cheek bones [and other features] found in criminals, savages and apes." See Little, "What Type of Criminal Are You?"

5. Flynn, "My Life in the Secret Service," October 4, 1924, 389–90; James B. Morrow, "Counterfeiters; Their Ways Told by New Chief of U.S. Secret Service," *Washington Herald*, January 12, 1913; William Flynn Sanders, e-mail message to author, April 26, 2021.

6. Flynn, "My Life in the Secret Service," October 4, 1924, 392–93; William Flynn Sanders, e-mail message to author, April 26, 2021; Mike Dash, *The First Family: Terror, Extortion, Revenge, Murder, and the Birth of the American Mafia* (New York: Random House, 2009), 13; Bob McCabe, *Counterfeiting and Technology: A History of the Long Struggle between Paper-Money Counterfeiters and Security Printing* (Atlanta: Whitman Publishing, 2016), 448.

7. Flynn, "My Life in the Secret Service," October 4, 1924, 393; William Flynn Sanders, e-mail message to author, April 26, 2021; Morrow, "Counterfeiters"; Hunt, "Nemesis of Counterfeiters," 48. There were two main types of prisoners held at the jail. One group consisted of persons placed there by U.S. magistrates for crimes against U.S. laws, including counterfeiting. A second group included those being held under civil process issued by judges of the state courts. See Prison Association of New York, *Fifty-First Annual Report of the Prison Association of New York: For the Year 1895* (Albany, NY: Wynkoop Hallenbeck Crawford Co., 1896), 95, https://books.google .com/books?id=29QJAAAAIAAJ&pg=PA95&lpg=PA95&dq=ludlow+jail+held +counterfeiters&source=bl&ots=sIQi2VcCct&sig=ACfU3U0K4NJWnowp M51iM_-tbx6OYQeSCw&hl=en&sa=X&ved=2ahUKEwiggYuNh-3vAhUe GDQIHYNLBpwQ6AEwEnoECBIQAw#v=onepage&q=ludlow%20jail%20 held%20counterfeiters&f=false. Many of the prisoners at the jail were debtors, even though debtors' prisons had been abolished by the federal government in 1833. A creditor who convinced a judge that a debtor was a flight risk could have the person locked up at the Ludlow Street Jail. See Eric Grundhauser, "The New York Prison That Doubled as a Clubhouse for Alimony Cheats," *Atlas Obscura*,

September 4, 2015, https://www.atlasobscura.com/articles/the-new-york-prison-that-doubled-as-a-clubhouse-for-alimony-cheats.

8. Hunt, "Nemesis of Counterfeiters," 47–48.

9. Hunt, "Nemesis of Counterfeiters," 48; Grundhauser, "The New York Prison"; "The Ludlow-Street Jail," *New York Times*, February 3, 1868 (emphasis in the original). One of the prisoners at the Ludlow Street Jail before Flynn began working there was Boss Tweed, who paid $75 per week for special quarters. He was also allowed by the jail authorities to regularly visit his home. During one of those visits, he escaped to Spain but was eventually caught and sent back to the United States in 1876. He died at the jail in 1878. See Lib Tietjen, "If You Do the Crime, You've Got to Do the Time," *Tenement Museum* (blog), https://www.tenement.org/blog/if-you-do-the-crime-youve-got-to-do-the-time/, and Grundhauser, "The New York Prison."

10. "Life in Ludlow-St. Jail," *New-York Tribune*, May 30, 1871; Grundhauser, "The New York Prison."

11. Prison Association, *Fifty-First Annual Report*, 95–96; Hunt, "Nemesis of Counterfeiters," 48–49.

12. "Tamsen Is in a Scrape," *World* (NY evening edition), May 13, 1895; "Tamsen for Contempt," *Brooklyn Citizen*, May 13, 1895; "Ten Favor M'Laughlin," *New York Times*, May 11, 1895; "Jail for Illingworth," *New York Times*, May 16, 1895; Hunt, "Nemesis of Counterfeiters," 48. The evening edition of the *New York World* sometimes went by *Evening World* on its front page and other times *The (Evening Edition) World*. The daily edition was simply *The World*. This is reflected in subsequent notes.

13. William Flynn Sanders, e-mail message to author, March 27, 2021; Hunt, "Nemesis of Counterfeiters," 48.

14. Flynn, "My Life in the Secret Service," October 4, 1924, 393–94; "Put under Big Bonds," *Chicago Tribune*, August 7, 1895; William Flynn Sanders, e-mail message to author, April 26, 2021.

15. McCabe, *Counterfeiting and Technology*, 191–92; "Brockway's Talent," *Boston Globe*, August 18, 1895; Flynn, "My Life in the Secret Service," October 4, 1924, 394; Ute Wartenberg Kagan, "Funny Money: The Fight of the US Secret Service against Counterfeit Money," *ANS Magazine* 9, no. 2 (Summer 2010): 18.

16. Flynn, "My Life in the Secret Service," October 4, 1924, 394; McCabe, *Counterfeiting and Technology*, 192; Lief Davisson, "What Are Electrotypes?," *The E-Sylum* 23, no. 12 (March 22, 2020), https://www.coinbooks.org/v23/esylum_v23n12a23.html; Glenn Fleishmann, "Reading the Reprintings: The Printer's Side," Medium.com, February 22, 2021, https://glennf.medium.com/reading

-the-reprintings-the-printers-side-b80797522ec4. For an excellent account of how criminals today utilize technology to their advantage, see Marc Goodman, *Future Crimes: Everything Is Connected, Everyone Is Vulnerable and What We Can Do about It* (New York: Doubleday, 2015).

17. McCabe, *Counterfeiting and Technology*, 200, 203; Kagan, "Funny Money," 18; Morrow, "Counterfeiters"; "Brockway an Old-Timer in Crime," *Chicago Tribune*, August 7, 1895; "Brockway, the Most Picturesque Criminal of the Age," *San Francisco Chronicle*, March 2, 1896.

18. William J. Flynn, "My Life in the Secret Service," *Flynn's*, October 25, 1924, 1048–49; McCabe, *Counterfeiting and Technology*, 207. In 1909, it became unlawful to possess counterfeit notes. See McCabe, *Counterfeiting and Technology*, 424n214.

19. Flynn, "My Life in the Secret Service," October 25, 1924, 1049–50; McCabe, *Counterfeiting and Technology*, 208, 210–13; "Expert Counterfeiter Captured," *St. Louis Globe-Democrat*, April 2, 1896; "Counterfeited with a Pen," *Boston Post*, April 3, 1896.

20. Morrow, "Counterfeiters."

21. Carol Leonnig, *Zero Fail: The Rise and Fall of the Secret Service* (New York: Random House, 2021), 14–15.

22. Leonnig, *Zero Fail*, 16; "150+ Years of History," United States Secret Service, https://www.secretservice.gov/about/history/150-years; McCabe, *Counterfeiting and Technology*, 216. President James Garfield was assassinated in 1881, but just like the Lincoln assassination, this one did not result in a permanent protective force being established for the president. See Leonnig, *Zero Fail*, 14–15.

23. McCabe, *Counterfeiting and Technology*, 170, 218, 418n115; "Catching Counterfeiters," U.S. Marshals Service, https://www.usmarshals.gov/history/counterfeit/counterfeit4.htm; "150+ Years of History."

24. McCabe, *Counterfeiting and Technology*, 219, 450; "Counterfeiters in the Employ of the Government," *New York Times*, June 28, 1867.

25. McCabe, *Counterfeiting and Technology*, 216, 229.

26. Flynn, "My Life in the Secret Service," October 4, 1924, 401.

27. Flynn, "My Life in the Secret Service," October 4, 1924, 401–2.

28. Flynn, "My Life in the Secret Service," October 4, 1924, 402.

29. Flynn, "My Life in the Secret Service," October 4, 1924, 402.

30. Hunt, "Nemesis of Counterfeiters," 49; "The 'Sherlock Holmes' of Bogus Coiners," *Hampton's Magazine* 24, no. 6 (June 1910): 862, https://books.google.com/books?id=ROsZAQAAIAAJ&pg=PA862&lpg=PA862&dq=%22william

+j.+flynn%22+counterfeiters&source=bl&ots=B7G8z1L6T0&sig=ACfU3U0t
KfK_Ry0Hyo0lEG-bBJVRJEW4Yg&hl=en&sa=X&ved=2ahUKEwi-7O
_Sv6vvAhV-JzQIHXIjBGc4FBDoATAJegQIBBAD#v=onepage&q=%22wil
liam%20j.%20flynn%22%20counterfeiters&f=false; "Head Sleuth Quits His
Job," *Morning Tribune* (Tampa, FL), June 11, 1901; William J. Flynn, "The Man
the Government Couldn't Catch," *New York Herald*, March 26, 1922.

31. "Passed the Spurious," *Pittsburgh Commercial Gazette*, December 14,
1899; "M'Cauley Denies He Is a Coiner," *Pittsburg Press*, December 14, 1899.
The *Pittsburg* [*sic*] *Press*, like several other publications at that time, did not
use the letter "h" at the end of the city's name. See Patricia Lowry, "The Next
Page/Are Yinz from Pittsburg?," *Pittsburgh Post-Gazette*, July 17, 2011, https://
www.post-gazette.com/opinion/Op-Ed/2011/07/17/The-Next-Page-Are-yinz
-from-Pittsburg/stories/201107170206.

32. "Passed the Spurious"; "M'Cauley Denies He Is a Coiner."

33. William J. Flynn, "My Life in the Secret Service," *Flynn's*, October 11,
1924, 626.

34. Larry B. Sheafe, "The United States Secret Service: An Administrative
History" (unpublished manuscript, 1983), 28–30, https://www.governmentat
tic.org/25docs/USSSadminHistSheafeUnpub_1983.pdf; "To Succeed Chief
Hazen," *Evening Star* (Washington, D.C.), February 26, 1898; Chad B. News-
wander, "Presidential Security: Bodies, Bubbles, & Bunkers" (PhD diss., Virginia
Polytechnic Institute and State University, 2009), 94.

35. RG 87, DRA, Hazen, vol. 11, May 3, 1901.

36. RG 87, DRA, Hazen, vol. 11, May 5, 1901; "William P. Hazen Resigns,"
New York Times, May 28, 1901; "Refused to Go to Buffalo," *Boston Globe*, May 28,
1901. McKinley was assassinated while attending the Pan-American Exposition
in Buffalo. He was greeting visitors when Czolgosz approached him as if to shake
his hand but instead shot him with a .32-caliber pistol, which was wrapped in
a handkerchief in his right hand. See Jeffrey D. Simon, *Lone Wolf Terrorism:
Understanding the Growing Threat* (Amherst, NY: Prometheus Books, 2013),
160. There was a Secret Service agent unofficially traveling with McKinley, even
though the service was still not authorized to perform presidential protection
duties. That agent was supposed to stand by McKinley's side as he greeted visitors, but he moved farther away when the head of the exposition requested that
he be allowed to stand next to the president. See Leonnig, *Zero Fail*, 15–16.

37. Simon, *Lone Wolf Terrorism*, 162; "'Shoving the Queer': Professional
Counterfeiters," *Anglophenia* (blog), BBC America, July 15, 2013, https://www
.bbcamerica.com/blogs/shoving-the-queer-counterfeit-new-york--1015430.

38. "Bank of England Forgers," *Sun* (NY), January 2, 1903; William J. Flynn, "Headquarters Gossip," *Flynn's Weekly*, July 10, 1926, 797; Flynn, "My Life in the Secret Service," October 11, 1924, 636.

39. "Bank of England Forgers"; Flynn, "My Life in the Secret Service," October 11, 1924, 636–37.

40. William J. Flynn, "The Adventures of the Queen of Counterfeiters," *Pittsburg Press*, August 6, 1911.

41. Hunt, "Nemesis of Counterfeiters," 49–50; "Stella Frauto's Band," *New York Times*, November 28, 1902; "Last of Bad Gang of Counterfeiters Taken," *Buffalo Review*, November 28, 1902; "Counterfeiters Caught," *Sun* (Baltimore), November 28, 1902.

42. "Last of Bad Gang."

43. "Last of Bad Gang"; "Counterfeiters Caught"; Hunt, "Nemesis of Counterfeiters," 49–50.

44. Hunt, "Nemesis of Counterfeiters," 50.

CHAPTER 2: BRINGING DOWN THE GODFATHER

1. Mike Dash, *The First Family: Terror, Extortion, Revenge, Murder, and the Birth of the American Mafia* (New York: Random House, 2009), 46–47; Thomas Hunt, "Nemesis of Counterfeiters: William J. Flynn," *Informer: The Journal of American Mafia History* 3, no. 2 (April 2010): 36; "Origins of the Mafia," History.com, updated May 28, 2019, https://www.history.com/topics/crime/origins-of-the-mafia.

2. Dash, *The First Family*, 47–48; "Origins of the Mafia."

3. Dash, *The First Family*, 48–49.

4. Joseph Bruno, "Joe Morello and the Black Handers," Legends of America, https://www.legendsofamerica.com/20th-blackhand/; Thomas Hunt, "*Sinistro*: The Underworld Career of Giuseppe Morello (1867–1930)," The American Mafia: The History of Organized Crime in the United States, http://mafiahistory.us/a029/f_morello.html; "The Origins of the Most Famous and Weird Superstitions in Italy," LearnAmo.com, https://learnamo.com/en/popular-italian-beliefs; Dash, *The First Family*, 51. Morello was nicknamed "One Finger Jack" by the Secret Service. See David Critchley, *The Origin of Organized Crime in America: The New York City Mafia, 1891–1931* (New York: Routledge, 2009), 39.

5. Dash, *The First Family*, 51–55.

6. Dash, *The First Family*, 57; Critchley, *The Origin of Organized Crime in America*, 38.

7. Dash, *The First Family*, xxix, 56–58, 353; Hunt, "*Sinistro*"; Bruno, "Joe Morello."

8. Dash, *The First Family*, 58–60; Hunt, "*Sinistro*"; Bruno, "Joe Morello."

9. Bruno, "Joe Morello"; Dash, *The First Family*, 50, 60, 61–62, 70, 118.

10. Dash, *The First Family*, 70; "The Depression of 1893," Vassar College, http://projects.vassar.edu/1896/depression.html.

11. Dash, *The First Family*, 71–75, 118; Hunt, "*Sinistro*"; Thomas Hunt, "Witnesses for the Defense," *Informer: The Journal of American Mafia History* 3, no. 2 (April 2010): 29–30; "Giuseppe Morello," Time Note, https://timenote.info/en /Giuseppe-Morello.

12. Dash, *The First Family*, 101–3; Bruno, "Joe Morello."

13. Dash, *The First Family*, 102–4, 109–10; Bruno, "Joe Morello." Morello was also believed to be responsible for the disappearance and likely murder of his maid, Mollie Callahan, whose body was never found. Callahan was told never to enter one of the rooms in Morello's apartment (where the counterfeiting machinery was stored), but she apparently did and was killed to prevent her from going to the police with that information. See Dash, *The First Family*, xxxvii, 105–6, and Hunt, "*Sinistro*."

14. Hunt, "*Sinistro*."

15. Hunt, "*Sinistro*"; William J. Flynn, "My Life in the Secret Service," *Flynn's*, October 25, 1924, 1067–68. The English translation of the Italian word *lupo* is "wolf," hence Lupo's moniker "Lupo the Wolf." Another explanation is that he was so ruthless and predatory that the nickname perfectly fit him. See Dash, *The First Family*, 114.

16. "Ignazio Lupo," GangRule, https://www.gangrule.com/biographies /ignazio-lupo; Dash, *The First Family*, 114; Mike Dickson, "Ignazio Lupo— Implicated in the Early 1900's Barrel Murders," American Mafia History, April 27, 2014, https://americanmafiahistory.com/ignazio-lupo/#:~:text=From%20 an%20early%20age%20he,attacked%20him%20with%20a%20knife. While Lupo is usually referred to as "Ignazio Lupo" or simply "Lupo the Wolf," some accounts of his life identify him as "Ignazius Lupo," "Ignazio Saietta," "Lupo Saietta," and "Ignazio Lupo Saietta."

17. Dickson, "Ignazio Lupo"; Hunt, "Witnesses for the Defense," 25, 27; "Ignazio Lupo," GangRule; Dash, *The First Family*, 114.

18. Hunt, "Witnesses for the Defense," 25; Dash, *The First Family*, 115; "Ignazio Lupo," GangRule; "Ignazio Lupo: Biography," FAMpeople.com, May 19, 2019, https://fampeople.com/cat-ignazio-lupo.

19. Bruno, "Joe Morello"; Walter S. Bowen and Harry Edward Neal, *The United States Secret Service* (Philadelphia: Chilton Company, 1960), 37; Mike La Sorte, "La Mano Nera (The Black Hand)," AmericanMafia.com, http://www.americanmafia.com/Feature_Articles_425.html.

20. Bowen and Neal, *The United States Secret Service*, 37–38.

21. Bowen and Neal, *The United States Secret Service*, 37; Dash, *The First Family*, 78–79; Gaetano D'Amato, "The 'Black Hand' Myth," *The North American Review* 187, no. 629 (April 1908): 544, 548; Stephan Talty, *The Black Hand: The Epic War between a Brilliant Detective and the Deadliest Secret Society in American History* (Boston: Houghton Mifflin Harcourt, 2017), 71; La Sorte, "La Mano Nera." According to D'Amato, the name "Black Hand" originated in Spain and referred to a criminal society active there in the late nineteenth century.

22. Bruno, "Joe Morello"; Dash, *The First Family*, 79.

23. William J. Flynn, *The Barrel Mystery* (New York: The James A. McCann Company, 1919), 28. For Flynn, Black Handers were not just extortionists. "When I say Black Handers," he wrote, "I mean also counterfeiters." See Flynn, *The Barrel Mystery*, 8.

24. Bowen and Neal, *The United States Secret Service*, 38–39.

25. Dash, *The First Family*, 120–21; Bowen and Neal, *The United States Secret Service*, 38–39.

26. Dash, *The First Family*, 120–21; Bowen and Neal, *The United States Secret Service*, 38–39; Flynn, *The Barrel Mystery*, 9.

27. Dash, *The First Family*, 122–23; Dickson, "Ignazio Lupo"; Hunt, "Witnesses for the Defense," 33n23.

28. "Passed Counterfeit Money," *Yonkers Statesman* (Yonkers, NY), January 2, 1903; Hunt, "Nemesis of Counterfeiters," 50; Flynn, *The Barrel Mystery*, 18.

29. Flynn, *The Barrel Mystery*, 19–21; Hunt, "Nemesis of Counterfeiters," 50. While Flynn spelled the name of one of the suspects as "DePriema," Hunt spells it "DePrima," and Dash spells it "Di Priemo."

30. Flynn, *The Barrel Mystery*, 21.

31. Dash, *The First Family*, 125–26.

32. Dash, *The First Family*, 1–3; Flynn, *The Barrel Mystery*, 9. In testimony several years later during his trial for counterfeiting charges, Lupo said he thought he sold the tavern sometime in 1902. See Hunt, "Witnesses for the Defense," 27.

33. Dash, *The First Family*, 3–4.

34. Dash, *The First Family*, 5.

35. Flynn, *The Barrel Mystery*, 4–5; Dash, *The First Family*, 5–6.

36. Flynn, *The Barrel Mystery*, 5; Dash, *The First Family*, 6–8; "'Barrel' Murder Mystery," *Seattle Star*, April 16, 1903; "Barrel Murder," *Times-Democrat* (Lima, OH), April 17, 1903; "Barrel Murder Mystery," *Buffalo Evening Times*, April 18, 1903; "Mafia Suspects Held," *Sun* (Baltimore), April 17, 1903; "Arrests in Barrel Mystery Case Made," *San Francisco Examiner*, April 18, 1903; "Police Are Certain They Have Slayers," *World* (NY evening edition), April 16, 1903.

37. Dash, *The First Family*, 11–12; Flynn, *The Barrel Mystery*, 7–8.

38. RG 87, DRA, Flynn, vol. 9, April 12–14, 1903; Dash, *The First Family*, 15–19; Flynn, *The Barrel Mystery*, 8–10.

39. Dash, *The First Family*, 18–21; Flynn, *The Barrel Mystery*, 10–11; RG 87, DRA, Flynn, vol. 9, April 14, 1903; William J. Flynn, "Black Hand Inner Secrets Laid Bare by William J. Flynn, Chief of the U.S. Secret Service: The Famous Barrel Murder Mystery," *Washington Post*, April 19, 1914.

40. Dash, *The First Family*, 19–20; Flynn, "Black Hand Inner Secrets." Flynn's concern about the color of Madonia's suit is puzzling since the doomed man could have worn a brown suit on the evening of April 12, when Flynn and his agents saw him, and a blue suit on April 13, the night before he was murdered (at around three in the morning on April 14). At times, Flynn implied that he saw him on the night of April 13 and that there was no time for him to change clothes before he was murdered several hours later. "The suit of the dead man was described as blue, while I remembered him to be clothed in brown," Flynn wrote. "Of course, he might have changed his clothes before meeting his death, but this was not likely." See Flynn, "Black Hand Inner Secrets." There is also a report by one of Flynn's agents indicating that the Secret Service agents saw Madonia on the afternoon of April 13. "We identified the body [in the morgue] as that of the man we saw in company of Morrello [*sic*] et al. during the afternoon of the 13th," the agent wrote in his daily report. See RG 87, DRA, Flynn, vol. 9, April 15, 1903.

41. Dash, *The First Family*, 20–21; RG 87, DRA, Flynn, vol. 9, April 14–15, 1903.

42. Dash, *The First Family*, 22–23.

43. Dash, *The First Family*, 23–25; Flynn, "Black Hand Inner Secrets"; Flynn, *The Barrel Mystery*, 10–12; RG 87, DRA, Flynn, vol. 9, April 15, 1903.

44. RG 87, DRA, Flynn, vol. 9, April 15, 1903; Dash, *The First Family*, 26.

45. Flynn, "Black Hand Inner Secrets."

46. Flynn, "Black Hand Inner Secrets"; Flynn, *The Barrel Mystery*, 13–14.

47. Flynn, "Black Hand Inner Secrets"; Flynn, *The Barrel Mystery*, 14–15.

48. Flynn, *The Barrel Mystery*, 16–17; Flynn, "Black Hand Inner Secrets." The revenge killing was not the work of DePriema, as he was still in the Sing Sing prison at the time of the murder. See Flynn, *The Barrel Mystery*, 22.

49. Flynn, "Black Hand Inner Secrets"; Brent Sidney Roberts, "'Steady Hammer': Origins of American Counterterrorism in the Dime Novel World of William J. Flynn" (PhD diss., Montana State University, 2020), 132, 134.

50. Talty, *The Black Hand*, xiv; "Plea from Detectives," *New York Times*, April 30, 1905.

51. Dash, *The First Family*, 9; Talty, *The Black Hand*, xiv, 10, 16–17; Andrew Paul Mele, *The Italian Squad: How the NYPD Took Down the Black Hand Extortion Racket* (Jefferson, NC: McFarland, 2020), 14–15; Anna Maria Corradini, *Joe Petrosino, a 20th Century Hero: A Documented Account of His Assassination in Palermo* (Palermo: Provincia Regionale di Palermo, 2009), 25–26.

52. Talty, *The Black Hand*, 2–3; Mele, *The Italian Squad*, 5.

53. Talty, *The Black Hand*, 3–4 (emphasis in the original).

54. Talty, *The Black Hand*, 4–10; Mele, *The Italian Squad*, 11–13; Corradini, *Joe Petrosino*, 23–25.

55. Talty, *The Black Hand*, 10–12; Mele, *The Italian Squad*, 13; Corradini, *Joe Petrosino*, 24.

56. Corradini, *Joe Petrosino*, 26; Talty, *The Black Hand*, 12–13, 46; Mele, *The Italian Squad*, 13; "Wife Murder," *Boston Post*, February 21, 1897; "Found in New York," *Boston Globe*, March 27, 1897; "Three Years After," *Times-Tribune* (Scranton, PA), September 12, 1895.

57. "Wore Green Whiskers on Sunday," *Sun* (NY), April 16, 1894; "Actor Israel behind Bars," *World* (NY evening edition), April 16, 1894; "Jottings about Town," *Sun* (NY), April 17, 1894; "Violated the Sunday Theatrical Law," *New York Times*, April 16, 1894; Batya Miller, "Enforcement of the Sunday Closing Laws on the Lower East Side, 1882–1903," *American Jewish History* 91, no. 2 (June 2003): 269.

58. "Wore Green Whiskers"; "Actor Israel behind Bars."

59. "Wore Green Whiskers"; "Violated the Sunday Theatrical Law"; "Actor Israel Behind Bars."

60. Talty, *The Black Hand*, 16; Mele, *The Italian Squad*, 13–14.

61. Mele, *The Italian Squad*, 15–17; Talty, *The Black Hand*, 41–42; Joe Avella, "A Martyr to Duty: Remembering Giuseppe 'Joe' Petrosino, the Original 'Untouchable,'" Buhner.com, 2003, http://www.buhner.com/petrosino.html.

62. Talty, *The Black Hand*, 40; Mele, *The Italian Squad*, 17.

63. Talty, *The Black Hand*, 44; Mele, *The Italian Squad*, 17.

64. Talty, *The Black Hand*, 96, 121–22, 241.

65. Dash, *The First Family*, 182; Talty, *The Black Hand*, 125; "Ruined by Lupo, the Mafia Leader," *New York Times*, March 17, 1909.

66. Lieutenant Joseph Petrosino, "The 'Black Hand' and Its Methods," *Daily Sentinel* (Junction City, KS), February 20, 1908.

67. Talty, *The Black Hand*, 166, 172.

68. Dash, *The First Family*, 212, 219–20; Talty, *The Black Hand*, 186.

69. Talty, *The Black Hand*, 150–52, 165–66, 173.

70. Dash, *The First Family*, 213; Mele, *The Italian Squad*, 75; Talty, *The Black Hand*, 173–74.

71. Dash, *The First Family*, 213–14; Talty, *The Black Hand*, 174–75, 182–83; Mele, *The Italian Squad*, 75–77.

72. Mele, *The Italian Squad*, 75–77; Corradini, *Joe Petrosino*, 42; Dash, *The First Family*, 211, 215, 219; Talty, *The Black Hand*, 187; "New Secret Service to Fight Black Hand," *New York Times*, February 20, 1909; "Bingham Gets His Fund," *Sun* (NY), February 20, 1909; "Bingham's Secret Service Started," *New York Herald*, February 20, 1909. The *Herald*'s story also ran in its European edition, which was printed in Paris and distributed throughout Europe. The story was then picked up by the Naples newspaper *Il Mattino* and published in several other Italian newspapers. Petrosino's "secret" mission was thus known throughout Italy. He learned that his cover had been blown when he met up in Padula with his brother, who showed him the article from yet another Italian newspaper, *Il Pungolo*. See Dash, *The First Family*, 215, 219, and Talty, *The Black Hand*, 187. It appears that *L'Araldo Italiano* might have revealed Petrosino's mission on February 9, the day he set sail for Italy. See Dash, *The First Family*, 219.

73. Mele, *The Italian Squad*, 77–80; Dash, *The First Family*, 216–17; Talty, *The Black Hand*, 186–87, 190, 191.

74. Talty, *The Black Hand*, 192; Corradini, *Joe Petrosino*, 114.

75. Talty, *The Black Hand*, 192, 197–98; Dash, *The First Family*, 221.

76. Dash, *The First Family*, 221–22.

77. Talty, *The Black Hand*, 206; Mele, *The Italian Squad*, 86; "War on Black Hand in All America for Murder of Petrosino," *World* (NY evening edition), March 13, 1909.

78. Corradini, *Joe Petrosino*, 162–63, 205.

79. Mele, *The Italian Squad*, 89–90; Corradini, *Joe Petrosino*, 196–97, 207–8, 260–62; Dash, *The First Family*, 220, 230; Critchley, *The Origin of Organized Crime in America*, 64.

80. Mele, *The Italian Squad*, 92; Dash, *The First Family*, 226–27; Corradini, *Joe Petrosino*, 124–25, 178, 255.

81. Mele, *The Italian Squad*, 88, 91, 95; Talty, *The Black Hand*, 211–12, 220; Dash, *The First Family*, 367; Owen Moritz, "Apple Sauce," *Daily News* (NY), May 29, 1987; Howard Thompson, "'Pay or Die' at Warner," *New York Times*, May 27, 1960.

82. Flynn, *The Barrel Mystery*, 34.

83. Flynn, *The Barrel Mystery*, 24; Dash, *The First Family*, 236.

84. "A Dabbler in Revolutions," *Sun* (NY), September 11, 1906; "George B. Boynton, 'The War Maker,' Tells His Adventures," *New York Times*, June 11, 1911.

85. "A Dabbler in Revolutions"; Hunt, "Nemesis of Counterfeiters," 51–52; William J. Flynn, "Headquarters Gossip," *Flynn's Weekly*, June 26, 1926, 475; "Nip Plan to Coin Money for Rebels," *Standard Union* (Brooklyn, NY), August 23, 1906; "Finance a Big Revolution with Counterfeit Cash," *World* (NY evening edition), August 22, 1906; "Ready to Make Coin to Beat Pres. Castro," *Brooklyn Citizen*, Aug. 23, 1906; "Pardon for Boynton," *New York Times*, January 31, 1907; "Bad Money and Revolt," *New York Times*, September 19, 1906; "Working to Finance Venezuelan Revolution Counterfeiters Were Arrested in New York," *Houston Post*, August 23, 1906.

86. "Nip Plan to Coin Money for Rebels"; "Came Back to Go to Jail," *Sun* (NY), October 23, 1906; Hunt, "Nemesis of Counterfeiters," 52.

87. "Bogus Bolivar Plot Foiled," *Chicago Daily Tribune*, August 23, 1906; Hunt, "Nemesis of Counterfeiters," 52; Flynn, "Headquarters Gossip," June 26, 1926, 480; "Came Back to Go to Jail"; "Working to Finance Venezuelan Revolution"; "Nip Plan to Coin Money for Rebels"; "Pardon for Boynton."

88. "Witte Has Arrived," *Washington Post*, August 8, 1905; "Russia Resolved Not to Pay an Indemnity to Japan," *Buffalo Courier*, August 8, 1905.

89. Dash, *The First Family*, 235–36; Bowen and Neal, *The United States Secret Service*, 39.

90. Dash, *The First Family*, 190–91, 230, 237–38; Bowen and Neal, *The United States Secret Service*, 41; Thomas Hunt, *Wrongly Executed? The Long-Forgotten Context of Charles Sberna's 1939 Electrocution* (Whiting, VT: Seven•Seven•Eight, 2016), 73.

91. Dash, *The First Family*, 234–35, 245; Giuseppe Calicchio et al., Plaintiffs-in-Error, (Defendants Below) v. the United States, Defendant-in-Error, (Plaintiff Below), Brief for the United States, 15 (2nd Cir. Ct. App.), U.S. Secret Service files; Hunt, *Wrongly Executed?*, 74; Flynn, *The Barrel Mystery*, 32, 33–34,

38–42, 163–65; "The Morello and Lupo Trial," GangRule, https://www.gang rule.com/events/the-morello-lupo-trial-1910.

92. Dash, *The First Family*, 245–51; Hunt, *Wrongly Executed?*, 75.

93. Dash, *The First Family*, 246–47; Bowen and Neal, *The United States Secret Service*, 44–45.

94. Dash, *The First Family*, 245–51; Hunt, *Wrongly Executed?*, 75.

95. Dash, *The First Family*, xxviii, 250, 258; "The Morello and Lupo Trial"; RG 87, DRA, Flynn, vol. 28, November 15, 1909.

96. Bowen and Neal, *The United States Secret Service*, 45.

97. RG 87, DRA, Flynn, vol. 28, November 15, 1909.

98. William J. Flynn, "Confession of 'Comito,' Tool of the Black Hand," *Idaho Statesman*, May 10, 1914; Dash, *The First Family*, 253–54.

99. Dash, *The First Family*, 184–86, 253–54; "W. J. Flynn to John E. Wilkie, February 15th, 1910," RG 87, GC; Bowen and Neal, *The United States Secret Service*, 41–43.

100. Flynn, *The Barrel Mystery*, 72–75 (emphasis in the original).

101. Dash, *The First Family*, 234–35, 252–53; Flynn, *The Barrel Mystery*, 168–70.

102. Dash, *The First Family*, 254, 259–60; "Bogus Money Trial," *New-York Tribune*, January 27, 1910; "Sicilian Dagger for Henkel," *Sun* (NY), January 27, 1910.

103. "Comito Fears Sicilians," *Sun* (NY), January 29, 1910; "Accused Italian Angry; Tells about Comrades," *Buffalo Courier*, February 2, 1910; "Comito a Nimble Witness," *New York Times*, February 1, 1910; "Didn't Like Lawyer's Face," *New York Times*, February 2, 1910.

104. "Comito a Nimble Witness"; "Guards at Trial," *New-York Tribune*, February 1, 1910; Bowen and Neal, *The United States Secret Service*, 47; "W. J. Flynn to John E. Wilkie."

105. "W. J. Flynn to John E. Wilkie"; Giuseppe Calicchio et al. v. United States, 21; Hunt, "Nemesis of Counterfeiters," 53.

106. "Lupo to Prison for 30 Years," *Sun* (NY), February 20, 1910; "30 Years for 'Wolf,'" *Washington Post*, February 20, 1910; "150 Years in All for the Lupo Gang," *New York Times*, February 20, 1920.

107. "Lupo to Prison for 30 Years"; "30 Years for 'Wolf'"; Dash, *The First Family*, 261–63; "150 Years in All for the Lupo Gang."

108. Dash, *The First Family*, 262–63; "150 Years in All for the Lupo Gang"; "The Morello and Lupo Trial."

109. "Black Hand Manacled at Last," *New York Times*, April 3, 1910.

110. "Counterfeiters Guilty; Get Heavy Sentences," *Brooklyn Daily Eagle*, February 20, 1910; "Letter from John E. Wilkie, Chief to William J. Flynn, Operative S.S. Division, New York, N.Y.," February 22, 1910, RG 87, GC.

111. Flynn, *The Barrel Mystery*, 264. Similar to how Morello and Lupo were tried and sentenced for counterfeiting activities and not murder and extortion, the notorious gangster Al Capone was sentenced to a long prison term in 1931 for income tax evasion rather than for bootlegging and murder, which he had engaged in during Prohibition in the 1920s. See Kelly Phillips Erb, "Al Capone Convicted on This Day in 1931 after Boasting, 'They Can't Collect Legal Taxes from Illegal Money,'" *Forbes*, October 17, 2020, https://www.forbes.com/sites/kellyphillipserb/2020/10/17/al-capone-convicted-on-this-day-in-1931-after-boasting-they-cant-collect-legal-taxes-from-illegal-money/?sh=34c6ba161435; John J. Binder, *Al Capone's Beer Wars: A Complete History of Organized Crime in Chicago during Prohibition* (Amherst, NY: Prometheus Books, 2017), 241; and Jonathan Eig, *Get Capone: The Secret Plot That Captured America's Most Wanted Gangster* (New York: Simon & Schuster Paperbacks, 2010), 343–67.

112. Dash, *The First Family*, xxiii, 267, 274.

113. Hunt, *Wrongly Executed?*, 78–80, 92–94; Dash, *The First Family*, xxi–xxii, 337–39, 363–64; Thomas Hunt, "Mafia Boss of Bosses Despairs in Prison," *Informer: The Journal of American Mafia History* 3, no. 2 (April 2010): 42–43.

114. Dash, *The First Family*, 268–69; Flynn, *The Barrel Mystery*, 45–46. Dash points out that it is not known whether Comito ever reunited with his wife or remained with Katrina.

115. "Started as Tinsmith," *Boston Globe*, November 18, 1910; James B. Morrow, "Counterfeiters; Their Ways Told by New Chief of U.S. Secret Service," *Washington Herald*, January 12, 1913.

CHAPTER 3: A THANKLESS JOB

1. "Lexow Committee Report," *New York Times*, January 18, 1895; Daniel Czitrom, "The Origins of Corruption in the New York City Police Department," *Time*, June 28, 2016, https://time.com/4384963/nypd-scandal-history/.

2. "Lexow Committee Report"; Andrew Paul Mele, *The Italian Squad: How the NYPD Took Down the Black Hand Extortion Racket* (Jefferson, NC: McFarland, 2020), 13–14, 52–53; Robert McNamara, "Theodore Roosevelt and the New York Police Department," ThoughtCo., updated June 19, 2019, https://www.thoughtco.com/theodore-roosevelt-ny-police-department-1773515; Dexter Marshall, "Roosevelt Has Brains," *Washington Times*, July 7, 1895.

3. Marshall, "Roosevelt Has Brains"; Mele, *The Italian Squad*, 13–14, 52–53; Stephan Talty, *The Black Hand: The Epic War between a Brilliant Detective and the Deadliest Secret Society in American History* (Boston: Houghton Mifflin Harcourt, 2017), 15–16; Bernard Whalen and Jon Whalen, *The NYPD's First Fifty Years: Politicians, Police Commissioners, & Patrolmen* (Lincoln, NE: Potomac Books, 2014), 40.

4. Mele, *The Italian Squad*, 53; Richard Zacks, *Island of Vice: Theodore Roosevelt's Quest to Clean Up Sin-Loving New York* (New York: Anchor Books, 2012), 108–10; Ian Harvey, "The Story of Theodore Roosevelt and the New York Police Department," Vintage News, February 2, 2017, https://www.thevintagenews.com/2017/02/02/the-story-of-theodore-roosevelt-and-the-new-york-police-department/?chrome=1&A1c=1.

5. Zacks, *Island of Vice*, 356–57, 360–62; "William J. Flynn," *Metropolitan Magazine*, April 1911, 72; Theodore Roosevelt, "Municipal Administration: The New York Police Force," *The Atlantic*, September 1897, https://www.theatlantic.com/magazine/archive/1897/09/municipal-administration-the-new-york-police-force/519849/.

6. Harvey, "The Story of Theodore Roosevelt"; Whalen and Whalen, *The NYPD's First Fifty Years*, 1–3; Czitrom, "The Origins of Corruption."

7. Whalen and Whalen, *The NYPD's First Fifty Years*, 8–9; Zacks, *Island of Vice*, 360.

8. Whalen and Whalen, *The NYPD's First Fifty Years*, xvii, xviii, xix, 1.

9. Zacks, *Island of Vice*, 365.

10. "U.S. Secret Service Head Sees Gaynor," *New York Times*, April 19, 1910.

11. "U.S. Secret Service Head Sees Gaynor."

12. RG 87, DRA, Flynn, vol. 9, April 14, 1903; Arthur W. Towne, "Mayor Gaynor's Police Policy and the Crime Wave in New York City," *Journal of Criminal Law and Criminology* 2, no. 3 (May 1911–March 1912): 375–76.

13. "William J. Gaynor," Historical Society of the New York Courts, https://history.nycourts.gov/biography/william-j-gaynor/; "Gaynor a Puzzle to Friend and Foe," *New York Times*, September 12, 1913; Robert M. Thornton, "William Jay Gaynor: Libertarian Mayor of New York," Foundation for Economic Education, March 1, 1970, https://fee.org/articles/william-jay-gaynor-libertarian-mayor-of-new-york/.

14. Jay Maeder, "The Story of William Gaynor, the Only New York Mayor Ever Gunned Down in Office," *New York Daily News*, August 14, 2017, https://www.nydailynews.com/new-york/story-william-gaynor-nyc-mayor-gunned-article-1.802037; Lately Thomas, *The Mayor Who Mastered New York: The Life*

and Opinions of William J. Gaynor (New York: William Morrow & Company, 1969), 159–60, 184; William L. Chenery, "So This Is Tammany Hall!," *Atlantic Monthly*, September 1924, 310.

15. "Biographical Sketch" (repr., *Evening Sun* [NY], June 26, 1911) in *Some of Mayor Gaynor's Letters and Speeches* (New York: Greaves Publishing Company, 1913), 13; Thomas, *The Mayor Who Mastered New York*, 290–91; Maeder, "The Story of William Gaynor."

16. "Know Your Mayors: William Jay Gaynor," Bowery Boys, March 4, 2008, https://www.boweryboyshistory.com/2008/03/know-your-mayors-william-jay -gaynor.html; Maeder, "The Story of William Gaynor"; "Gaynor a Puzzle to Friend and Foe"; *Some of Mayor Gaynor's Letters and Speeches*, 26, 32–33.

17. Whalen and Whalen, *The NYPD's First Fifty Years*, 67–68; "Flynn Is to Give New York a Real Detective Force," *New York Times*, October 30, 1910; "Backed by Real Detective Experience, W. J. Flynn, Head of City Service, Brings Terror to Evildoers," *Brooklyn Daily Eagle*, December 18, 1910; "New York Bad Place for Crooks Now," *The Leader* (Guthrie, OK), October 26, 1910; "Flynn Revolutionizes the Detective Bureau," *New-York Tribune*, November 18, 1910.

18. "Models Detective Force on Secret Service," *Brooklyn Citizen*, November 11, 1910; "Flynn Revolutionizes the Detective Bureau"; William J. Flynn, "My Life in the Secret Service," *Flynn's*, November 1, 1924, 28–29; "Flynn Is to Give New York a Real Detective Force." Bill Bratton faced a similar challenge when he became commissioner of the NYPD in 1994. "The entire culture of the New York Police Department needed to be transformed," Bratton wrote. "We would concentrate on rooting out corruption by recruiting investigators from leaders within the ranks, by training supervisors to see signs of trouble and rewarding commanders for finding it." See William Bratton, *Turnaround: How America's Top Cop Reversed the Crime Epidemic*, with Peter Knobler (New York: Random House, 1998), 195.

19. "New York Police in Big Shakeup," *Boston Globe*, November 18, 1910; Whalen and Whalen, *The NYPD's First Fifty Years*, 68; "Secret Service Methods in New York's Police System," *New York Times*, February 26, 1911; Flynn, "My Life in the Secret Service," November 1, 1924, 29; "Models Detective Force on Secret Service"; "Flynn Revolutionizes the Detective Bureau."

20. "Many Sleuths Are Shifted," *Bridgeport Evening Farmer* (Bridgeport, CT), November 19, 1910; "Flynn Revolutionizes the Detective Bureau"; "Flynn Is to Give New York a Real Detective Force"; Flynn, "My Life in the Secret Service," November 1, 1924, 29; "Flynn Inaugurates New Detective Plan," *New York Times*, November 18, 1910; "Cropsey and Flynn at Odds; Don't Speak," *New York Times*, February 12, 1911.

21. Talty, *The Black Hand*, 97–98.

22. "Get Kidnappers and Their Victim," *Fall River Evening News* (Fall River, MA), December 9, 1910; "Flynn's Men Get Kidnapper Gang," *New York Times*, December 9, 1910. The *New York Times* story states that Longo was snatched in front of his cousin Michael Rizzo's home. In another story in the *New York Times*, Rizzo, who was also kidnapped, told police later that he was taken at the same time as Longo while the two boys were playing in front of Rizzo's grandfather's house. See "Rizzo Boy Freed by Kidnappers," *New York Times*, December 10, 1910.

23. "Get Kidnappers and Their Victim"; "Flynn's Men Get Kidnapper Gang."

24. "Flynn's Men Get Kidnapper Gang."

25. "Flynn's Men Get Kidnapper Gang"; "Police Reserves Guard Italian Gang Members from Angry Crowds," *Brooklyn Daily Eagle*, December 9, 1910; "Get Kidnappers and Their Victim." One newspaper account states that it was an anonymous letter, not a person Flynn knew, that revealed the location of the kidnapped boys. See "Get Kidnappers and Their Victim."

26. "Flynn's Men Get Kidnapper Gang."

27. "Flynn's Men Get Kidnapper Gang"; "Grand Jury Indicts Alleged Kidnappers," *Brooklyn Daily Eagle*, December 13, 1910; "Woman Kidnapper Quickly Convicted," *New York Times*, December 21, 1910.

28. "Rizzo Boy Freed by Kidnappers."

29. "Police Reserves Guard Italian Gang Members from Angry Crowds."

30. "Punishing Kidnappers," *York Daily* (York, PA), December 31, 1910. There is no record of what happened to the rest of the group that was arrested, although it may be that many of them were held as material witnesses. See "Quickly Convicted Woman Kidnapper," *Camden Post-Telegram* (Camden, NJ), December 21, 1910.

31. "Punishing Kidnappers."

32. Whalen and Whalen, *The NYPD's First Fifty Years*, 68–69; Brent Sidney Roberts, "'Steady Hammer': Origins of American Counterterrorism in the Dime Novel World of William J. Flynn" (PhD diss., Montana State University, 2020), 237–39; "Criminals Threaten Police Official," *Steinauer Star* (Steinauer, NE), February 2, 1911.

33. "Life's Detective Yarns Are Dull, Says William J. Flynn," *Rutland Daily Herald* (Rutland, VT), May 26, 1922.

34. William J. Flynn, "Headquarters Gossip," *Flynn's*, July 4, 1925, 959–60.

35. Allen Churchill, "The Girl Who Never Came Back," *American Heritage*, August 1960, https://www.americanheritage.com/girl-who-never-came-back; Flynn, "Headquarters Gossip," July 4, 1925, 959.

36. Churchill, "The Girl Who Never Came Back"; Flynn, "Headquarters Gossip," July 4, 1925, 959.

37. Churchill, "The Girl Who Never Came Back."

38. Churchill, "The Girl Who Never Came Back."

39. Churchill, "The Girl Who Never Came Back."

40. Flynn, "Headquarters Gossip," July 4, 1925, 960; "New York's Mystery—Miss Dorothy Arnold," *Times-Democrat* (Pawnee, OK), March 2, 1911; "Millionaire Will Pay Big Reward," *Bridgeport Evening Farmer* (Bridgeport, CT), January 26, 1911. The spelling of "clew" this way (instead of "clue") was common at the time.

41. Flynn, "Headquarters Gossip," July 4, 1925, 960; Churchill, "The Girl Who Never Came Back"; "New York's Mystery."

42. Churchill, "The Girl Who Never Came Back"; Flynn, "Headquarters Gossip," July 4, 1925, 960.

43. "New York Police Problems," *Boston Evening Transcript*, May 3, 1911; "Flynn's Men Catch Gamblers in Traps," *New York Times*, December 20, 1910.

44. "New York Police Problems"; "Flynn's Men Catch Gamblers in Traps."

45. "Flynn's Men Catch Gamblers in Traps."

46. "Flynn's Men Catch Gamblers in Traps."

47. "Flynn's Men Catch Gamblers in Traps."

48. "Flynn Harried into Quitting the Police," *New York Times*, April 28, 1911; "Raid Big Gambling House in Harlem," *New York Times*, March 3, 1911.

49. "Flynn Harried into Quitting the Police"; "New York Police Problems"; "Uneasy Is Ruler of Police Force," *Brooklyn Daily Times*, March 25, 1911; "Cropsey Mad with Flynn because Secret Service Is Kept Secret from Him," *World* (NY evening edition), February 11, 1911; "Cropsey and Flynn in Clash over Police," *Brooklyn Daily Eagle*, February 11, 1911.

50. "Gaynor Rebukes Head of Police," *New York Times*, February 27, 1911; "Flynn Harried into Quitting the Police."

51. "Flynn Harried into Quitting the Police."

52. "Flynn Harried into Quitting the Police"; "Declares New York Police Force To Be 'Crooked Lay-Out," *Buffalo Courier*, April 28, 1911.

53. "Flynn Harried into Quitting the Police"; "Flynn Is Glad to Quit His 'Thankless Job,'" *Brooklyn Daily Times*, April 27, 1911; Thomas Hunt, "Nemesis of Counterfeiters: William J. Flynn," *Informer: The Journal of American Mafia History* 3, no. 2 (April 2010): 54; "Exit Flynn," *New-York Tribune*, April 28, 1911.

54. "Gang Leader Taken," *Washington Post*, October 10, 1911; Hunt, "Nemesis of Counterfeiters," 54; "Escapes Captors Drowns Himself," *Montgomery Times*, July 14, 1911.

55. Hunt, "Nemesis of Counterfeiters," 54–55.

56. "Italian Crimes Baffle Police," *New York Times*, August 31, 1911; Whalen and Whalen, *The NYPD's First Fifty Years*, 70; New York City Board of Aldermen, *Report of the Special Committee of the Board of Aldermen of the City of New York, Appointed August 5, 1912 to Investigate the Police Department, Submitted June 10, 1913* (London: Forgotten Books, 2018), 3; "Cropsey Had Quit Several Days Ago; Waldo Gets the Job," *World* (NY evening edition), May 23, 1911; "Pinkerton Man Takes Flynn's 'Thankless Job,'" *Buffalo Evening News*, May 1, 1911.

57. "Italian Crimes Baffle Police."

58. Mike Dash, *Satan's Circus: Murder, Vice, Police Corruption and New York's Trial of the Century* (New York: Three Rivers Press, 2007), 140; Whalen and Whalen, *The NYPD's First Fifty Years*, 75; New York City Board of Aldermen, *Report of the Special Committee*, 6.

59. Whalen and Whalen, *The NYPD's First Fifty Years*, 75; New York City Board of Aldermen, *Report of the Special Committee*, 6; Dash, *Satan's Circus*, 142; Sam Roberts, "100 Years after a Murder, Questions about a Police Officer's Guilt," *City Room* (blog), *New York Times*, July 15, 2012, https://cityroom.blogs.nytimes.com/2012/07/15/100-years-after-a-murder-questions-about-a-police-officers-guilt/.

60. Whalen and Whalen, *The NYPD's First Fifty Years*, 76–78; Dash, *Satan's Circus*, 176–78, 281–82, 342–44; Richard F. Snow, "American Characters: Charles Becker," *American Heritage*, December 1978, https://www.americanheritage.com/charles-becker; Roberts, "100 Years after a Murder."

61. Snow, "American Characters"; Dash, *Satan's Circus*, 142; "Tombs Inmate Trio Tripped Up 'Killer Cop,'" excerpt from Mark S. Gado, "Killer Cop," Crime Magazine, 1999, http://www.correctionhistory.org/html/chronicl/tombs/killercop2.html.

62. "Flynn Coming Back to Aid Aldermen," *New York Times*, August 22, 1912; New York City Board of Aldermen, *Report of the Special Committee*, 1.

63. "Reward Offered for Gun Men," *News-Journal* (Lancaster, PA), August 22, 1912; "List of Names Is Made Public," *Kane Republican* (Kane, PA), August 28, 1912; Hunt, "Nemesis of Counterfeiters," 55; "William J. Flynn Quits the Curran Committee," *Sun* (NY), November 16, 1912; "Flynn Quits Committee," *New York Times*, November 16, 1912; New York City Board of Aldermen, *Report of the Special Committee*. Reporters went to Flynn's home in Manhattan to ask

him why he was quitting the Curran Committee. After first stating that he had intended to stay with the committee for only a few months at the most, he gave the reporters his real reason. "My accounts have been held up in the Mayor's office," he said. "If I had no other reason for leaving my present job that would have been sufficient. It is plain that I cannot afford to work for nothing and then pay the expenses of the aldermanic investigating committee, too. The city owes me about $2,200 in all. Up to date my salary owed me is about $1,500, and besides that I have spent from my own pocket about $800. Yes, sir, I would leave on that account if for no other reason." See "Flynn Quits Committee," *New-York Tribune*, November 16, 1912.

CHAPTER 4: ON THE TRAIL OF GERMAN SPIES AND SABOTEURS

1. Walter S. Bowen, "U.S. Secret Service: A Chronicle" (unpublished manuscript, 1955), U.S. Secret Service files, 439.

2. Bowen, "U.S. Secret Service," 439–40; Walter S. Bowen and Harry Edward Neal, *The United States Secret Service* (Philadelphia: Chilton Company, 1960), 162; *Hearings before the Subcommittee of the House Committee on Appropriations, Second Session*, 63rd Cong. 232, 1915 Legislative, Executive, and Judicial Appropriation Bill (statement of William J. Flynn, Secret Service Chief, January 20, 1914).

3. "Why Counterfeiters Can No Longer Sleep," *Evening Times-Star and Alameda Daily Argus* (Alameda, CA), February 12, 1913; Bowen, "U.S. Secret Service," 442.

4. Bowen, "U.S. Secret Service," 441–43, 460.

5. Bowen, "U.S. Secret Service," 452–54.

6. "Black Hand Secrets Revealed by Chief of Secret Service," *Idaho Sunday Statesman*, June 28, 1914; "June 28, 1914," National WWI Museum and Memorial, https://www.theworldwar.org/learn/wwi/june28; L. Noble, "Sarajevo 1914," Cambridge University Library, https://www.lib.cam.ac.uk/collections/depart ments/germanic-collections/about-collections/spotlight-archive/sarajevo-1914; Howard Blum, *Dark Invasion: 1915: Germany's Secret War and the Hunt for the First Terrorist Cell in America* (New York: Harper, 2014); Heribert Von Feilitzsch, *The Secret War on the United States in 1915: A Tale of Sabotage, Labor Unrest and Border Troubles* (Amissville, VA: Henselstone Verlag, 2015).

7. Jeanette Lamb, "Black Hand: The Secret Group Who Set Fire to Europe and Initiated World War I," HistoryCollection.com, November 20, 2018, https://historycollection.com/secret-group-set-fire-europe-initiated-ww1/2/; Sarah Pruitt, "How a Wrong Turn Started World War I," History.com,

updated August 31, 2018, https://www.history.com/news/how-a-wrong-turn-started-world-war-i.

8. Pruitt, "How a Wrong Turn Started World War I"; Editors of Encyclopaedia Britannica, "Gavrilo Princip: Slavic Nationalist," Britannica, https://www.britannica.com/biography/Gavrilo-Princip; Lamb, "Black Hand"; "Italy Enters World War I," National WWI Museum and Memorial, https://www.theworldwar.org/learn/wwi/italy. Princip was convicted and sentenced to twenty years in prison. He did not receive the death penalty because he was nineteen years old at the time of the assassination, and under Austro-Hungarian law, a person had to be at least twenty to be executed. He died of tuberculosis while in prison in 1918. See Pruitt, "How a Wrong Turn Started World War I."

9. "President Wilson's Declaration of Neutrality," WWI Document Archive, https://wwi.lib.byu.edu/index.php/President_Wilson%27s_Declaration_of_Neutrality.

10. "What You Need to Know about the British Naval Blockade of the First World War," Imperial War Museums, https://www.iwm.org.uk/history/what-you-need-to-know-about-the-british-naval-blockade-of-the-first-world-war; Von Feilitzsch, *The Secret War on the United States*, xix; Heribert Von Feilitzsch, *The Secret War Council: The German Fight against the Entente in America in 1914* (Amissville, VA: Henselstone Verlag, 2015), xxii–xxiii, 30.

11. Blum, *Dark Invasion*, 41; "Imperial Germany's Sabotage Operations in the U.S.," in *A Counterintelligence Reader, Volume One: American Revolution to World War II*, ed. Frank J. Rafalko (2011), https://irp.fas.org/ops/ci/docs/ci1/ch3c.htm; Von Feilitzsch, *The Secret War Council*, 11–12; Thomas A. Reppetto, *Battleground New York City: Countering Spies, Saboteurs, and Terrorists since 1861* (Washington, D.C.: Potomac Books, 2012), 37. Von Feilitzsch argues that it was Dr. Heinrich F. Albert, not von Bernstorff, who was designated as the head of the secret intelligence group. See Von Feilitzsch, *The Secret War on the United States*, 13, and Von Feilitzsch, *The Secret War Council*, vii, 11, 15–16.

12. Blum, *Dark Invasion*, 69–70; Reppetto, *Battleground New York City*, 38. According to Von Feilitzsch, Albert was not made commercial attaché until 1915. See Von Feilitzsch, *The Secret War Council*, xxiii.

13. Von Feilitzsch, *The Secret War on the United States*, 13; Von Feilitzsch, *The Secret War Council*, 11, 15; Ernest Wittenberg, "The Thrifty Spy on the Sixth Avenue El," *American Heritage*, December 1965, https://www.americanheritage.com/thrifty-spy-sixth-avenue-el.

14. Von Feilitzsch, *The Secret War on the United States*, 13–15; Blum, *Dark Invasion*, 70–71; John Price Jones, *The German Spy in America: The Secret Plot-*

ting of German Spies in the United States and the Inside Story of the Sinking of the Lusitania (London: Hutchinson & Co., 1917), 207, https://books.google.com /books?id=sbzvaaaamaaj&printsec=frontcover&source=gbs_ge_summary _r&cad=0#v=onepage&q&f=false; William J. Flynn, "'My Ten Biggest Man-Hunts'—told by Chief W. J. Flynn," *New York Herald*, January 22, 1922.

15. Von Feilitzsch, *The Secret War on the United States*, 121–24; Von Feilitzsch, *The Secret War Council*, 157, 161; William G. McAdoo, *Crowded Years: The Reminiscences of William G. McAdoo* (Boston: Houghton Mifflin, 1931), 322; "Imperial Germany's Sabotage Operations in the U.S."; "George Sylvester Viereck Asks 'Who Is to Blame?,'" *The Fatherland*, no. 27, RG 65, OG, M1085, Fold3, NARA.

16. Von Feilitzsch, *The Secret War on the United States*, 1–3, 252–57. According to Blum, the German agents in the United States received the green light to begin a sabotage campaign earlier than January 1915. "On November 28, 1914," Blum writes, "new marching orders arrived from Berlin. A secret cable instructed: 'It is necessary to hire through third parties who stand in no relations to the official representatives of Germany agents for arranging explosions on ships bound for enemy countries." See Blum, *Dark Invasion*, 91. German saboteurs plotted an attack in Canada even earlier than this. The plan was to blow up the Welland Canal in Ontario, a twenty-six-mile waterway connecting Lake Ontario with Lake Erie that served as a major shipping lane for grains and corn during World War I. The attack, however, never occurred, as von Papen canceled it one week before it was to take place in late September 1914. He apparently learned that the Canadians had deployed a large force to protect the canal in case of sabotage. See Von Feilitzsch, *The Secret War Council*, 110, 121.

17. Von Feilitzsch, *The Secret War on the United States*, 32. The Germans produced many "cigar bombs," which were incendiary devices made of lead, shaped like a cigar, and designed to cause fires aboard ships and burn cargo. The inside of the device was divided by a copper disc that separated two compartments of chemicals. One "chemical which has a rapid corrosive effect on copper filled the upper compartment. When it had eaten through the disk it came into contact with the chemical in the lower compartment. The combination produced instantly a flame as hot as a tiny fragment of the sun. The acid did not begin to work on the copper until one broke off a little knob at the upper end. Then it became a time bomb, the time—from two days to a week—being regulated by the thickness or thinness of the copper disk." These devices also melted completely after ignition, leaving virtually no evidence behind. See Von Feilitzsch, *The Secret War on the United States*, 27–29.

18. Von Feilitzsch, *The Secret War on the United States*, 3, 32–33.

19. Von Feilitzsch, *The Secret War on the United States*, xvi, 74–75, 210; Blum, *Dark Invasion*, 219–23, 359; Michael Warner, "The Kaiser Sows Destruction: Protecting the Homeland the First Time Around," *Studies in Intelligence* 46, no. 1 (2002), https://www.cia.gov/static/5b90ec45fb53185a0c2e0de82d42c1c5/The-Kaiser-Sows-Destruction.pdf. In another incident during this period, a mentally unstable German American named Erich Muenter attempted to assassinate the powerful and influential banker J. P. Morgan on July 3, 1915, at his home on Long Island. He claimed that he wanted to end the role the Morgan family was playing in financing the war. Morgan was shot but not seriously injured. The day before, Muenter had placed a bomb underneath the switchboard of a public phone at the U.S. Capitol in Washington, D.C. The bomb exploded, destroying the Senate Reception Room, but did not injure anybody. Muenter hanged himself while in jail after the assassination attempt at the Morgan home. See Beverly Gage, *The Day Wall Street Exploded: A Story of America in Its First Age of Terror* (New York: Oxford University Press, 2009), 22–23, 106, and Jeffrey D. Simon, *America's Forgotten Terrorists: The Rise and Fall of the Galleanists* (Lincoln, NE: Potomac Books, 2022), 211–12n37.

20. William J. Flynn, "How We Trapped the Mysterious Lt. Fay'—Chief Flynn," *New York Herald*, February 26, 1922; Von Feilitzsch, *The Secret War on the United States*, 151; *Counter-Espionage Detail, United States Secret Service, Treasury Department, 1915–1918*, report submitted by Frank Burke to Frank J. Wilson, Chief, December 7, 1938, U.S. Secret Service files, 37; Blum, *Dark Invasion*, 258–60.

21. Von Feilitzsch, *The Secret War on the United States*, 152–55; Thomas J. Tunney, *Throttled! The Detection of the German and Anarchist Bomb Plotters* (Boston: Small, Maynard & Company, 1919), 148; *Counter-Espionage Detail*, 38; Blum, *Dark Invasion*, 255.

22. "Breitung Ignorant of Plot, Uncle Says," *New York Times*, November 10, 1915. Fay was convicted of sabotage and sentenced to eight years in the U.S. Penitentiary in Atlanta. He escaped in August 1916 but was captured two years later in Spain and sent back to the United States. See "Fay Captured in Spain," *New York Times*, August 16, 1918.

23. Von Feilitzsch, *The Secret War on the United States*, 61–70; Editors of Encyclopaedia Britannica, "Lusitania: British Ship," Britannica, https://www.britannica.com/topic/Lusitania-British-ship; Wittenberg, "The Thrifty Spy."

24. Blum, *Dark Invasion*, 339; McAdoo, *Crowded Years*, 323–24; Bowen and Neal, *The United States Secret Service*, 84–85; Wittenberg, "The Thrifty Spy."

25. Wittenberg, "The Thrifty Spy"; William J. Flynn, "My Life in the Secret Service," *Flynn's*, November 8, 1924, 254; Blum, *Dark Invasion*, 339–40; McAdoo, *Crowded Years*, 323–24; Bowen and Neal, *The United States Secret Service*, 85.

26. Bowen and Neal, *The United States Secret Service*, 85; McAdoo, *Crowded Years*, 324; Wittenberg, "The Thrifty Spy"; "Age Ends Career in Secret Service," *New York Times*, May 31, 1942; Blum, *Dark Invasion*, 340. For an excellent account of Tunney's pursuit of the German saboteurs, see Blum, *Dark Invasion*.

27. "A Wireless Detective in Real Life," *Wireless Age*, September 1915, 872–74; Charles E. Apgar, "Making the Records from Sayville," *Wireless Age*, September 1915, 877–78; "Charles E. Apgar, Radio Expert, 85," *New York Times*, August 19, 1950; Lynn Conley, "Charles Emory Apgar—'The Wireless Wizard,'" Apgar Family Association, September 18, 2011, http://www.apgarfamily.org/node/28.

28. "A Wireless Detective in Real Life," 872–74; Apgar, "Making the Records from Sayville," 877–78; "Charles Emory Apgar"; Dr. Grant Wythoff, "The Invention of Wireless Cryptography," Brewminate.com, May 25, 2019, https://brewminate.com/the-invention-of-wireless-cryptography/; Wittenberg, "The Thrifty Spy."

29. Apgar, "Making the Records from Sayville," 877–78; Wittenberg, "The Thrifty Spy"; "A Wireless Detective in Real Life," 873.

30. *Counter-Espionage Detail*, 27; Wittenberg, "The Thrifty Spy"; Jones, *The German Spy in America*, 100.

31. Bowen and Neal, *The United States Secret Service*, 85.

32. McAdoo, *Crowded Years*, 324–25; *Counter-Espionage Detail*, 13.

33. McAdoo, *Crowded Years*, 325; *Counter-Espionage Detail*, 13.

34. McAdoo, *Crowded Years*, 325–26; *Counter-Espionage Detail*, 14.

35. McAdoo, *Crowded Years*, 326–27; *Counter-Espionage Detail*, 14–15; Bowen and Neal, *The United States Secret Service*, 86–87.

36. McAdoo, *Crowded Years*, 327; *Counter-Espionage Detail*, 15; Bowen and Neal, *The United States Secret Service*, 87–88.

37. McAdoo, *Crowded Years*, 327; *Counter-Espionage Detail*, 15; Bowen and Neal, *The United States Secret Service*, 88; Arthur Nielsen, "1915 Seventy-Five Years Ago," *American Heritage*, July/August 1990, https://www.americanheritage.com/1915-seventy-five-years-ago-2#.

38. Wittenberg, "The Thrifty Spy"; McAdoo, *Crowded Years*, 328; *Counter-Espionage Detail*, 16; Von Feilitzsch, *The Secret War on the United States*, 211–12.

39. Wittenberg, "The Thrifty Spy"; McAdoo, *Crowded Years*, 327.

40. Wittenberg, "The Thrifty Spy"; McAdoo, *Crowded Years*, 328–29; Bowen and Neal, *The United States Secret Service*, 88–89; "Imperial Germany's Sabotage Operations in the U.S."

41. Wittenberg, "The Thrifty Spy"; Von Feilitzsch, *The Secret War on the United States*, 108–13; Bowen and Neal, *The United States Secret Service*, 89; McAdoo, *Crowded Years*, 329; "Imperial Germany's Sabotage Operations in the U.S."

42. *Counter-Espionage Detail*, 10–11; Michael Digby, *Burn, Bomb, Destroy: The German Sabotage Campaign in North America 1914–1917* (Havertown, PA: Casemate Publishers, 2021), 98; Bowen, "U.S. Secret Service," 476–77; Bowen and Neal, *The United States Secret Service*, 89–90; Wittenberg, "The Thrifty Spy." Germany had additional plans for an invasion of the United States as early as 1897. See "The German Plan to Invade America," *American Heritage*, November/December 2002, https://www.americanheritage.com/german-plan-invade-america.

43. "Imperial Germany's Sabotage Operations in the U.S."; Wittenberg, "The Thrifty Spy"; Bowen and Neal, *The United States Secret Service*, 90–91; Nielsen, "1915 Seventy-Five Years Ago."

44. McAdoo, *Crowded Years*, 328; Bowen and Neal, *The United States Secret Service*, 91.

45. "How Germany Has Worked in U.S. to Shape Opinion, Block the Allies and Get Munitions for Herself, Told in Secret Agents' Letters," *World* (NY), August 15, 1915; Wittenberg, "The Thrifty Spy"; Von Feilitzsch, *The Secret War on the United States*, 212–17; "Imperial Germany's Sabotage Operations in the U.S."; "A Case for Prompt Action," *Brooklyn Daily Eagle*, August 16, 1915; "Insult to the American People," *New York Evening Globe* (date not found). After the story appeared in the *World* on August 15, a meeting was held that night in Brooklyn by members of the Kriegerbund, a society of German army veterans living in the United States. Threats were made against the newspaper. One member called for the bombing of the *World*'s headquarters building in Manhattan, while another called for the assassination of Ralph Pulitzer, the paper's publisher, to serve "as a warning to the other newspapers to leave Germany alone." The more conservative members of the group, however, took control of the meeting and prevented further discussion of taking violent action against the newspaper. See "Miscellaneous Reports, Sunday, August 15, 1915," National Civic Federation records, Box 454, Reel 405, Manuscripts and Archives Division, New York Public Library, Astor, Lenox, and Tilden Foundations.

46. Wittenberg, "The Thrifty Spy"; "Imperial Germany's Sabotage Operations in the U.S."; Von Feilitzsch, *The Secret War on the United States*, 13, 223–24.

47. "Spy Squad Plans Fail To Mature," *San Francisco Examiner*, August 18, 1915; "Secret Service Men Have Proof Germans Violate Neutrality," *Austin American* (Austin, TX), August 18, 1915; "Have Proof of Strike Inciting," *Washington Herald*, August 18, 1915.

48. McAdoo, *Crowded Years*, 324–37, 330.

49. Jones, *The German Spy in America*, 55; McAdoo, *Crowded Years*, 330.

50. Von Feilitzsch, *The Secret War on the United States*, 243; Blum, *Dark Invasion*, 231–32, 411–12; Elke Weesjes with Phil Nerges, "100 Years of Terror: The Black Tom Explosion and the Birth of U.S. Intelligence Services," *Natural Hazards Observer* 40, no. 7 (October 31, 2016), https://hazards.colorado.edu /article/100-years-of-terror-the-black-tom-explosion-and-the-birth-of-u-s-in telligence-services-1. German intrigue after the Albert papers were publicized also included attempts to poison horses and mules being shipped to England for use in the war. See Von Feilitzsch, *The Secret War on the United States*, xi, 232–41, and Blum, *Dark Invasion*, 267–72, 384, 403–7, 409–11.

51. Simon, *America's Forgotten Terrorists*, 72; Gage, *The Day Wall Street Exploded*, 108; McAdoo, *Crowded Years*, 367–68; Von Feilitzsch, *The Secret War on the United States*, xxii–xiii; Blum, *Dark Invasion*, 416. A bomb went off at one of these Preparedness Day parades in San Francisco on July 22, 1916, killing ten people and injuring forty others. German agents were not considered suspects. Instead, two labor leaders were framed for the bombing. The perpetrators were never discovered. See Simon, *America's Forgotten Terrorists*, 73–76.

52. Blum, *Dark Invasion*, 416–18; Evan Andrews, "The Secret History of the Zimmermann Telegram," History.com, updated November 20, 2018, https://www.history.com/news/the-secret-history-of-the-zimmermann-tele gram#:~:text=No%20one%20in%20the%20United,the%20German%20minis ter%20to%20Mexico; McAdoo, *Crowded Years*, 368; "U.S. Entry into World War I, 1917," Office of the Historian, United States Department of State, https://history.state.gov/milestones/1914-1920/wwi.

53. Charles H. McCormick, *Hopeless Cases: The Hunt for the Red Scare Terrorist Bombers* (Lanham, MD: University Press of America, 2005), 44, 46; J. A. Baker, "In Re Hansen Neutrality Matter," September 9, 1915, RG 65, OG, M1085, Fold3, NARA.

54. John F. Fox Jr., "Bureaucratic Wrangling over Counterintelligence, 1917–18," *Studies in Intelligence* 49, no. 1 (March 2005): 13–16.

55. Fox, "Bureaucratic Wrangling over Counterintelligence," 14; McCormick, *Hopeless Cases*, 44; "Berlin Backed Sabotage Here, Lansing Shows," *New York Times*, October 11, 1917; Mike Dash, *The First Family: Terror, Extortion,*

Revenge, Murder, and the Birth of the American Mafia (New York: Random House, 2009), 349–50. The 1917 Espionage Act gave the Justice Department the authority to prosecute individuals suspected of violations related to espionage, subversion, and other matters. See Fox, "Bureaucratic Wrangling over Counterintelligence," 14.

56. "Chief Flynn Quits Secret Service; May Head Police," *New York Times*, December 23, 1917; "Hands Tied in Spy Service, Flynn Asserted; Quit after Vain Plea for Co-operation," *New York Times*, January 4, 1918; "W. J. Flynn to Secretary of the Treasury," November 30, 1917, U.S. Secret Service files. It is possible that Flynn was forced out of the Secret Service due to the Hale episode and the Bielaski report. See Dash, *The First Family*, 350, and McCormick, *Hopeless Cases*, 44. Flynn, however, was a favorite of Treasury Secretary McAdoo, so it is unlikely that McAdoo pressured Flynn into retirement. Fox presents the interesting theory that Flynn resigned in order to bring attention to the problems in the U.S. intelligence effort and the need for a coordinated intelligence agency headed by the Secret Service. See Fox, "Bureaucratic Wrangling over Counterintelligence," 15.

57. John W. Harrington, "United Secret Service Needed, Asserts Flynn, Star Sleuth," *Sun* (NY), January 13, 1918. There were reports that after Flynn resigned from the Secret Service, he had talks with the newly elected mayor of New York, John Hylan, about becoming commissioner of the NYPD. Nothing, however, materialized from those talks. See McCormick, *Hopeless Cases*, 45, and "Chief Flynn Quits Secret Service."

58. Harrington, "United Secret Service Needed." It is not clear what the "obvious reasons" were for Flynn keeping it secret that it was Frank Burke who stole the briefcase. One possibility is that not doing so would have exposed Burke to retaliation by German agents in the United States or even possible legal action for committing a crime (theft). But it is unlikely that a Secret Service hero would have been prosecuted in U.S. courts.

59. Simon, *America's Forgotten Terrorists*, 129–30; "Flynn, Here, Bares Workings of Vast German Spy System in United States," *Los Angeles Times*, April 7, 1918. Flynn was president of an organization formed after the war named "Real Men of America." It consisted of prominent individuals from New York who had done patriotic and effective service for the country during World War I and afterward. It was a secretive organization that held no public meetings. The group discussed among themselves the current state of affairs in the nation and what each of them could contribute to uncovering plots or any type of activity harmful to the United States. When a reporter asked one of the members about

the meaning of the group's name, the member replied, "We're all regular fellows, good Americans, real men. Why not call [our group] the 'Real Men of America'?" See "14 Real Men of America Have a Mystery Dinner," *New York Herald*, January 31, 1920, and William Flynn Sanders, e-mail message to author, June 10, 2021, October 13, 2022, and October 14, 2022.

60. "King Baggot Joins Whartons," *Moving Picture World*, December 1, 1917, 1304; Barbara Tepa Lupack, *Silent Serial Sensations: The Wharton Brothers and the Magic of Early Cinema* (Ithaca, NY: Cornell University Press, 2020), 208; "King Baggot, 68, Early Film Star," *New York Times*, July 13, 1948.

61. Lupack, *Silent Serial Sensations*, 208–11, 218; William J. Flynn, *The Eagle's Eye: A True Story of the Imperial German Government's Spies and Intrigues in America from Facts Furnished by William J. Flynn, Recently Retired, Chief of the U.S. Secret Service, Novelized by Courtney Ryley Cooper* (New York: The McCann Company, 1919).

62. Lupack, *Silent Serial Sensations*, 12–13, 209–10, 214; William J. Hilliar, "Films Reviewed: The Eagle's Eye," *Billboard*, January 26, 1918, 66.

63. Lupack, *Silent Serial Sensations*, 214–17.

64. Lupack, *Silent Serial Sensations*, 218, 223; Olivia B. Waxman, "People Longing for Movie Theaters during the 1918 Flu Pandemic Feels Very Familiar in 2021," *Time*, March 4, 2021, https://time.com/5940086/1918-pandemic-covid-19-movie-theaters-history/; "At the Grand Today and Tomorrow," *Times Recorder* (Zanesville, OH), November 6, 1918; "The Rex Monday," *St. Petersburg Daily Times* (St. Petersburg, FL), December 1, 1918; Ashley Halsey III, "The Flu Can Kill Tens of Millions of People. In 1918, That's Exactly What It Did," *Washington Post*, January 27, 2018, https://www.washingtonpost.com/news/retropolis/wp/2018/01/27/the-flu-can-kill-tens-of-millions-of-people-in-1918-thats-exactly-what-it-did/; "Wharton Studio History: Ithaca and the Silver Screen," Wharton Studio Museum, https://whartonstudiomuseum.org/wharton-studio-history/.

65. "Foiled Spies Plan Against U.S.—Special Agent Flynn Traces German Plots," *San Francisco Examiner*, April 30, 1918; William J. Flynn, "The Eagle's Eye," *State Journal* (Lansing, MI), May 4, 1918; William J. Flynn, "The Eagle's Eye," *El Paso Morning Times*, May 5, 1918; William J. Flynn, "The Eagle's Eye," *Atlanta Constitution*, September 1, 1918; Brent Sidney Roberts, "'Steady Hammer': Origins of American Counterterrorism in the Dime Novel World of William J. Flynn" (PhD diss., Montana State University, 2020), 298–99; "WM. J. Flynn Gets a Job," *Muncie Morning Star*, September 9, 1918; "Flynn Made Chief Railroad Detective," *Sun* (NY), September 15, 1918; Frederic J. Haskin, "A New National

Police Force," *Muncie Sunday Star*, May 4, 1919; A. Cloyd Gill, "U.S. Railroad Police Head Has World's Longest Beat," *Washington Times*, May 18, 1919.

66. Haskin, "A New National Police Force"; Gill, "U.S. Railroad Police Head."

CHAPTER 5: THE RED SCARE

1. "Clear and Present Danger: A. Mitchell Palmer Goes Hunting for Bolsheviks," *Lapham's Quarterly*, Spring 2014, https://www.laphamsquarterly.org/revolutions/clear-and-present-danger. Flynn was the first head of the BI to use the title "director."

2. "Bruce Bielaski, Justice Aide, Dies," *New York Times*, February 20, 1964; Brent Sidney Roberts, "'Steady Hammer': Origins of American Counterterrorism in the Dime Novel World of William J. Flynn" (PhD diss., Montana State University, 2020), 315; "Clews to 'Red' Who Dynamited Palmer House Are Discovered; Wide War Begun on Radicals," *Washington Post*, June 4, 1919; "Flynn to Direct Search for Reds," *New York Times*, June 4, 1919.

3. The discussion of the Galleanists is drawn from Jeffrey D. Simon, *America's Forgotten Terrorists: The Rise and Fall of the Galleanists* (Lincoln, NE: Potomac Books, 2022), 9–128. The followers of Galleani have also been referred to by some scholars and others as "Galleanisti."

4. "Department of Justice's Dragnet for 'Reds,' Rapidly Spread in Determined War on Anarchy," *Evening Star* (Washington, D.C.), June 4, 1919; "U.S. Is Organizing Greatest Force of Detectives," *Pasadena Post* (Pasadena, CA), September 25, 1919; "Make A Clean Job of It," *Olean Evening Times* (Olean, NY), June 5, 1919.

5. "Bomb Plotters Sought on Ships by N.Y. Officials," *Evening World* (NY), June 6, 1919; "Department of Justice's Dragnet for 'Reds'"; "Flynn Drafts Many Secret Service and Other Aids [*sic*] in Man Hunt," *Sun* (NY), June 5, 1919. BI agents were also placed in round-the-clock surveillance of Palmer's summer home in Stroudsburg, Pennsylvania. The presence of the attorney general there worried the townspeople. "The entire town of Stroudsburg has been in a ferment of fear and apprehension lest Bolshevists or I.W.W.'s attempt an attack," an agent reported. "The newspapers of the vicinity carried headlines and editorials on the subject, and the authorities and citizens appealed to the Attorney General asking that the Department of Justice use every effort to avert such a catastrophe." See J. A. Brann, "In Re: Protection of Person and Property of A. Mitchell Palmer; Esq., Attorney General of the U.S.," July 18, 1919, RG 65, OG, M1085, Fold3, NARA.

6. Roberts, "'Steady Hammer,'" 334–35; Beverly Gage, *The Day Wall Street Exploded: A Story of America in Its First Age of Terror* (New York: Oxford Uni-

versity Press, 2009), 127. The reorganization plan called for dividing the country into sixty-five districts, with agents assigned permanently to each one. In those districts, "working in cooperation with them will be operatives who have a roving commission. The necessity of any one investigation will be met by a shifting and concentration of operatives sufficient to meet the requirements of the case in hand. The network of operatives from coast to coast will be greatly enlarged and strengthened under the reorganization program." Flynn also brought new blood into the BI. Of these, "many among the new operatives are young men who have shown great promise in their previous work. Women operatives are also included in the reorganization." See "U.S. Is Organizing Greatest Force of Detectives."

7. "Flynn on Trail of Local Reds in Bomb Plots," *Brooklyn Daily Times*, June 8, 1919.

8. Paul Avrich, *Sacco and Vanzetti: The Anarchist Background* (Princeton, NJ: Princeton University Press, 1991), 81, 149. Avrich points out that both in style and in content, the flyers were similar to the *Go-Head!* flyers distributed in Massachusetts earlier in the year. Even the name used to sign the leaflets, "The Anarchist Fighters," recalled the name used to sign the *Go-Head!* flyers ("The American Anarchists").

9. Simon, *America's Forgotten Terrorists*, 131; Avrich, *Sacco and Vanzetti*, 155. Almost a year later, the New Jersey branch of the BI compared the style of writing in the flyer with letters that Luigi Galleani had written in the past and found enough similarities to conclude that Galleani was the author of *Plain Words*. See Simon, *America's Forgotten Terrorists*, 223n26.

10. Avrich, *Sacco and Vanzetti*, 154–56, 171–73; Simon, *America's Forgotten Terrorists*, 133, 135–36.

11. "Summary Report in Re Bomb Explosions of June 2, 1919, Massachusetts Investigation," May 13, 1920, File Number 211205-x, BI, FOIA; J. F. McDevitt, "Re: Bomb Explosions—June 2nd—Pro Prensa Society—Genaro Pazos— E. Paredes: Lugio [*sic*] Galleni [*sic*]," October 3, 1919, Case Number 360086, RG 65, BS, M1085, Fold3, NARA; "Summary Report in Re Bomb Explosions of June 2, 1919. New Jersey Investigation," May 25, 1920, File Number 211205-x, BI, FOIA; Simon, *America's Forgotten Terrorists*, 133, 135. The Boston office indicated in a May 13, 1920, summary (see the first citation entry in this note) that it wrote to the New York office on June 19, 1919, that Galleani had to know about the bombings.

12. Avrich, *Sacco and Vanzetti*, 167; Charles H. McCormick, *Hopeless Cases: The Hunt for the Red Scare Terrorist Bombers* (Lanham, MD: University Press of America, 2005), 43; Gage, *The Day Wall Street Exploded*, 128; Lona Manning,

"9/16: Terrorists Bomb Wall Street," Sam Houston State University, Fall 2012, https://www.shsu.edu/his_rtc/2012_Fall/1302_Wall_St_Bombing.pdf. For an excellent biography of Hoover, see Beverly Gage, *G-Man: J. Edgar Hoover and the Making of the American Century* (New York: Viking, 2022).

13. Avrich, *Sacco and Vanzetti*, 167–68; Gage, *G-Man*, 61–62.

14. Adam Hochschild, *American Midnight: The Great War, a Violent Peace, and Democracy's Forgotten Crisis* (New York: Mariner Books, 2022), 280; Tim Weiner, *Enemies: A History of the FBI* (New York: Random House, 2012), 29–32, 34; Gage, *The Day Wall Street Exploded*, 120; Gage, *G-Man*, 79–80; Avrich, *Sacco and Vanzetti*, 168, 174–75; Simon, *America's Forgotten Terrorists*, 142; "Arrests Are Made Here in Round-Up for Red Plotting," *Evening Star* (Washington, D.C.), November 8, 1919; Regin Schmidt, *Red Scare: FBI and the Origins of Anticommunism in the United States, 1919–1943* (Copenhagen: Museum Tusculanum Press, 2000), 275–76; Ann Hagedorn, *Savage Peace: Hope and Fear in America, 1919* (New York: Simon & Schuster, 2007), 413–14.

15. Paul Avrich and Karen Avrich, *Sasha and Emma: The Anarchist Odyssey of Alexander Berkman and Emma Goldman* (Cambridge, MA: Belknap Press of Harvard University Press, 2012), 1–4; Weiner, *Enemies*, 24.

16. Weiner, *Enemies*, 31–32; "249 Reds Sail for Russia on Anarchist Ark," *Washington Times*, December 21, 1919; Hagedorn, *Savage Peace*, 413.

17. Weiner, *Enemies*, 34–35; Robert K. Murray, *Red Scare: A Study in National Hysteria, 1919–1920* (Minneapolis: University of Minnesota Press, 1955), 213; Simon, *America's Forgotten Terrorists*, 145–46.

18. Murray, *Red Scare*, 219; Avrich, *Sacco and Vanzetti*, 176; Simon, *America's Forgotten Terrorists*, 146–47. Post later wrote a scathing account of the Palmer Raids. See Louis F. Post, *The Deportations Delirium of Nineteen-Twenty: A Personal Narrative of an Historic Official Experience* (Chicago: Charles H. Kerr & Company, 1923). For a superb discussion of Post and his role in the deportation cases, see Hochschild, *American Midnight*, 305–10, 317–18, 323–25.

19. "Red Backbone Broken by Raid Says Official," *Los Angeles Evening Express*, January 3, 1920; Simon, *America's Forgotten Terrorists*, 132–33, 136–37, 146; Avrich, *Sacco and Vanzetti*, 180–81, 197; Gage, *The Day Wall Street Exploded*, 213.

20. Avrich, *Sacco and Vanzetti*, 181–83.

21. Gage, *The Day Wall Street Exploded*, 213–14; Simon, *America's Forgotten Terrorists*, 133.

22. McCormick, *Hopeless Cases*, 58–59; Avrich, *Sacco and Vanzetti*, 184–85.

23. Avrich, *Sacco and Vanzetti*, 184–85; McCormick, *Hopeless Cases*, 57–58; *Hearings before the [House] Committee on Rules*, 66th Cong., 2nd Sess., pt. 1, 162 ("Attorney General A. Mitchell Palmer on Charges Made against Department of Justice by Louis F. Post and Others," June 1, 1920).

24. *Hearings before the [House] Committee on Rules*, 162; McCormick, *Hopeless Cases*, 59; Avrich, *Sacco and Vanzetti*, 191–92.

25. Avrich, *Sacco and Vanzetti*, 192; McCormick, *Hopeless Cases*, 59.

26. Avrich, *Sacco and Vanzetti*, 192.

27. Avrich, *Sacco and Vanzetti*, 193.

28. Gage, *The Day Wall Street Exploded*, 214; Avrich, *Sacco and Vanzetti*, 193. Salsedo's widow, Maria, brought a suit for $100,000 against Palmer, Flynn, and BI agents, charging them with causing her husband's death. She lost the suit, and the U.S. Circuit Court of Appeals affirmed the decision. The court ruled that Salsedo's suicide was "not a result naturally and reasonably to be expected from the acts of misconduct alleged to have been committed by the defendants." See Avrich, *Sacco and Vanzetti*, 194, and "Nobody Held Liable for Causing Suicide," *New York Herald*, February 19, 1922.

29. W. Ralph Palmera, "Report of Special Agent W. Ralph Palmera, In Re: 'A Stormo' (The Alarm) Andrea Salsedo," August 13, 1920, RG 65, BS, M1085, Fold3, NARA; Simon, *America's Forgotten Terrorists*, 191. Agent Palmera of the BI wrote that "a stormo" means "the alarm," but other translations have it as "to the flock."

30. "Red's Death Plunge, 14 Stories, Bares Long Bomb Trial," *New York Times*, May 4, 1920.

31. *Hearings before the [House] Committee on Rules*, 163. Shortly after Salsedo's suicide, Elia was brought to Ellis Island for deportation hearings and then deported to Italy in August. According to McCormick, Elia's "continued presence was a public relations liability [for the Justice Department]. The sooner he was gone [it was reasoned] the sooner Salsedo's death could be forgotten. Deporting him would at least rid the country of a dangerous Galleanist and keep him away from inquiring reporters." See McCormick, *Hopeless Cases*, 64.

32. *Hearings before the [House] Committee on Rules*, 163; Gage, *The Day Wall Street Exploded*, 214.

33. Hochschild, *American Midnight*, 313–14, 321–23, 327–28; Simon, *America's Forgotten Terrorists*, 148–49; McCormick, *Hopeless Cases*, 64. Extraordinary security measures were put in place everywhere in anticipation of May Day riots. In Boston, the police set up seven machine guns manned by military veterans in

various parts of the city, with some of the guns mounted on automobiles. In New York, the eleven-thousand-man police force was kept on duty, and guards were positioned at railway stations, bridges, and the homes of prominent individuals. See "Reds' May Day Plot Failure, Federal View," *Pittsburgh Gazette Times*, May 1, 1920, and "Gotham Swarming with Dept. of Justice Agents," *Lewiston Saturday Journal* (Lewiston, ME), May 1, 1920.

34. Allan L. Damon, "The Great Red Scare," *American Heritage*, February 1968, https://www.americanheritage.com/great-red-scare; Simon, *America's Forgotten Terrorists*, 150; "Palmer Plans to Keep Post," *Washington Herald*, July 31, 1920; "Veteran U.S. Sleuth Resigns Post to Take Shipping Board Berth," *Washington Times*, July 30, 1920.

35. Gage, *G-Man*, 88; "Summary of 'The FBI in Our Open Society,' a Book by Harry and Bonaro Overstreet," GovernmentAttic.org, July 3, 2008, https://www.governmentattic.org/docs/FBI_In_Our_Open_Society_1953.pdf, 3.

36. Damon, "The Great Red Scare."

37. "'Confession' and Lost City at the Orpheum," *Yonkers Herald* (Yonkers, NY), August 26, 1920; "Coming To-Morrow—Tuesday," *Oneonta Daily Star* (Oneonta, NY), August 2, 1920; William J. Flynn, "The Barrel Mystery," *Buffalo Sunday Times*, July 25, 1920.

38. David C. Rapoport, *Waves of Global Terrorism: From 1879 to the Present* (New York: Columbia University Press, 2022), 103.

CHAPTER 6: LAST HURRAH

1. "Memorandum in Re: Explosion at J. P. Morgan's Office" (reported by Agent Scully, New York office, 7:15 p.m.), September 16, 1920, File Number 61-5, BI, FOIA.

2. "Graphic Story by Girl of Terrors of Explosion and the Scenes of Death," *Evening World* (NY), September 16, 1920.

3. "Graphic Story by Girl."

4. "Graphic Story by Girl"; Jeffrey D. Simon, *America's Forgotten Terrorists: The Rise and Fall of the Galleanists* (Lincoln, NE: Potomac Books, 2022), 162; Beverly Gage, *The Day Wall Street Exploded: A Story of America in Its First Age of Terror* (New York: Oxford University Press, 2009), 1.

5. "Women and Girls Do Heroic Work among Injured," *News* (NY), September 17, 1920; Simon, *America's Forgotten Terrorists*, 162–63. One of the nearby hospitals placed an advertisement the next day in all the major New York

newspapers, pleading with the business community to contribute funds so they could improve their facilities to handle the next emergency:

It Happened
And We Couldn't Handle All of the Injured
It Can Happen Again
Help Us So We Can Help You!

Yesterday a catastrophe struck home—you know the story—the dead and the wounded lying helpless on the street waiting, begging for help that had to be summoned from all over the city—some even dying on their way in cabs, trucks and ambulances to distant hospitals.

All because WE couldn't even crowd them all under one roof. All because, through want of funds, through want of thought by business men, the most populous and congested "Wall Street" district has not had adequate hospital protection.

What has happened, can happen again. We are appealing NOW to the business and financial interests of the "Wall Street" district to help us make our equipment adequate to protect THEM and THEIR employees and to succor them in moment of need.

Give and give liberally. It is for your own protection, for your own benefit.

Whether your limit is $1.00 or $10,000, open your purse and send contributions to THE BROAD STREET HOSPITAL.

See Advertisement, *New York Times*, September 17, 1920; Advertisement, *Sun and New York Herald*, September 17, 1920; and Advertisement, *New York Tribune*, September 17, 1920. The *New-York Tribune* dropped the hyphen from its name beginning with the April 16, 1914, issue.

6. "Quick Response by Organized and Volunteer Workers in Relief Work," *New York Times*, September 17, 1920.

7. Lona Manning, "9/16: Terrorists Bomb Wall Street," Sam Houston State University, Fall 2012, https://www.shsu.edu/his_rtc/2012_Fall/1302_Wall_St_Bombing.pdf; "Hospitals Rush Aid to Victims," *New York Times*, September 17, 1920; "Another Bomb Victim," *Los Angeles Times*, September 27, 1920; "Amelia Newton 'Minnie' Huger," Find a Grave, https://www.findagrave.com/memorial/146599761/amelia-newton-huger; "34 Dead in Blast, 16 from BKLYN-L.I., 53 in Hospitals," *Brooklyn Daily Eagle*, September 18, 1920.

8. Simon, *America's Forgotten Terrorists*, 161–62.

9. "Explosion Killed 17-Year-Old Boy on His Birthday," *Evening World* (NY), September 17, 1920; Gage, *The Day Wall Street Exploded*, 146.

10. "Quick Response"; "Crowds Jam Streets of Financial District in Wild Effort to Reach Scene of Explosion," *News* (NY), September 17, 1920; "Greatest Store of Gold in One Place in World Near Explosion Scene," *St. Louis Post-Dispatch*, September 17, 1920; "Soldiers Withdrawn," *Buffalo Courier*, September 17, 1920; "U.S. Troops on Scene within Forty Minutes," *New York Tribune*, September 17, 1920; RG 87, DRA, New York, vol. 70, September 16, 1920; Gage, *The Day Wall Street Exploded*, 19–20, 132, 168. It wasn't just the crowds possibly breaking into the buildings that the Treasury Department was worried about. When William Moran, chief of the Secret Service, learned about the explosion, he directed his New York office to immediately send agents to the scene and begin an investigation on the theory that the Sub-Treasury Building and the Assay Office might have been targets if the explosion was caused by a bomb. See RG 87, DRA, New York, vol. 70, September 16, 1920.

11. "Quick Response"; Gage, *The Day Wall Street Exploded*, 150–51; Charles H. McCormick, *Hopeless Cases: The Hunt for the Red Scare Terrorist Bombers* (Lanham, MD: University Press of America, 2005), 69–70; Simon, *America's Forgotten Terrorists*, 166–67; "It's Business As Usual Today in Wall Street," *Buffalo Evening Times*, September 17, 1920.

12. Simon, *America's Forgotten Terrorists*, 166–67; Bernard Whalen and Jon Whalen, *The NYPD's First Fifty Years: Politicians, Police Commissioners, & Patrolmen* (Lincoln, NE: Potomac Books, 2014), 113; "Wall Street Bombing 1920," FBI, https://www.fbi.gov/history/famous-cases/wall-street-bombing-1920.

13. "Nation-Wide Plot Feared at Capital," *New York Tribune*, September 17, 1920; "Flynn Checks Up on All Radicals in Federal Probe," *News* (NY), September 17, 1920; "Bomb Plot, Not an Accident, Say Officials," *Sun and New York Herald*, September 17, 1920; Gage, *The Day Wall Street Exploded*, 125, 133.

14. Gage, *The Day Wall Street Exploded*, 141–42.

15. Simon, *America's Forgotten Terrorists*, 164–65.

16. Gage, *The Day Wall Street Exploded*, 138; McCormick, *Hopeless Cases*, 125.

17. Gage, *The Day Wall Street Exploded*, 138; McCormick, *Hopeless Cases*, 125; Howard Blum, "American Dynamite," *Vanity Fair*, September 1, 2008, https://www.vanityfair.com/culture/2008/09/blum-excerpt200809; William R. Hunt, *America's Sherlock Holmes: The Legacy of William Burns* (Guilford, CT: Lyons Press, 2019), 1–4. Hunt's book was originally published in 1990 with a differ-

ent title. See *Front-Page Detective: William J. Burns and The Detective Profession, 1880–1930* (Bowling Green, OH: Bowling Green State University Press, 1990).

18. Hunt, *America's Sherlock Holmes*, 4–5, 13, 27, 28–67; "W. J. Burns Dead; Famous Detective," *New York Times*, April 15, 1932; McCormick, *Hopeless Cases*, 125; Gage, *The Day Wall Street Exploded*, 138.

19. Gage, *The Day Wall Street Exploded*, 137, 138–39; Hunt, *America's Sherlock Holmes*, 69–70, 119; "W. J. Burns Dead."

20. Hunt, *America's Sherlock Holmes*, 68.

21. Geoffrey Cowan, *The People v. Clarence Darrow: The Bribery Trial of America's Greatest Lawyer* (New York: Times Books/Random House, 1993), 87; Jeffrey D. Simon, *The Terrorist Trap: America's Experience with Terrorism* (Bloomington: Indiana University Press, 1994), 40–41; Gage, *The Day Wall Street Exploded*, 88–89; Howard Blum, *American Lightning: Terror, Mystery, the Birth of Hollywood, and the Crime of the Century* (New York: Crown Publishers, 2008), 87.

22. Hunt, *America's Sherlock Holmes*, 75–80; Simon, *The Terrorist Trap*, 40–41; Gage, *The Day Wall Street Exploded*, 89.

23. Simon, *The Terrorist Trap*, 41; Hunt, *America's Sherlock Holmes*, 84; Gage, *The Day Wall Street Exploded*, 89, 137.

24. Hunt, *America's Sherlock Holmes*, 138–40, 195; "W. J. Burns Dead"; McCormick, *Hopeless Cases*, 127.

25. Gage, *The Day Wall Street Exploded*, 141; Simon, *America's Forgotten Terrorists*, 166; Hunt, *America's Sherlock Holmes*, 195.

26. Simon, *America's Forgotten Terrorists*, 166; "Detective Burns Says Police Have Enough Evidence to Find Bombers in Ten Days," *Washington Times*, September 17, 1920. Burns later summoned reporters to his home to state that he had been approached by a group of ex-servicemen who wanted to hire him to find the perpetrators of the attack, but he said he had not yet decided if he would accept the assignment. See Hunt, *America's Sherlock Holmes*, 195–96, and "Ex-Service Men Organize to Seek Punishment of Reds," *New York Times*, September 18, 1920.

27. "Detective Burns Says Police Have Enough Evidence"; Gage, *The Day Wall Street Exploded*, 148.

28. "Blast Looked for, Flynn Told Friend," *Washington Times*, September 17, 1920; "Telephone Message from Mr. Flynn, 10:25 pm," September 16, 1920, File Number 61-5, BI, FOIA; "City to Pay $10,000 Reward; Grand Jury Starts Inquiry," *Evening World* (NY), September 17, 1920.

29. C. J. Scully, "Memorandum for Director W. J. Flynn, In Re: Wall Street Explosion," October 18, 1920, File Number 61-5, BI, FOIA; Charles A. Sloan, "Long Arm of U.S. Picking Up Bomb Suspects, *Chicago Tribune*, September 19, 1920; "Five Anarchists Sought by Flynn," *New York Times*, September 19, 1920; Paul Avrich, *Sacco and Vanzetti: The Anarchist Background* (Princeton, NJ: Princeton University Press, 1991), 206. A few years later, Flynn wrote that "it was the Galleani Reds who conceived and carried out the Wall street outrage." He even suggested that Galleani had orchestrated the plot from Italy. "I learned from sources too impressive and reliable to be disbelieved that it was Galleani who not only sowed the seed that grew into the attack upon Wall street but he plotted the thing and forwarded his suggestions to America," Flynn also wrote. See Simon, *America's Forgotten Terrorists*, 165, and William J. Flynn, "On the Trail of the Anarchist Band—Chief Flynn," *New York Herald*, March 5, 1922.

30. "Circulars Clue to Plot," *New York Times*, September 18, 1920.

31. Simon, *America's Forgotten Terrorists*, 163–65; Avrich, *Sacco and Vanzetti*, 206; "To Put Down Terrorists," *New York Times*, September 18, 1920; "Flynn Hastens to Scene," *Los Angeles Times*, September 17, 1920; "William J. Flynn Will Run Down Conspirators," *Richmond Times-Dispatch* (Richmond, VA), September 17, 1920; Investigator, "Arrests of Bomb Plotters Near," *Daily News* (NY), September 18, 1920. While news of the bombing and the investigations naturally dominated the media, there were of course other events to report. One newspaper, however, either without realizing it or demonstrating an incredible insensitivity to those who lost loved ones in the blast, used the following headline to report baseball scores on the same page it had stories about the bombing: "New York Weeps as Yankee World Series Chance Fades; Dodgers, Giants Still In." See *Buffalo Courier*, September 19, 1920.

32. "Memorandum in Re: Explosion at J. P. Morgan's Office" (reported by Division Superintendent Lamb, New York office, 10:40 p.m.), September 16, 1920, BI, FOIA; Avrich, *Sacco and Vanzetti*, 205–6; "Death List Now 33, Many Hurt May Die," *Buffalo Evening News*, September 17, 1920; G. O. Holdridge to Hon. William J. Flynn, October 15, 1920, File Number 61-5, BI, FOIA; Simon, *America's Forgotten Terrorists*, 163, 167–68.

33. "Statement of Glover S. Way, 32 Hawthorne Avenue, East Orane [*sic*], N.J. Re Explosion on Wall Street," September 20, 1920, File Number 61-5, BI, FOIA; J. S. Johnson, "Statement of J. J. Dobbyn, Manager Hollister Lynn & Walton, 7 Wall Street, NY City," September 21, 1920, File Number 61-5, BI, FOIA; Gage, *The Day Wall Street Exploded*, 133, 172; "Review and Outlook:

Dynamite for Wall Street," *Wall Street Journal*, September 17, 1920; Simon, *America's Forgotten Terrorists*, 167.

34. "Memorandum of Telephone Information from Mr. Lamb, at New York, to Mr. Neale" (reported by Greene, 4:30 p.m.), September 17, 1920, File Number 61-5-211205-2x, BI, FOIA.

35. Nathan Ward, "The Fire Last Time," *American Heritage*, November/December 2001, https://www.americanheritage.com/fire-last-time; Avrich, *Sacco and Vanzetti*, 206–7; Gage, *The Day Wall Street Exploded*, 225–26, 243; W. J. Flynn to Postmaster, February 25, 1921, File Number 61-5, BI, FOIA; P-137, "In Re: Wall Street Bomb Explosion," December 20, 1920, File Number 211205-375, BI, FOIA; P-137, "In Re: Wall Street Bomb Explosion," December 22, 1920, File Number 211205-379, BI, FOIA; P-137, "In Re: Wall Street Bomb Explosion," January 7, 1921, File Number 211205-421, BI, FOIA; George J. Starr, "In Re: Wall Street Explosion," November 6, 1925, File Number 61-5, BI, FOIA.

36. "Circulars Clue to Plot"; "Dragnet Spread to Bag Radicals," *Indianapolis News*, September 18, 1920; "Detectives Seek Driver of Death Wagon; 35 Slain," *Oklahoma City Times*, September 18, 1920; Gage, *The Day Wall Street Exploded*, 171-72, 215; Avrich, *Sacco and Vanzetti*, 206; Simon, *America's Forgotten Terrorists*, 163.

37. Scully, "Memorandum for Director W. J. Flynn"; Roy S. Hall, "Wall Street Bomb," October 20, 1920, File Number 61-5, BI, FOIA.

38. "Memorandum in Re: Explosion in J. P. Morgan's Office" (reported by Division Superintendent Lamb, New York office, 9:25 p.m.), September 16, 1920, File Number 61-5, BI, FOIA; M. J. Davis, "Summary, Wall Street Explosion of September 16th, in Re: Dupont or Dittmer Wagon Alleged to Be in Vicinity," September 16–20, 1920, File Number 61-5, BI, FOIA; D. C. Devlin, "In Re: Wall Street Explosion—September 16, 1920," September 18, 1920, File Number 61-5, BI, FOIA; Scully, "Memorandum for Director W. J. Flynn"; McCormick, *Hopeless Cases*, 70–71; Gage, *The Day Wall Street Exploded*, 143–44, 147.

39. Scully, "Memorandum for Director W. J. Flynn"; "Quantity of Blasting Gelatin January 1st to Date," September 30, 1920, File Number 61-5, BI, FOIA; H. W. Hess, "Wall Street Explosion. New York City," November 26, 1920, File Number 61-5, BI, FOIA; W. B. Poole, "Explosion, Wall Street, NYC., Sept. 16, 1920," File Number 211205-374, BI, FOIA; McCormick, *Hopeless Cases*, 83–85.

40. Scully, "Memorandum for Director W. J. Flynn."

41. "Enright Satisfied with Police Work on Bomb Mystery," *Brooklyn Daily Eagle*, September 27, 1920.

42. Simon, *America's Forgotten Terrorists*, 169; McCormick, *Hopeless Cases*, 77–79.

43. Simon, *America's Forgotten Terrorists*, 169–70; R. B. Spencer, "Wall Street Explosion—New York City" (summary report), October 5, 1921, File Number 61-5, BI, FOIA; McCormick, *Hopeless Cases*, 77–79.

44. Simon, *America's Forgotten Terrorists*, 168–69; Gage, *The Day Wall Street Exploded*, 175–77; McCormick, *Hopeless Cases*, 77; "Memorandum in Re: Explosion at J. P. Morgan's Office" (reported by Agent Scully, New York office, 7:15 p.m.); "Memorandum of Telephone Information from Mr. Lamb."

45. G. J. Cystal, "In Re Bomb Explosion," September 16, 1920, File Number 61-5, BI, FOIA; J. F. McAuley, "Bomb Explosion New York City Sept. 16, 1920," September 20, 1920, File Number 61-5, BI, FOIA; Harold L. Scott, "Bomb Explosion, New York City," September 20, 1920, File Number 61-5, BI, FOIA.

46. Elbert E. Leib to Wm. J. Flynn, September 18, 1920, File Number 61-5, BI, FOIA; "Circulars Put into Mail Box before Blast," *Indianapolis Star*, September 18, 1920; Director to Elbert E. Leib, Esq., September 22, 1920, File Number 61-5, BI, FOIA.

47. Hunt, *America's Sherlock Holmes*, 196–97.

48. William P. Hazen to Hon. William J. Flynn, October 18, 1920, File Number 61-5, BI, FOIA.

49. Simon, *America's Forgotten Terrorists*, 192; Gage, *The Day Wall Street Exploded*, 226.

50. Gage, *The Day Wall Street Exploded*, 226–28; McCormick, *Hopeless Cases*, 108–9; Simon, *America's Forgotten Terrorists*, 192–93.

51. Gage, *The Day Wall Street Exploded*, 228; McCormick, *Hopeless Cases*, 108–9; Hunt, *America's Sherlock Holmes*, 199; Simon, *America's Forgotten Terrorists*, 191–93. Galleani, for unknown reasons, decided to turn himself in at the prison in Turin in October 1922. It is not known where he was while he was on the run from the authorities. See Antonio Senta, *Luigi Galleani: The Most Dangerous Anarchist in America*, trans. Andrea Asali with Sean Sayers (Chico, CA: AK Press, 2019), 197–99, and Simon, *America's Forgotten Terrorists*, 193.

52. Gage, *The Day Wall Street Exploded*, 228–29; McCormick, *Hopeless Cases*, 109; Hunt, *America's Sherlock Holmes*, 199, 209, 204.

53. "Flynn to Keep Post," *New York Times*, March 2, 1921; "Harding Agreed on Burns as Secret Service Head," *Sun* (Baltimore), March 12, 1921.

54. W. J. Flynn to Honorable H. M. Daugherty, April 4, 1921, File Number 61-5-437, BI, FOIA; W. J. Flynn to Postmaster; Gage, *The Day Wall Street Exploded*, 242–43; "U.S. Is on Trail of Man Who Caused Wall St. Tragedy,"

New York Herald, March 31, 1921. In his letter to Daugherty, Flynn, without mentioning DeGrazio, said the photos were the result "of an examination of several hundred photographs of anarchists, from which two were selected by the only witness we have who can identify the driver." In the circular to the police chiefs and postmaster, Flynn wrote that the "composite photograph of the driver of the horse and wagon [was] . . . identified by the Blacksmith who shod the horse on the day previous to the explosion, and it is also identified by another man." Flynn did not state who that other man was. See W. J. Flynn to Honorable H. M. Daugherty and also W. J. Flynn to Postmaster. The *Herald* did not publish the composite photograph of the suspect. Other newspapers, however, did. See "Bomb 'Composite' Brings Arrest," *New Castle Herald* (New Castle, PA), June 2, 1921, and "'Composite' Brings Bomb Arrest," *Pittston Gazette* (Pittston, PA), May 25, 1921.

55. W. J. Flynn to Honorable H. M. Daugherty; Gage, *The Day Wall Street Exploded*, 244–46; McCormick, *Hopeless Cases*, 111–12.

56. "Memorandum from Director W. J. Flynn, by telephone from New York, N.Y." (2 p.m.), April 22, 1921, File Number 61-5, BI, FOIA; Gage, *The Day Wall Street Exploded*, 246, 249–50; McCormick, *Hopeless Cases*, 112.

57. McCormick, *Hopeless Cases*, 112–13; Gage, *The Day Wall Street Exploded*, 246, 250–51; "Identification of Bomb Suspect Is Weak, Says Flynn," *New York Tribune*, April 28, 1921.

58. "Bayonne, N. J. Suspect Seen in Wall St.," *Buffalo Commercial*, May 19, 1921; McCormick, *Hopeless Cases*, 109, 117–18; Gage, *The Day Wall Street Exploded*, 251–52. There have been many different spellings of De Filippis's name in newspapers and other accounts of his story. These include "De Filippo," "De Fillipos," "De Fillippis," and "Di Filipos." The name is also similar to that of a Galleanist, Salvatore De Filippis, which might have added to the belief that he was involved with the Wall Street bombing.

59. Richard J. Butler and Joseph Driscoll, *Dock Walloper: The Story of "Big Dick" Butler* (New York: G. P. Putnam's Sons, 1933), 133–34, https://archive.org /stream/dockwalloperstor00butlrich/dockwalloperstor00butlrich_djvu.txt; "W. J. Burns Chosen Chief U.S. Sleuth," *Evening Star* (Washington, D.C.), August 18, 1921; Gage, *The Day Wall Street Exploded*, 261.

60. "Flynn Booted Out," *Every Evening* (Wilmington, DE), August 20, 1921; "W. J. Burns Drops Eight of Flynn's Appointees," *Standard Union* (Brooklyn, NY), August 30, 1921. Another newspaper editorial stated that "Mr. Flynn should not be lost to the service. It would be harmful to the personnel of the department to reward such a man with dismissal. There is always a big place for a

big man and such a place should be found for William J. Flynn." The newspaper also wished Flynn and Burns could get along and work together: "Both [Flynn and Burns] have merits that co-operatively would make of them a remarkable team for the promotion of thoroughness and efficiency." See "Flynn and Burns," *Boston Post*, August 22, 1921.

61. "Naming of Burns May Take Crime Bureau from N.Y.," *Evening World* (NY), August 19, 1921; "Burns Starts Secret Service School Here," *New York Tribune*, September 13, 1921; Gage, *The Day Wall Street Exploded*, 262–63.

62. McCormick, *Hopeless Cases*, 131. One of the early investigations launched by Burns after becoming BI director involved putting Edwin Fischer under surveillance. He was the former tennis star who had warned friends weeks before the Wall Street bombing to stay away from the area on September 15, one day before the explosion. This surveillance went forward despite the fact that Flynn and his agents had quickly dismissed Fischer's predictions as just the lucky guess of an emotionally disturbed individual who had no knowledge of an impending attack. It might have been yet another attempt by Burns to embarrass and discredit Flynn if he could prove some connection between Fischer and the bombing. He was not successful. See Burns to Hanrahan, October 4, 1921, File Number 21105-685, BI, FOIA, and W. J. West, "Bomb Explosion, Wall Street, New York City, September 16, 1920," October 7, 1921, File Number 211205-674, BI, FOIA.

63. "Burns Sees Soviet Hand in Explosion," *Pittsburgh Post*, September 28, 1920; Editors of Encyclopaedia Britannica, "Third International," Britannica, https://www.britannica.com/topic/Third-International.

64. Gage, *The Day Wall Street Exploded*, 268, 281–82; McCormick, *Hopeless Cases*, 132; Dr. Stanislow Gulkowske to Mr. William J. Burns, n.d., File Number 61-5, BI, FOIA.

65. McCormick, *Hopeless Cases*, 132–33; Gage, *The Day Wall Street Exploded*, 283–84; Simon, *America's Forgotten Terrorists*, 172; "Clear Up Mystery of Wall Street Tragedy," *Pittsburg Daily Headlight* (Pittsburg, KS), December 17, 1921.

66. McCormick, *Hopeless Cases*, 133, 138; Gage, *The Day Wall Street Exploded*, 288; Simon, *America's Forgotten Terrorists*, 172.

67. Gage, *The Day Wall Street Exploded*, 321; McCormick, *Hopeless Cases*, 140–41; Simon, *America's Forgotten Terrorists*, 232n48.

68. Simon, *America's Forgotten Terrorists*, 172–73.

69. "Memorandum, L. E. Short to Mr. McGuire, Wall Street Explosion—1920," March 13, 1959, File Number 61-5, BI, FOIA; "Memorandum,

Mr. Tavel to J. W. Marshall, Wall Street Explosion," May 23, 1969, File Number 61-5, BI, FOIA.

70. Simon, *America's Forgotten Terrorists*, 173; Avrich, *Sacco and Vanzetti*, 64, 103, 207.

71. Simon, *America's Forgotten Terrorists*, 174; Edward Houlton James, "The Story of Mario Buda before the Jury of the World" (typescript, February 21, 1928), Sandor Teszler Library Archives and Special Collections, Wofford College, Spartanburg, SC, 4; Avrich, *Sacco and Vanzetti*, 204–7; Gage, *The Day Wall Street Exploded*, 325–26; David C. Rapoport, *Waves of Global Terrorism: From 1879 to the Present* (New York: Columbia University Press, 2022), 103.

72. Avrich, *Sacco and Vanzetti*, 208, 245n32; Paul Avrich, *Anarchist Voices: An Oral History of Anarchism in America* (Oakland, CA: AK Press, 2005), 132–33; Simon, *America's Forgotten Terrorists*, 175; Mike Davis, *Buda's Wagon: A Brief History of the Car Bomb* (London: Verso, 2007), 2; Gage, *The Day Wall Street Exploded*, 325–26; Kenyon Zimmer, *Immigrants against the State: Yiddish and Italian Anarchism in America* (Urbana: University of Illinois Press, 2015), 152; Bruce Watson, *Sacco and Vanzetti: The Men, the Murders, and the Judgment of Mankind* (New York: Viking, 2007), 77; Bruce Watson, "Prime Suspect," *New York Times*, March 18, 2009; Nunzio Pernicone, "Luigi Galleani and Italian Anarchist Terrorism in the United States," *Studi Emigrazione/Etudes Migrations* 30, no. 111 (1993): 469–70; Jeffrey D. Simon, "The Forgotten Terrorists: Lessons from the History of Terrorism," *Terrorism and Political Violence* 20, no. 2 (April–June 2008): 206–8.

73. "Life's Detective Yarns Are Dull, Says William J. Flynn," *Rutland Daily Herald* (Rutland, VT), May 26, 1922.

CHAPTER 7: LONGING FOR THE OLD DAYS

1. Beverly Gage, *The Day Wall Street Exploded: A Story of America in Its First Age of Terror* (New York: Oxford University Press, 2009), 321–22; "Flynn Organizes a Detective Bureau," *Yonkers Herald* (Yonkers, NY), October 3, 1921; "W. J. Flynn Organizes a Detective Agency," *New York Herald*, October 3, 1921; Charles H. McCormick, *Hopeless Cases: The Hunt for the Red Scare Terrorist Bombers* (Lanham, MD: University Press of America, 2005), 118; Regin Schmidt, *Red Scare: FBI and the Origins of Anticommunism in the United States, 1919–1943* (Copenhagen: Museum Tusculanum Press, 2000), 53.

2. Emily W. Leider, *Dark Lover: The Life and Death of Rudolph Valentino* (New York: Farrar, Straus and Giroux, 2003), 206–7, 226–27; Hadley Hall

Meares, "Unlucky Star: The Brief, Bombastic Life of Rudolph Valentino," *Vanity Fair*, September 14, 2021, https://www.vanityfair.com/hollywood/2021/09/rudolph-valentino-biography-death.

3. Famous Players-Lasky Corporation, Plaintiff-Respondent, against Rodolph Valentino, Defendant-Appellant, Appeal from Order, I (Supr. Ct., App. Div., 1st Dpt. Dec. 1, 1922), 348–53; Leider, *Dark Lover*, 224–25. Valentino was known by several different first names, including "Rodolph," "Rodolfo," "Rudy," and "Rudolph." The latter name was the more popular one.

4. G. P. T. Ryall, "New York Turf Writer Tells of Trip Aboard Train of Equine King," *Courier-Journal* (Louisville, KY), May 8, 1922; Tom Hall, "Morvich Became First Cal-Bred to Win Kentucky Derby," *BloodHorse*, September 1, 2021, https://www.bloodhorse.com/horse-racing/articles/252881/morvich-became-first-cal-bred-to-win-kentucky-derby; "Morvich Reaches Louisville Safely," *New York Times*, May 8, 1922.

5. "Arrests Reveal $100,000 Bond Robbery Clew," *New York Tribune*, December 23, 1922; "Porters Obtain $100,000," *Cincinnati Enquirer*, December 24, 1922.

6. William J. Flynn, "'My Ten Biggest Man-Hunts'—Told by Chief W. J. Flynn," *New York Herald*, January 22, 1922; McCormick, *Hopeless Cases*, 118–19.

7. Flynn, "'My Ten Biggest Man-Hunts.'"

8. William J. Flynn, "'My Ten Biggest Man-hunts'—Told by Chief W. J. Flynn, Story II," *New York Herald*, January 29, 1922.

9. William J. Flynn, "'My Ten Biggest Man-Hunts'—Told by Chief W. J. Flynn, Case III," *New York Herald*, February 5, 1922; William J. Flynn, "'How We Caught the Gunrunner'—Chief Flynn, Case IV," *New York Herald*, February 12, 1922; William J. Flynn, "On the Trail of the Anarchist Band—Chief Flynn, Case VII," *New York Herald*, March 5, 1922.

10. William J. Flynn, "The Man the Government Couldn't Catch—Chief Flynn, Case X," *New York Herald*, March 26, 1922.

11. Flynn, "The Man the Government Couldn't Catch."

12. Flynn, "The Man the Government Couldn't Catch."

13. Flynn, "The Man the Government Couldn't Catch."

14. Flynn, "The Man the Government Couldn't Catch."

15. Brent Sidney Roberts, "'Steady Hammer': Origins of American Counterterrorism in the Dime Novel World of William J. Flynn" (PhD diss., Montana State University, 2020), 385–95; William J. Flynn and George Barton, "The Adventures of Peabody Smith, IV.—The Persistence of Percival Jayne," *Argosy-Allstory Weekly*, November 18, 1922, 245.

16. William J. Flynn, "My Life in the Secret Service," *Flynn's*, October 4, 1924, 387–402.

17. Flynn, "My Life in the Secret Service," October 4, 1924, 387–88.

18. "Flynn's (Weekly) (Detective) (Fiction) (Magazine)," Galactic Central, http://www.philsp.com/mags/flynns.html; "The Literary Market," *Editor* 67, no. 2 (October 11, 1924): I–II.

19. Agatha Christie, "Traitor Hands," *Flynn's*, January 31, 1925, 273–326; David Morris, "Insights: Agatha Christie's 'Traitor Hands' & Flynn's Weekly," Collecting Christie, September 8, 2021, https://www.collectingchristie.com/post/flynns; Mel Gussow, "Mignon Eberhart, Novelist, 97; Blended Mystery and Romance," *New York Times*, October 9, 1996; Mignon Good Eberhart, "The Dark Corridor," *Flynn's*, December 5, 1925, 481–516.

20. "The Press: Flynn's," *Time*, September 29, 1924, https://content.time.com/time/subscriber/article/0,33009,719238,00.html; Richard Enright, "Vultures of the Dark," *Flynn's*, September 20, 1924.

21. William J. Flynn, "Headquarters Gossip," *Flynn's*, March 28, 1925, 617; William J. Flynn, "Headquarters Gossip," *Flynn's*, July 18, 1925, 320; Roberts, "'Steady Hammer,'" 376–77.

22. Henry Leverage, ed., "Dictionary of the Underworld," *Flynn's*, March 7, 1925, 191; Henry Leverage, ed., "Dictionary of the Underworld," *Flynn's*, March 21, 1925, 511–12.

23. *Flynn's Weekly Detective Fiction*, May 26, 1928.

24. Mike Dash, *The First Family: Terror, Extortion, Revenge, Murder, and the Birth of the American Mafia* (New York: Random House, 2009), 352–53; William Flynn Sanders, e-mail message to author, March 23, 2021, and April 2, 2021; "William J. Flynn, Long of Secret Service, Is Dead," *New York Herald Tribune*, October 15, 1928. Family quarrels over running the detective agency endured long after Flynn's death. Flynn's other children believed that they had a right to the business and that Veronica and Elmer had stolen it from them. "I can now well understand Veronica's nervousness every time I went into the office," William W. Flynn Jr. wrote to his sister Jane and her husband (Cal) in 1954, "and her telling me that Jane and Kathleen (another sister) were snooping around and she feared they might try to get a part of the agency. What a lovely family!" William also wrote that Veronica failed to pay the storage fee for her parents' household effects and therefore lost them. (See William Flynn Sanders, e-mail message to author, July 19, 2022.)

25. "William J. Flynn, Long of Secret Service"; Roberts, "'Steady Hammer,'" 396.

26. "W. J. Flynn, Noted Detective, Dead," *New York Times*, October 15, 1928; "Chief William J. Flynn," *Daily Times and Mamaroneck Paragraph* (Mamaroneck, NY), October 15, 1928; "William J. Flynn, Detective, Is Dead," *Tampa Daily Times*, October 15, 1928; "William J. Flynn Succumbs; Was War-Time Commander of Federal Secret Service," *Cincinnati Enquirer*, October 15, 1928.

27. "William J. Flynn," *Des Moines Register*, October 17, 1928; "Secret Service," *Brooklyn Daily Eagle*, October 18, 1928.

28. "Rites for Flynn Attended by 1,000," *Daily News* (NY), October 17, 1928; Dash, *The First Family*, 367.

29. Flynn, "My Life in the Secret Service," October 4, 1924, 388; Dash, *The First Family*, 367.

CHAPTER 8: AN INCORRUPTIBLE PUBLIC SERVANT

1. "William J. Flynn, Long of Secret Service, Is Dead," *New York Herald Tribune*, October 15, 1928.

2. William J. Flynn, *The Barrel Mystery* (New York: The James A. McCann Company, 1919), 264; "An American Sherlock Holmes," *Philadelphia Inquirer*, October 16, 1928.

3. Adam Hochschild, *American Midnight: The Great War, a Violent Peace, and Democracy's Forgotten Crisis* (New York: Mariner Books, 2022), 280; Beverly Gage, *G-Man: J. Edgar Hoover and the Making of the American Century* (New York: Viking, 2022), 79–80, 88; Jeffrey D. Simon, *America's Forgotten Terrorists: The Rise and Fall of the Galleanists* (Lincoln, NE: Potomac Books, 2022), 150; Tim Weiner, *Enemies: A History of the FBI* (New York: Random House, 2012), 34; Richard Gid Powers, *Secrecy and Power: The Life of J. Edgar Hoover* (New York: Free Press, 1987), 67; "An American Sherlock Holmes." The letter from Hoover to Seldes was placed in the *Congressional Record* in 1949. See "Proceedings and Debates of the 80th Congress, Second Session, Volume 94—Part 1, January 6, 1948, to February 19, 1948," 80 Cong. Rec. 124 (daily ed. January 13, 1948).

4. Simon, *America's Forgotten Terrorists*, 103; Bill Bratton and Peter Knobler, *The Profession: A Memoir of Policing in America* (New York: Penguin Books, 2022), 35–36; Beverly Gage, *The Day Wall Street Exploded: A Story of America in Its First Age of Terror* (New York: Oxford University Press, 2009), 26–27.

5. Gage, *The Day Wall Street Exploded*, 127–28; Brent Sidney Roberts, "'Steady Hammer': Origins of American Counterterrorism in the Dime Novel World of William J. Flynn" (PhD diss., Montana State University, 2020), 306–7.

6. "A Byte Out of History: How the FBI Got Its Name," FBI, March 24, 2006, https://archives.fbi.gov/archives/news/stories/2006/march/fbiname_022 406; William Flynn Sanders, e-mail message to author, March 23, 2021.

7. "Proceedings and Debates of the Sixty-Sixth Congress, First Session," Sundry Civil Appropriations Bill, 66 Cong. Rec. 1514–15 (daily ed. June 21, 1919).

8. James B. Morrow, "Counterfeiters; Their Ways Told by New Chief of U.S. Secret Service," *Washington Herald*, January 12, 1913; Roberts, "'Steady Hammer,'" 307.

9. "Flynn's Daughter Also Detective," *Spokane Daily Chronicle* (Spokane, WA), February 28, 1931; Gordon Sinclair, "Female Detective Scorns Investigating Men's Past," *Border Cities Star* (Windsor, ON, Canada), October 22, 1934; "Flynn Organizes a Detective Bureau," *Yonkers Herald* (Yonkers, NY), October 3, 1921; "Automat Unions Call Walkout in New York," *Chattanooga Daily Times* (Chattanooga, TN), August 7, 1937; "Strikebreakers Balk at $9 Day, Join Pickets," *Times Union* (Brooklyn, NY), March 3, 1936.

10. Thomas Hunt, "Nemesis of Counterfeiters: William J. Flynn," *Informer: The Journal of American Mafia History* 3, no. 2 (April 2010): 64; "Mrs. William J. Flynn," *New York Times*, April 24, 1937; William Flynn Sanders, e-mail message to author, March 23, 2021.

11. "William J. Flynn, Long of Secret Service."

Bibliography

Apgar, Charles E. "Making the Records from Sayville." *Wireless Age*, September 1915, 877–80.

Avrich, Paul. *Anarchist Voices: An Oral History of Anarchism in America*. Oakland, CA: AK Press, 2005.

———. *Sacco and Vanzetti: The Anarchist Background*. Princeton, NJ: Princeton University Press, 1991.

Avrich, Paul, and Karen Avrich. *Sasha and Emma: The Anarchist Odyssey of Alexander Berkman and Emma Goldman*. Cambridge, MA: Belknap Press of Harvard University Press, 2012.

Binder, John J. *Al Capone's Beer Wars: A Complete History of Organized Crime in Chicago during Prohibition*. Amherst, NY: Prometheus Books, 2017.

Blum, Howard. "American Dynamite." *Vanity Fair*, September 2008. https://www.vanityfair.com/culture/2008/09/blum-excerpt200809.

———. *American Lightning: Terror, Mystery, the Birth of Hollywood, and the Crime of the Century*. New York: Crown Publishers, 2008.

———. *Dark Invasion: 1915, Germany's Secret War and the Hunt for the First Terrorist Cell in America*. New York: Harper, 2014.

Bowen, Walter S. "U.S. Secret Service: A Chronicle." Unpublished manuscript, 1955. U.S. Secret Service files.

Bowen, Walter S., and Harry Edward Neal. *The United States Secret Service*. Philadelphia: Chilton Company, 1960.

Bratton, Bill, and Peter Knobler. *The Profession: A Memoir of Policing in America*. New York: Penguin Books, 2022.

Bratton, William. *Turnaround: How America's Top Cop Reversed the Crime Epidemic*. With Peter Knobler. New York: Random House, 1998.

Bruno, Joseph. "Joe Morello and the Black Handers." *Legends of America*. https://www.legendsofamerica.com/20th-blackhand/.

Butler, Richard J., and Joseph Driscoll. *Dock Walloper: The Story of "Big Dick" Butler*. New York: G. P. Putnam's Sons, 1933. https://archive.org/stream /dockwalloperstor00butlrich/dockwalloperstor00butlrich_djvu.txt.

"Catching Counterfeiters." U.S. Marshals Service. https://www.usmarshals.gov /history/counterfeit/counterfeit4.htm.

Chenery, William L. "So This Is Tammany Hall!" *The Atlantic Monthly*, September 1924, 310–19.

Christie, Agatha. "Traitor Hands." *Flynn's*, January 31, 1925, 273–326.

Churchill, Allen. "The Girl Who Never Came Back." *American Heritage*, August 1960. https://www.americanheritage.com/girl-who-never-came-back.

"Clear and Present Danger: A. Mitchell Palmer Goes Hunting for Bolsheviks." *Lapham's Quarterly*, Spring 2014. https://www.laphamsquarterly.org/revo lutions/clear-and-present-danger.

Conley, Lynn. "Charles Emory Apgar—'The Wireless Wizard.'" Apgar Family Association. http://www.apgarfamily.org/node/28.

Corradini, Anna Maria. *Joe Petrosino, a 20th Century Hero: A Documented Account of His Assassination in Palermo*. Palermo: Provincia Regionale di Palermo, 2009.

Cowan, Geoffrey. *The People v. Clarence Darrow: The Bribery Trial of America's Greatest Lawyer*. New York: Times Books/Random House, 1993.

Critchley, David. *The Origin of Organized Crime in America: The New York City Mafia, 1891–1931*. New York: Routledge, 2009.

Czitrom, Daniel. "The Origins of Corruption in the New York City Police Department." *Time*, June 28, 2016. https://time.com/4384963/nypd-scan dal-history/.

D'Amato, Gaetano. "The 'Black Hand' Myth." *North American Review* 187, no. 629 (April 1908): 543–49.

Damon, Allan L. "The Great Red Scare." *American Heritage*, February 1968. https://www.americanheritage.com/great-red-scare.

Dash, Mike. *The First Family: Terror, Extortion, Revenge, Murder, and the Birth of the American Mafia*. New York: Random House, 2009.

———. *Satan's Circus: Murder, Vice, Police Corruption and New York's Trial of the Century*. New York: Three Rivers Press, 2007.

Davis, Mike. *Buda's Wagon: A Brief History of the Car Bomb*. London: Verso, 2007.

Davisson, Lief. "What Are Electrotypes?" *E-Sylum* 23, no. 12 (March 22, 2020). https://www.coinbooks.org/v23/esylum_v23n12a23.html.

Digby, Michael. *Burn, Bomb, Destroy: The German Sabotage Campaign in North America 1914–1917*. Havertown, PA: Casemate Publishers, 2021.

Eberhart, Mignon Good. "The Dark Corridor." *Flynn's*, December 5, 1925, 481–516.

Eig, Jonathan. *Get Capone: The Secret Plot That Captured America's Most Wanted Gangster*. New York: Simon & Schuster Paperbacks, 2010.

Erb, Kelly Phillips. "Al Capone Convicted on This Day in 1931 after Boasting, 'They Can't Collect Legal Taxes from Illegal Money.'" *Forbes*, October 17, 2020. https://www.forbes.com/sites/kellyphillipserb/2020/10/17/al-ca pone-convicted-on-this-day-in-1931-after-boasting-they-cant-collect-le gal-taxes-from-illegal-money/?sh=34c6ba161435.

Flynn, William J. *The Barrel Mystery*. New York: The James A. McCann Company, 1919.

———. *The Eagle's Eye: A True Story of the Imperial German Government's Spies and Intrigues in America from Facts Furnished by William J. Flynn, Recently Retired, Chief of the U.S. Secret Service, Novelized by Courtney Ryley Cooper*. New York: The James A. McCann Company, 1919.

———. "Headquarters Gossip." *Flynn's Weekly*, June 26, 1926, 474–80.

———. "My Life in the Secret Service." *Flynn's*, October 4, 1924, 387–402.

Fox, John F., Jr. "Bureaucratic Wrangling over Counterintelligence, 1917–18." *Studies in Intelligence* 49, no. 1 (March 2005): 9–17.

Gage, Beverly. *The Day Wall Street Exploded: A Story of America in Its First Age of Terror*. New York: Oxford University Press, 2009.

———. *G-Man: J. Edgar Hoover and the Making of the American Century*. New York: Viking, 2022.

Goodman, Marc. *Future Crimes: Everything Is Connected, Everyone Is Vulnerable and What We Can Do about It*. New York: Doubleday, 2015.

Grundhauser, Eric. "The New York Prison That Doubled as a Clubhouse for Alimony Cheats." *Atlas Obscura*, September 4, 2015. https://www.atlasob scura.com/articles/the-new-york-prison-that-doubled-as-a-clubhouse -for-alimony-cheats.

Hagedorn, Ann. *Savage Peace: Hope and Fear in America, 1919*. New York: Simon & Schuster, 2007.

Hall, Tom. "Morvich Became First Cal-Bred to Win Kentucky Derby." *Blood-Horse*, September 1, 2021. https://www.bloodhorse.com/horse-racing/arti cles/252881/morvich-became-first-cal-bred-to-win-kentucky-derby.

Harvey, Ian. "The Story of Theodore Roosevelt and the New York Police Department." Vintage News. February 2, 2017. https://www.thevintagenews.com /2017/02/02/the-story-of-theodore-roosevelt-and-the-new-york-police -department/?chrome=1&A1c=1.

Hochschild, Adam. *American Midnight: The Great War, a Violent Peace, and Democracy's Forgotten Crisis*. New York: Mariner Books, 2022.

Hunt, Thomas. "Nemesis of Counterfeiters: William J. Flynn." *Informer: The Journal of American Mafia History* 3, no. 2 (April 2010): 47–68.

———. "*Sinistro*: The Underworld Career of Giuseppe Morello (1867–1930)." The American Mafia: The History of Organized Crime in the United States. http://mafiahistory.us/a029/f_morello.html.

———. *Wrongly Executed? The Long-Forgotten Context of Charles Sberna's 1939 Electrocution*. Whiting, VT: Seven•Seven•Eight, 2016.

Hunt, William R. *America's Sherlock Holmes: The Legacy of William Burns*. Guilford, CT: Lyons Press, 2019.

"Imperial Germany's Sabotage Operations in the U.S." In *A Counterintelligence Reader, Volume One: American Revolution to World War II*, edited by Frank J. Rafalko. 2011. https://irp.fas.org/ops/ci/docs/ci1/ch3c.htm.

Jones, John Price. *The German Spy in America: The Secret Plotting of German Spies in the United States and the Inside Story of the Sinking of the Lusitania*. London: Hutchinson & Co., 1917. https://books.google.com/books?id=s bzvaaaamaaj&printsec=frontcover&source=gbs_ge_summary_r&cad=0 #v=onepage&q&f=false.

Kagan, Ute Wartenberg. "Funny Money: The Fight of the U.S. Secret Service against Counterfeit Money." *ANS Magazine* 9, no. 2 (Summer 2010). http://numismatics.org/magazine/wp-content/uploads/sites/2/ansmaga zinesummer10opt.pdf.

Leider, Emily W. *Dark Lover: The Life and Death of Rudolph Valentino*. New York: Farrar, Straus and Giroux, 2003.

Leonnig, Carol. *Zero Fail: The Rise and Fall of the Secret Service*. New York: Random House, 2021.

Lupack, Barbara Tepa. *Silent Serial Sensations: The Wharton Brothers and the Magic of Early Cinema*. Ithaca, NY: Cornell University Press, 2020.

Manning, Lona. "9/16: Terrorists Bomb Wall Street." Sam Houston State University. Fall 2012. https://www.shsu.edu/his_rtc/2012_Fall/1302_Wall_St _Bombing.pdf.

McAdoo, William G. *Crowded Years: The Reminiscences of William G. McAdoo*. Boston: Houghton Mifflin Company, 1931.

McCabe, Bob. *Counterfeiting and Technology: A History of the Long Struggle between Paper-Money Counterfeiters and Security Printing*. Atlanta: Whitman Publishing, 2016.

McCormick, Charles H. *Hopeless Cases: The Hunt for the Red Scare Terrorist Bombers*. Lanham, MD: University Press of America, 2005.

Meares, Hadley Hall. "Unlucky Star: The Brief, Bombastic Life of Rudolph Valentino." *Vanity Fair*, September 14, 2021. https://www.vanityfair.com/hollywood/2021/09/rudolph-valentino-biography-death.

Mele, Andrew Paul. *The Italian Squad: How the NYPD Took Down the Black Hand Extortion Racket*. Jefferson, NC: McFarland & Company, 2020.

Miller, Batya. "Enforcement of the Sunday Closing Laws on the Lower East Side, 1882–1903." *American Jewish History* 91, no. 2 (June 2003): 269–86.

Murray, Robert K. *Red Scare: A Study in National Hysteria, 1919–1920*. Minneapolis: University of Minnesota Press, 1955.

Newswander, Chad B. "Presidential Security: Bodies, Bubbles, & Bunkers." PhD diss., Virginia Polytechnic Institute and State University, 2009. https://vtechworks.lib.vt.edu/bitstream/handle/10919/77042/etd-04182009-110718_Presidential_ewswander_ETD.pdf?sequence=1&isAllowed=y.

Nielsen, Arthur. "1915 Seventy-Five Years Ago." *American Heritage*, July/August 1990. https://www.americanheritage.com/1915-seventy-five-years-ago-2#.

"150+ Years of History." United States Secret Service. https://www.secretservice.gov/about/history/150-years.

Pernicone, Nunzio. "Luigi Galleani and Italian Anarchist Terrorism in the United States." *Studi Emigrazione/Etudes Migrations* 30, no. 111 (1993): 469–89.

Post, Louis. F. *The Deportations Delirium of Nineteen-Twenty: A Personal Narrative of an Historic Official Experience*. Chicago: Charles H. Kerr & Company, 1923.

Powers, Richard Gid. *Secrecy and Power: The Life of J. Edgar Hoover*. New York: Free Press, 1987.

Rapoport, David C. *Waves of Global Terrorism: From 1879 to the Present*. New York: Columbia University Press, 2022.

Reppetto, Thomas A. *Battleground New York City: Countering Spies, Saboteurs, and Terrorists since 1861*. Washington, D.C.: Potomac Books, 2012.

Roberts, Brent Sidney. "'Steady Hammer': Origins of American Counterterrorism in the Dime Novel World of William J. Flynn." PhD diss., Montana State University, 2020.

Roosevelt, Theodore. "Municipal Administration: The New York Police Force." *The Atlantic*, September 1897. https://www.theatlantic.com/magazine/archive/1897/09/municipal-administration-the-new-york-police-force/519849/.

Schmidt, Regin. *Red Scare: FBI and the Origins of Anticommunism in the United States, 1919–1943*. Copenhagen: Museum Tusculanum Press, 2000.

Senta, Antonio. *Luigi Galleani: The Most Dangerous Anarchist in America*. Translated by Andrea Asali with Sean Sayers. Chico, CA: AK Press, 2019.

Sheafe, Larry B. "The United States Secret Service: An Administrative History." Unpublished manuscript, 1983. https://www.governmentattic.org/25docs /USSSadminHistSheafeUnpub_1983.pdf.

Simon, Jeffrey D. *America's Forgotten Terrorists: The Rise and Fall of the Galleanists*. Lincoln, NE: Potomac Books, 2022.

———. "The Forgotten Terrorists: Lessons from the History of Terrorism." *Terrorism and Political Violence* 20, no. 2 (April–June 2008): 195–214.

———. *Lone Wolf Terrorism: Understanding the Growing Threat*. Amherst, NY: Prometheus Books, 2013.

———. *The Terrorist Trap: America's Experience with Terrorism*. Bloomington: Indiana University Press, 1994.

Snow, Richard F. "American Characters: Charles Becker." *American Heritage*, December 1978. https://www.americanheritage.com/charles-becker.

Talty, Stephan. *The Black Hand: The Epic War between a Brilliant Detective and the Deadliest Secret Society in American History*. Boston: Houghton Mifflin Harcourt, 2017.

Thomas, Lately. *The Mayor Who Mastered New York: The Life and Opinions of William J. Gaynor*. New York: William Morrow & Company, 1969.

Towne, Arthur W. "Mayor Gaynor's Police Policy and the Crime Wave in New York City." *Journal of Criminal Law and Criminology* 2, no. 3 (May 1911– March 1912): 375–80.

Tunney, Thomas J. *Throttled! The Detection of the German and Anarchist Bomb Plotters*. Boston: Small, Maynard & Company, 1919.

Von Feilitzsch, Heribert. *The Secret War Council: The German Fight against the Entente in America in 1914*. Amissville, VA: Henselstone Verlag, 2015.

———. *The Secret War on the United States in 1915: A Tale of Sabotage, Labor Unrest and Border Troubles*. Amissville, VA: Henselstone Verlag, 2015.

Warner, Michael. "The Kaiser Sows Destruction: Protecting the Homeland the First Time Around." *Studies in Intelligence* 46, no. 1 (2002). https:// www.cia.gov/static/5b90ec45fb53185a0c2e0de82d42c1c5/The-Kaiser -Sows-Destruction.pdf.

Watson, Bruce. *Sacco and Vanzetti: The Men, the Murders, and the Judgment of Mankind*. New York: Viking, 2007.

Weesjes, Elke, with Phil Nerges. "100 Years of Terror: The Black Tom Explosion and the Birth of U.S. Intelligence Services." *Natural Hazards Observer* 40, no.

7 (October 31, 2016). https://hazards.colorado.edu/article/100-years-of-ter
ror-the-black-tom-explosion-and-the-birth-of-u-s-intelligence-services-1.

Weiner, Tim. *Enemies: A History of the FBI*. New York: Random House, 2012.

Whalen, Bernard, and Jon Whalen. *The NYPD's First Fifty Years: Politicians, Police Commissioners, & Patrolmen*. Lincoln, NE: Potomac Books, 2014.

"Wharton Studio History: Ithaca and the Silver Screen." Wharton Studio Museum. https://whartonstudiomuseum.org/wharton-studio-history/.

Wittenberg, Ernest. "The Thrifty Spy on the Sixth Avenue El." *American Heritage*, December 1965. https://www.americanheritage.com/thrifty-spy -sixth-avenue-el.

Zacks, Richard. *Island of Vice: Theodore Roosevelt's Quest to Clean Up Sin-Loving New York*. New York: Anchor Books, 2012.

Zimmer, Kenyon. *Immigrants against the State: Yiddish and Italian Anarchism in America*. Urbana: University of Illinois Press, 2015.

INDEX